W9-AGI-862

Tax Planning 2005

For You and Your Family

Prepared by

Editors-in-Chief

Wayne L. Tunney, FCA
Toronto

Sandra Bussey, CA
Waterloo

Editor

Joseph Petrie, BA
Toronto

Contributing KPMG Editors

Carol Bethune, MA
Toronto

Chantal Buote, LL.B., M.Fisc.
Montréal

George W. Denier, FCA
Toronto

Georgina Dimopoulos, CA
Toronto

Benita Loughlin, CA
Vancouver

Marianne Gray, BMgt, CA
Lethbridge

Deborah A. MacPherson, CA, CFP
Hamilton

Michele A. Wood-Tweel, CA, CFP
Halifax

THOMSON

CARSWELL

Library and Archives Canada has catalogued this publication as follows:

Tax planning for you and your family

Annual.
Began publication with issue for 1997.
Issued also in French under title: Vous, votre famille et le fisc.
ISSN 1207-5957
ISBN 0-459-28091-0 (2005 edition)

1. Tax planning — Canada — Popular works — Periodicals. 2. Income tax — Canada — Popular works — Periodicals. I. KPMG (Firm) II. Carswell Company

KE5759.Y43 2000-   343.7105'2'05   C96-900735-3
KF6297.ZA2 T39

Printed in Canada.

Composition: Computer Composition of Canada Inc.

THOMSON
——————★——————™
CARSWELL

One Corporate Plaza   **Customer Relations:**
2075 Kennedy Road   Toronto: 416-609-3800
Toronto, Ontario M1T 3V4   Elsewhere in Canada/U.S.:   1-800-387-5164
                                              Fax: 1-416-298-5082

Overview

Table of Contents

Foreword

Many Canadians do not give much thought to how they can reduce their taxes until it's time to file their tax returns each spring. By then, many tax saving opportunities may be lost. Filing your tax return is essentially a once-a-year accounting to the government to settle up your taxes owing or refund due for the previous year. It is the tax planning steps that you take throughout each year that will save the most money at tax time and in the years to come.

In this book our tax and financial planning professionals set out the most common rules and tax planning techniques that are currently available to individuals, but our emphasis is on tax planning aimed at minimizing your family's overall tax bill. A few hours invested in reading this book can pay off substantially in tax savings and in the organization of your financial affairs.

What exactly is tax planning?

Tax planning is a perfectly legitimate activity. You are entitled to arrange your affairs, within the limits of the law, so that you pay a minimum amount of tax.

Tax evasion is a different story. Evasion is illegal. You are evading tax if you fail to report income or if you misstate facts so as to claim deductions or credits to which you are not entitled. If you evade tax, you will be subject to interest, penalties, fines and possibly imprisonment as well as being required to pay the tax owing.

Tax avoidance is the somewhat nebulous activity of using the tax system in a way in which it was not intended. The *Income Tax Act* contains a general anti-avoidance rule (GAAR), which can apply to avoidance activities. If you misuse or abuse the provisions of the Act, you may run into GAAR. The line between tax planning and tax avoidance is not always clear.

This book cannot replace your tax adviser

The income tax system is constantly changing. If you thought you knew the rules a couple of years ago, you may find they have been modified. We also cannot predict what changes are in store for the future. Information in this book is current to July 15, 2004, and reflects the law and publicly-announced proposals for changes as of that date.

This book deals only in general terms. The Canadian tax system is extremely complex, far more than the book makes it appear. The details fill volumes, not a single book. If you carry on your own business, or manage a corporation, you will benefit greatly from personalized tax advice. Even if your affairs are relatively simple, you should consult a qualified tax professional (not just a tax return preparer). You will likely find the savings far outweigh the fees.

Bruce Flexman
Canadian Managing Partner - Tax
KPMG LLP

Tips for achieving your financial goals

- Create a financial plan and stick to it (1.1)
- Define your short-, medium- and long-term goals (1.1.1)
- Track your net worth and cash flow, and set an annual growth target (1.1.2 and 1.1.3)
- Save systematically by "paying yourself first" (1.1.3)
- Build an investment strategy that suits your unique circumstances and needs (1.1.4)
- Set benchmarks for measuring the performance of your investment portfolio and your investment manager (1.1.4)
- Contribute up to $2,000 annually to an RESP and earn a 20% government grant (1.2.1)
- Encourage your children to invest the money they earn (1.2.2)
- Think about using RRSP funds for a down payment on your first home under the Home Buyers' Plan (1.2.3)
- Increase the frequency of your mortgage payments to reduce your mortgage interest (1.2.3)
- Plan to minimize capital gains tax on dispositions of vacation homes (1.2.4)
- Set up an emergency fund or line of credit (1.3.1)
- Make sure you have adequate insurance and a current will (1.3.2 and 1.3.3)
- Consider a power of attorney (1.3.4)
- Shop around when choosing your financial and investment advisers (1.4)

In this chapter we offer a primer on financial planning with emphasis on the impact of taxes on your ability to meet your family's financial goals. We also point out tax planning ideas elsewhere in this book that may help you to achieve these goals. Given the importance of financial planning for your retirement, this area is discussed separately in Chapter 20.

1.1. Developing your financial plan

For many Canadians, at all stages in life, the very idea of financial planning is mystifying. It shouldn't be. Saving for retirement, financing your child's education or buying a house are within the reach of most of us—the purpose of financial planning is to clarify your objectives, set a realistic timetable for achieving them, and marshal your financial resources to support your plan. Of course, the process may require changing your expectations, paring down your current lifestyle or simply prioritizing expenses and making choices. But having a sound financial plan will likely ease your financial anxiety by giving you a realistic picture of your family's finances and a clear path for satisfying your goals.

In Canada, taxes are one of the biggest obstacles to the creation, maintenance and preservation of independent wealth. Tax planning to minimize your family's overall tax bill should be an integral part of your family's financial plan. The balance of this book is full of ideas about how to save taxes; the rest of this chapter is an overview of the financial planning framework in which your tax planning should take place.

1.1.1 Define your financial and lifestyle goals

| Create a financial plan and stick to it. |

Putting your dreams on paper is the first step toward realizing them. Start by setting down what you want and when you want it. If you have a spouse or domestic partner, compile your list together, compromising where necessary to make sure that you are both committed to the same objectives. You might also include your children and have them develop their own plan as a teaching exercise.

| Define your short-, medium- and long-term goals. |

While your list should take into account your family's well-being and future financial security, be sure to include any desired lifestyle-enhancing items like vacation homes, major renovations, luxury cars or swimming pools. If you want to take a sabbatical from work to spend time with your children or eventually start your own business, write it down. As part of this exercise, consider the discussion of building your investment strategy in 1.1.4, common financial goals in 1.2 and important financial safeguards in 1.3.

When you have completed your list, divide it into short-, medium- and long-term goals and rank them in order of priority within each section. Set down a timeframe for meeting each goal. Then do a bit of research and estimate the cost of achieving your goals, making sure to account for inflation. Don't let the numbers overwhelm you—over time the effects of compound growth can provide significant returns on your investments.

Nevertheless, you may need to revise your list by allowing more time to achieve a certain goal or by dropping items that are beyond your means.

As time goes by, your list will serve as a guide for directing your savings and investments and as an indicator of your progress. Since your personal and financial circumstances and goals are bound to change, it is important to revisit your list once or twice a year and revise it to reflect new priorities and achievements.

1.1.2 Track your net worth

Now that you have a better idea of where you want to go, the next step is to take a snapshot of where you are financially today—your net worth. Calculating your net worth is simply a matter of adding up your total assets (what you own) and total liabilities (what you owe), and then subtracting your liabilities from your assets. The resulting figure is the springboard for most aspects of financial management and planning.

It's also a good idea to separate your assets by ownership—whether your resources are owned by you, your spouse or jointly, can help in determining potential strategies for income splitting (see Chapter 5) and estate planning (see Chapter 21).

A close look at your assets will show you whether most of your assets are personal items, such as your home or your car, or investment assets, such as savings and shares. It should also indicate how liquid your assets are and help you determine if your investments are spread appropriately to balance expected rates of return with the degree of risk you are prepared to take (see 1.1.4).

Similarly, a close look at your liabilities may indicate whether your insurance coverage is adequate (see 1.3.2) and how your debts are affecting your bottom line. As we'll see in 7.2.3, interest incurred for personal reasons on credit cards, consumer loans and mortgages is not deductible for tax purposes, while interest on loans taken out to purchase income-generating investments or business income may be deductible. As a result, the interest on your consumer debts may cost you more than you make on your investments. Where possible, you should try to pay down your consumer debts, giving priority to those with the highest interest rates, and make sure that all loans you take out in the future are for a tax-deductible purpose.

> Track your net worth and cash flow, and set an annual growth target.

Updating your net worth calculation once or twice a year is a good way to track your financial health and progress toward achieving your financial goals. For example, if you are able to increase your net worth by 15% each year, your net worth will double every five years. Ways to increase your net worth include:

- improving the rate of return on your investments;
- investing more of your income by spending less on discretionary items and minimizing taxes; and
- reducing your debt by paying off your consumer loans and accelerating your mortgage and other debt payments.

1.1.3 Cash management and budgeting—the cornerstone of financial planning

The formula for accumulating the necessary funds to achieve your financial goals is no secret. Unless you expect to inherit money or win a lottery, the way to start building wealth is to save and regularly invest a portion of your income. Through the mathematical "miracle" of compounding, your investment assets can grow exponentially over time. So the more savings you have to invest and the longer they are invested, the greater your net worth will be.

One way to increase your net worth is to gain better control over your savings and expenses with a personal or family budget. List the amounts of money you expect to receive through your pay cheque or other sources and the amounts you pay out monthly for living expenses, such as mortgage payments, groceries and entertainment. This will allow you to realistically assess your cash flow and help you prioritize so you can spend your money where you need and want to.

Considering this information and any non-recurring expenses, set your budget for the next month or the remainder of the year. Once your budget is set, review it regularly for reasonableness and compare your actual spending against it.

Without making lifestyle changes, there is usually little you can do about your mortgage payments, car payments and other fixed expenses. However, the exercise of preparing—and sticking to—a budget will probably reveal opportunities to easily reduce your discretionary expenses such as travel, entertainment and gifts. Though not required, there are plenty of excellent software packages available that can help you create and monitor your family budget.

> Save systematically by "paying yourself first".

When preparing your budget, do not simply plan to save the amount left over at the end of each month—chances are there won't be as much left as you intended. Instead, get into the practice of saving a fixed amount of at least 10% of your income at the beginning of each month (or some other period) and using the balance for your expenses. Commonly known as the "pay yourself first" plan, this technique helps you to save systematically and to be less prone to making impulsive or needlessly expensive purchases. Although it may take you a few months to get used to having less cash readily available, you will probably be surprised at how quickly you will adjust. Consider having your financial institution automatically transfer your savings amount to a separate account or registered retirement savings plan (RRSP) (see Chapter 3) on a monthly or other regular basis.

1.1.4   Develop an appropriate investment strategy

Today's economic realities are forcing Canadians to take care of their own financial health. Even with professional advisers, most investors should take an active interest in their investment activities.

Modern investment wisdom suggests that it's not what you select but where you select it from. Known as "asset allocation", this process works as well for $100,000 as it does for $1 million. Simply put, asset allocation is the process of deciding how to invest a pool of resources among a broad array of assets.

> Build an investment strategy that suits your unique circumstances and needs.

It is typically considered the single most important part of managing a portfolio. According to Ibbotson Associates of Chicago, Illinois, over 90% of a portfolio's investment return is derived from the appropriate asset allocation mix. The actual securities selection contributes only 5% to 10% of the overall return.

Asset allocation has three levels. The first level entails selecting between asset classes: cash, fixed income and equities.

After that, a second level decision includes determining market exposure—in many cases, you would be wise to diversify your investments geographically. Canada represents less than 3% of the world's capitalization, and substantial investment opportunities are considered to exist beyond our borders. Most Canadians are satisfied with owning some U.S. stocks, but this usually doesn't allow for enough diversification because the North American markets strongly influence each other. Today, global investments are available through a variety of mutual funds. As we'll see in 3.1.7, there is a foreign content limit for registered retirement savings plans, but there are also several strategies for increasing your RRSP's participation in foreign markets above that level. There are no foreign content restrictions for non-registered investments.

Another level of asset allocation is deciding the currency exposure. For example, if you held U.S. funds in recent years while the U.S. currency was depreciating against the Canadian dollar, you may have made a nice profit, provided you converted to Canadian funds at a higher rate than you purchased the U.S. funds.

"Hedging" is an investment strategy through which an investor attempts to manage the various risks in a portfolio by holding different currencies in different markets that are expected to move in opposite directions. Since hedging transactions required sophisticated knowledge of global markets, many investors ignore this strategy. Many investors instead choose to achieve additional diversification by investing in a hedge fund.

Along with these three levels, asset allocation comes in two forms: strategic and tactical. Strategic asset allocation takes a long-term view and divides a portfolio among several asset classes according to the inherent risks and rewards of each asset. Tactical allocation consists of short-term market predictions that could last an hour or a day. This type of allocation often proves difficult because variables used in selecting the asset mix continually change and the portfolio must be adjusted to keep up with market movements. Other disadvantages may include higher fees, lack of liquidity in esoteric markets like precious metals, and the potential to misread economic signals.

While there is no perfect asset allocation for any one person, there are definitely inappropriate allocations. The following are some tips for getting the right mix.

Determine your objectives and risk tolerance—Before you make any investment decisions, determine your objectives and risk tolerance and decide your asset allocation. Risk tolerance is influenced by factors such as your age, your family situation and investor personality. For example, a 55-year-old with two dependent teenage children may have a dramatically different risk tolerance than an empty-nester or single person of the same age.

Risk tolerance should also reflect your ability to replace losses. A person with a high net worth can weather a loss of $50,000 in the market. But for the average retiree with a fixed pension and sustainable investment income, such a loss may be devastating. Asset allocation has to be a function of your investor profile and risk tolerance. If it's right, you should be able to sleep well in any market environment.

For a discussion of revising your investment strategy as you approach retirement, see 20.2.2.

Consider your total portfolio—Many investors make a classic mistake at the outset by separating their registered from non-registered investments; whether investments are in an RRSP or not is irrelevant to an asset allocation decision. Your total investment portfolio should be considered so that the right proportion of assets can be determined. Once the asset allocation is done, then you can decide, from a tax perspective, which investments are more effective to hold inside your RRSP.

Plan for a long horizon and stay on course—Once you have determined your asset allocation, plan to let your investments grow for at least five to seven years, long enough to go through a full market cycle. Average investors often make the mistake of buying what's hot because they think it's a great time to be in the market, then panic and sell as soon as the investment loses value. A disciplined approach to long-term asset allocation will probably give you higher returns in the long run.

Pay attention to fees—Be aware of management fees and commissions. A saving in fees of 1% per annum on a $100,000 investment earning a 6% annual return for 10 years could save you well over $15,000. You can't control the market, but you can control the fees and commissions you pay.

Inflation is a risk—Inflation is another factor you can't control, though you can plan for it. Depending on the rate of inflation, it can be a costly mistake to think of money in nominal terms instead of its real value. If your money isn't growing, you're losing it. Consider a $1,000 investment earning an average rate of return of 6% per year. After 10 years, the investment will be worth $1,790, but inflation will have eroded its real value. Assuming an annual inflation rate of 3%, this erosion will amount to $450 by the end of the tenth year, bringing the investment's real value down at that time to $1,340.

Rebalance annually—One of the most important steps in managing your investments is to regularly rebalance your portfolio according to your asset allocation. With discipline, this allows you to manage your investments for profit, by selling high and buying low.

For example, you may have decided originally that an investment mix of 40% in stocks and 60% in bonds met your objectives. However, due to a prosperous period in the economy, you find that the stock component of your portfolio grows to 55% while bonds now represent only 45% by value. In this case, the discipline of strategic asset allocation should force you to take profits and rebalance your original mix so that when the economy reverses—as it always does—you will be positioned to take advantage of the change.

Choose the right investment firm and monitor your investments' performance—Select an investment firm that fits your particular circumstances and needs and has consistently shown strong performance over the long-term, compared to its competitors. Your written

> Set benchmarks for measuring the performance of your investment portfolio and your investment manager.

investment policy should establish appropriate benchmarks that relate to your particular asset mix, such as market indices, to judge the performance of your investment portfolio and your investment manager. See 1.4 for general advice on choosing your professional advisers.

Don't try to outsmart the market—Focus your attention on getting the asset allocation right and then, within each asset class, try to keep your costs at a minimum. Make sure you are well diversified. Be consistent in your investment style and stick to your plan. Don't think that what happened in the past will happen in the future. In the financial market, history rarely repeats.

1.2   Some common financial goals

1.2.1   Planning for your children's education

Although post-secondary education may not be the route your child chooses, having a college degree or university diploma can greatly expand their range of occupational choices and will probably enhance their future earning power. But with government support for post-secondary institutions falling and tuition fees on the rise, putting a child through college or university is becoming increasingly costly. If your child decides to study outside Canada, the cost will increase exponentially. Most of us would be hard-pressed to finance these costs out of current income, so planning ahead is crucial.

Like any financial planning endeavour, decisions about funding your child's education should be made with an eye toward the effects of taxation. Below are a few common techniques for reducing your family's overall tax burden so that more funds will be available to finance your child's education.

> Contribute up to $2,000 annually to an RESP and earn a 20% government grant.

Registered Education Savings Plans (RESPs) can be effective education savings vehicles, especially due to the availability of Canada Education Savings Grants. Under this program, the government will provide a grant of 20% on the first $2,000 of annual contributions made in a year to an RESP, giving you an easy extra 20% return on your first $2,000 of contributions each year per beneficiary. For low- and middle-income families, the CESG grant will be even higher in 2005 and later years. The RESP rules are discussed at greater length in Chapter 4.

As an alternative to an RESP, you could invest in tax-efficient growth mutual funds in your child's name. Any income from these funds is normally taxed under the preferential rules for capital gains (see Chapter 6) or dividends (see Chapter 7). In addition, any capital gains distributed by the fund or on the sale of the fund will be taxable in your child's hands at your child's lower tax rate (or not taxed at all if his or her income is low enough). Until your child turns 18, the dividends and interest will be taxed in your hands due to the attribution rules discussed in 5.2.3; however, assuming you have selected a tax-efficient mutual fund, this will usually amount to a small proportion of the fund's overall return. Choosing a non-registered mutual fund provides some investment control and flexibility—there are no restrictions on the use of the funds and there is no limit on the amount that can be deposited annually.

If you receive Child Tax Benefit or Child Disability Benefit payments (see 2.3.1), consider depositing them to an account in your child's name. As with RESP funds, these deposits may add up to a significant investment over time and, since the anti-income splitting rules discussed in Chapter 5 don't apply, any investment income earned on the funds will be taxed in your child's hands, if at all. You may wish to withdraw the balance from the account annually and purchase higher-yielding investments on your child's behalf.

1.2.2 Encouraging your child to invest

If you have a child who works part-time (e.g., summer employment, paper route, etc.) with an income below the basic personal credit amount that can be earned tax-free ($8,012 for 2004—see 2.2), you might consider filing a tax return for him or her to report the earned income for RRSP purposes and allow the build up of an unused contribution limit, which may be of use in a later year when he or she becomes taxable (see 3.1.3). This can be especially useful when your child is in the teenage years and can expect to earn much more income in the future, since the unused deduction room can be carried forward indefinitely. If your child has cash available, he or she can contribute now to start enjoying tax-free investment growth but delay claiming the related tax deduction until a later year when your child has enough income to be taxable.

Instead of giving your child money which is easily spent, consider having him or her start an RRSP. The amount you can contribute may seem minimal—only 18% of the child's earned income from a summer or part-time job, plus the $2,000 lifetime overcontribution if the child turned 18 in the prior year (see 3.3.4). But the funds in the RRSP will enjoy tax-free compounding, which will accumulate significantly over time. For example, assuming a 6% rate of return, $1,000 a year invested in an RRSP each year beginning at age 16 will grow to $13,972 by the beginning of the year in which the child turns 22; at age 30, the RRSP will grow to $24,673, and if the annual contribution is made until the child retires at 65, the RRSP will be about $273,000.

To top up your child's earnings and help finance his or her education or other pursuits, consider lending your child, interest-free, an amount equal to what he or she earns over the year and would otherwise spend. Your child can use the loaned funds to pay for expenses such as tuition fees and invest his or her own income to earn investment income. That way, the anti-income splitting rules discussed in Chapter 5 will not attribute the investment income back to you and it will be taxed at your child's lower tax rate (or not taxed at all if his or her income is low enough). Later on, perhaps after graduating, your child can pay you back out of the invested funds, or keep the funds as "seed money" for their early working years. (This strategy is discussed in more detail in 5.3.11.)

> Encourage your children to invest the money they earn.

Chapter 5 discusses a number of techniques for splitting income with children. These strategies can significantly lower your family's overall tax burden and help your child become financially independent.

1.2.3 Buying a home

If you are renting your home, instead of buying, you may be missing out on a potential investment opportunity. A home can be a reliable hedge against inflation, a great retirement savings vehicle and a tax shelter—as we'll see in 6.4.2. If you own a home and sell it for a gain, the gain is usually tax-free as long as it has been your principal residence for income tax purposes.

So if you can afford to buy a home, don't rent. If you are renting while you are saving for a home, consider moving to less expensive rental accommodations and saving more toward your down payment. The sooner you start putting your money toward a mortgage instead of your landlord's pocket, the better off you will be. Below are a few tax planning and other issues for prospective home buyers to consider.

> Think about using RRSP funds for a down payment on your first home under the Home Buyers' Plan.

If you qualify, the Home Buyers' Plan can be a possible source of cash for financing your down payment. If you are saving to buy your first home, think about using your RRSP as your savings vehicle; under the Home Buyers' Plan discussed at 3.3.6, if you qualify, you can generally withdraw up to $20,000 as a loan from your RRSP to buy or build a home, without counting the withdrawal as income for tax purposes. You must then repay the loan, without interest, over 15 years starting in the second year following the year of withdrawal.

If you do plan to withdraw RRSP funds under the Home Buyers' Plan, consider making your RRSP contribution for the year at least 90 days before you make the withdrawal to preserve your ability to deduct the contribution amount. If you are depending on your RRSP for retirement income, you will want to forecast the decline in income that will result from the loss of the tax-free compounding when you withdraw a large chunk of RRSP funds now and pay it back over 15 years. See 3.3.6 for a more detailed discussion of the Home Buyers' Plan.

> Increase the frequency of your mortgage payments to reduce your mortgage interest.

Once you have a mortgage, consider making extra payments to reduce your interest costs. Based on a 25-year amortization period, your mortgage will be paid off at the same time whether you pay monthly or weekly and making extra payments can greatly reduce the amount of interest you'll pay over the life of your mortgage.

Accelerating your mortgage payment schedule doesn't necessarily mean that you will be shelling out any more cash than you do now. Here's the trick: figure out how much you can or want to pay each month and multiply that amount by 12. This is your annual payment. Then divide this number by 52 to determine the amount to pay weekly. Over the course of a year, your total mortgage payments will be identical, but more frequent payments will reduce your principal more quickly and reduce your overall interest cost.

Another way to save on mortgage interest is to maintain your original payment level when your mortgage comes up for renewal, even if interest rates have fallen. Also, each time you renew, consider increasing your payment by whatever you can commit—even an extra $50 or $100 will save you money in the long run.

1.2.4 Vacation properties

Plan to minimize capital gains tax on dispositions of vacation homes.

Buying a cottage, ski chalet or condo in Florida can provide years of enjoyment for your family. For a variety of reasons, a recreation property can also be a sound investment. You will probably save on your family's vacation costs. You may even find it easy to make up some of the property's costs by renting it out when your family is not using it. Market demand for desirable vacation properties (especially waterfront properties) within a reasonable drive from Canadian urban centres will probably remain steady, and, if historical trends continue, the value of your vacation home could rise significantly during the time you own it.

Whether you plan to keep the property in the family or sell it for future gain, bear in mind that capital gains tax (see 6.2.1) may apply on the difference between the property's cost when you bought it, plus improvements made, and its fair market value when you sell it or at the time of your death (or your spouse's death). The longer you own your cottage, the bigger the gain is likely to be.

To avoid leaving your survivors with a tax bill, which they may have to fund by selling the property, consider purchasing enough life insurance to fund the taxes that will arise on your death. You may be able to shelter some of the gain on the property's sale or on your death (or your spouse's) through the principal residence exemption (see 6.4.2). You may be able to protect future gains from tax by transferring the property to one of your children or to a family trust (see 5.3.7). Consider also our more general discussion of estate planning in Chapter 21.

If your vacation property is situated in the U.S. and you are a Canadian resident, the double hit of U.S. estate tax and Canadian income tax arising on death can carry a potentially high tax burden. The Canada-U.S. tax treaty may ease the potential for double taxation, but, as discussed at 19.4, some rather complex tax planning may be required and you should probably seek professional tax advice.

1.3 Preserving your family's financial security

The achievement of your financial goals can be delayed or derailed by unexpected changes of circumstance. Your family's financial plan should include measures to address risk and protect your family's financial security.

1.3.1 Do you have a line of credit and/or an emergency fund?

Set up an emergency fund or line of credit.

In today's business environment you cannot count on having a job for life. In addition to cash flow, job loss can affect your company-funded benefits and pension plan. Generally speaking, you should have an emergency fund large enough to handle the loss of a job for six months to one year. Canada Savings Bonds, money market or T-bill funds and cashable guaranteed investment certificates are good places to park emergency reserves.

Another way to provide an emergency fund is to establish a line of credit with your financial institution. Be careful to only use it when necessary, because the interest you'll incur will be non-deductible and you will have to repay it according to the line of credit's terms.

1.3.2 Do you have enough insurance?

Make sure you have adequate insurance and a current will.

Review your insurance needs with your financial advisers to determine the appropriate amount and form of your insurance coverage in various areas, including property loss, death, disability, sickness, personal liability and liquidity crisis.

A review should consider your need for life insurance. In the event of your death, life insurance may be critical for providing replacement income for your dependants and for funding your estate's tax and other liabilities. Life insurance plays many other important roles in estate planning. Some tax planning and other issues involving life insurance are discussed in 21.7.

One of your most valuable assets is your ability to earn income through employment or self-employment. Review your need for disability insurance—if you become disabled, the financial consequences can be devastating. Most disability insurance policies do not provide a level of income over and above what you need for basic ongoing living expenses. In the long-term, this could leave you without enough funds set aside for your retirement since disability income usually stops at age 65.

Make sure you have sufficient insurance to protect you from significant financial loss due to damage or destruction to your home, automobile or other personal assets. Without adequate coverage, the emotional trauma of such losses could be compounded by irreversible damage to your family's finances. Depending on your occupation or circumstances, you should also assess your need for other forms of insurance such as health and professional or director's liability coverage.

1.3.3 Is your will up-to-date?

Have you and your family members reviewed your wills within the past two years, or since there has been a change in your family circumstances? Are your wills effectively tax-structured? Remember that if you die intestate (without a will) your assets will be distributed according to provincial law, possibly differently from what you would have wished. Be sure to seek advice of a lawyer (or a notary in Québec) to ensure your will is legally valid and accurately reflects your wishes. You should also consult a tax adviser for assistance in reducing your estate's tax liability, including probate fees and U.S. estate tax.

For a more detailed discussion of the role of your will in planning for the orderly distribution of your estate and the minimization of taxes on death, see 21.2.

1.3.4 Do you have a power of attorney?

A power of attorney allows you to designate a person who will take control of your financial affairs if you become incapacitated due to illness or injury. If this happens and you do not have a power of attorney, control will yield to a provincial public trustee which may hamstring your family's ability to access your financial resources.

Powers of attorney are usually limited to decisions regarding your finances. In some provinces (including Ontario and Québec), you can empower a different person to make decisions about your health care and medical treatment.

> Consider a power of attorney.

Like your will, your power of attorney should be prepared with professional advice—consider having both drawn up at the same time.

Note that a power of attorney operates only while you are alive. Once you die your will takes over.

In some cases, a trust can be an effective alternative to a power of attorney—see 21.5.4.

1.4 Selecting your professional advisers

Financial planning is broad in scope and you may need advice from professionals with expertise in different areas. For some financial decisions, it will be worth the expense to invest in professional advice, whether from a lawyer, tax adviser, insurance broker, investment counsellor, or a personal financial adviser. And in some financial planning endeavours, such as estate planning, professional legal and tax advice is a must.

Given what's at stake—your family's finances—you should take the time to shop around for advisers who are knowledgeable and experienced in their fields and with whom you feel comfortable. When interviewing prospective advisers of any profession, be sure to cover the following topics:

Shop around when choosing your financial and investment advisers.

- Ask for client references, preferably from three or four people in circumstances similar to your own.
- Inquire into the professional's educational background, qualifications and level of experience.
- Ask whether the adviser belongs to any professional networks and associations to determine what sorts of resources are available to him or her.
- Make sure that you understand the fee arrangement.
- Be cautious of advisers whose objective may be to sell you investments, tax shelters, insurance or anything other than independent advice.

The level of your need for advisers will depend primarily on the complexity of your affairs and your own knowledge of financial matters. You will get better value for the fees you pay to your advisers if you spend some time up front educating yourself. After all, it's your money and you must ultimately take responsibility for its handling and performance.

If you have a spouse, be sure that he or she is acquainted with your advisers, since your spouse will need to deal with them in the event of your death or disability. It is also a good idea to keep an up-to-date list of your advisers' names and phone numbers in one place, perhaps in the same place as your will and list of assets.

CHAPTER 2

Tips for claiming tax deductions and credits

- The higher-income spouse should claim credits to reduce high-income provincial surtax (2.1.3)
- If you're unmarried and support a family member, don't miss out on the wholly dependent person credit (2.2.1)
- Working parents and students—claim your child care expenses (2.3.2)
- Take advantage of the tax credit for interest paid on student loans (2.4)
- If the Canada Revenue Agency (CRA) challenges your disability claim, consider objecting (2.5.1)
- Persons with disabilities—take advantage of the new deduction for disability supports needed to work or attend school (2.5.2)
- If you're separating, co-operate to minimize your joint tax bill (2.6)
- Aim to preserve pre-May 1, 1997 child support arrangements where practical (2.6)
- Combine your family's medical expenses on one return (2.7.1)
- Choose your own 12-month period for medical expense claims (2.7.1)
- Plan for the timing of your family's medical expense payments (2.7.1)
- Take advantage of Canada's generous tax break for political contributions (2.7.2)

In this chapter we describe how your tax bill is calculated and highlight some commonly available and sometimes overlooked deductions and credits that can be claimed on your income tax return, depending on your family status and personal circumstances.

2.1 Taxes, credits and deductions

2.1.1 Calculating your tax balance due or refund owing

To understand how deductions and credits work, you need to understand the basic tax calculation. We'll describe it briefly here. (For Québec residents, the provincial tax calculation is completely separate and not as described below. See Chapter 17.)

You start by adding up your various kinds of income: employment, business, interest, grossed-up dividends, taxable capital gains, and so on. This gives you **total income**. From this figure you subtract certain deductions, some of which we'll look at in this chapter, and reach **net income**. The net income figure is used for certain purposes later. Then some additional deductions are allowed, primarily losses carried forward from previous years, giving you **taxable income**.

You then calculate your **federal tax**, applying the federal **tax rates** and **brackets** to your taxable income using the formula shown on Schedule 1 of your tax return. Then you subtract various **non-refundable tax credits** (see 2.1.2), and certain others such as the dividend tax credit (see 7.1.1). This gives you **net federal tax**.

Your next step is to add your **provincial tax**. You compute your provincial tax in essentially the same way as your federal tax, using taxable income calculated for federal tax purposes but applying your province's tax brackets, rates and credits to your taxable income. Depending on the province, you may also have to add a provincial surtax and/or health care levy. Federal and provincial tax rates and brackets for 2004 are set out in Appendix I. Federal and provincial tax credits for 2004 are set out in Appendix II.

If you are self-employed, you may also be required to add your Canada Pension Plan (CPP) contribution on your self-employment income at this point.

Finally, you record all source deductions of tax (withheld by your employer, for example) and instalments paid, both of which are credited to your account. Along with these are the **refundable credits**— including the supplementary medical expense credit (see 2.7.1) and the employee or partner GST/HST rebate (see 2.9.4)—which are given the same treatment so that they can effectively be refunded to you even if you pay no tax for the year. (Some provinces also provide refundable tax credits.) The bottom line is your **balance due** or refund claimed, and that will be the cheque you send in by April 30 or receive when your return is assessed.

2.1.2 Deductions versus credits—what's the difference?

Before we get into the specific deductions and credits available, you need to understand the different effects of a deduction and a credit. You can refer back to the discussion in 2.1.1 as we go through this.

A **deduction** (or "write-off") reduces your taxable income, on which your federal tax is calculated. Bearing in mind that provincial tax rates and brackets vary, the combined effect of the federal and provincial taxes and provincial surtaxes means that, as long as you are still paying some tax, a deduction is worth about 24% where your taxable income is under $35,000; about 34% where it is between $35,000 and $70,000; about 41% where it is between $70,000 and $113,800; and about 45% where it is over $113,800.

In other words, a $100 write-off (of, say, deductible moving or child care expenses) is worth about $24 to $45 in tax savings, depending on your tax bracket.

A **credit**, on the other hand, is a direct reduction in tax; $100 of a credit such as the credit for political contributions (2.7.2 below) is worth exactly $100 to you.

There is a twist, however. Under the federal-provincial tax collection agreement, provinces can top up the federal amounts or add their own credits if they wish, but at minimum they must offer the same basic credits as those available federally (based on the credit's 1997 or current-year amount, whichever is less). As a result, the credits may be worth about 40% to 70% more, once you factor in the equivalent provincial credit. For example, for 2004, the maximum value of the basic personal credit (see 2.2.1) is $1,282 for federal purposes, but, if you live in Ontario, the value of the credit to you is actually $1,769, once the federal and provincial basic personal credit values are combined.

Finally, note the distinction between refundable and non-refundable credits. Because they are treated as having been paid by you, just like source withholdings and instalments, refundable credits are always worth what they say they are. Non-refundable credits, like deductions, become worthless once you reach the point of paying no tax at all for the year.

2.1.3 Transferring credits between spouses

Some of the non-refundable credits outlined below, such as charitable donations (see 8.1), can be transferred between spouses if not otherwise usable (see Schedule 2 of the T1 General Return).

Where you have a choice as to which spouse will claim certain credits, credits are worth slightly more to very high-income individuals in some provinces. That is because some provinces impose additional surtaxes on individuals with

> The higher-income spouse should claim credits to reduce high-income provincial surtax.

high basic provincial tax. For example, in Ontario in 2004, the provincial surtax is effectively an extra 20% of basic Ontario tax over $3,856 and an extra 36% of basic Ontario tax over $4,864.

If you are paying a surtax and your spouse is not, it is better for you to claim most of the credits that can be allocated between the two of you.

2.2 Personal, spousal and dependant credits

Every individual gets a basic federal credit, which allows you to receive a basic amount of income on a tax-free basis. In 2004, the basic federal credit is $1,282, which offsets the federal tax on your first $8,012 of income. (On your income tax return, you claim a "basic personal amount" of $8,012, which you later multiply by 16%.)

2.2.1 Spousal/partner and wholly dependent person credits

If you are married, you can claim a further federal credit of $1,089 if your spouse's income is under $680, or a reduced amount if your spouse has income between $680 and $7,484.

If you are single, widowed, divorced or separated, and you support another family member (such as a child) in your home, you can claim that person under the wholly dependent person credit. This will allow you the same claim as if that person were your spouse.

> If you're unmarried and support a family member, don't miss out on the wholly dependent person credit.

Common-law spouses and same-sex couples who meet certain criteria (below) are treated identically to legally married couples for all purposes relating to income tax. This means that the spousal credit can be claimed for a dependent common-law or same-sex spouse. It also means that a taxpayer who has a common-law or same-sex spouse cannot claim the wholly dependent person credit for a child.

Opposite-sex common-law spouses are treated as spouses if they are two people who "cohabit in a conjugal relationship", where either they have had a child together, or they have cohabited for at least 12 continuous months. Separation is not considered to terminate this "cohabiting" unless the couple separates for at least 90 days because of a breakdown in their relationship. Same-sex couples who have been living together for at least one year are treated the same under tax law as opposite-sex common-law couples.

2.3 Children

2.3.1 Child Tax Benefit

The "Child Tax Benefit" is an annual non-taxable benefit for low and moderate income families. The Child Tax Benefit is topped up with the National Child Benefit supplement, the federal government's contribution to the federal, provincial and territorial program to help protect benefits for low-income parents in the workforce.

As of July 2003, the government has introduced a Child Disability Benefit as an additional supplement to the Child Tax Benefit for low and moderate income families. The Child Disability Benefit is a non-taxable benefit paid for children who meet the eligibility for the disability tax credit (see 2.5.1).

Each province has additional programs and benefits available to aid lower-income families with the cost of raising children under age 18.

2.3.2 Child care expenses

For two-parent families, child care expenses can be deducted, usually by the spouse with the lower income, subject to various limitations. (The assumption is that the lower-income spouse would otherwise stay home with the children.) Single parents can deduct child care expenses from their own income, subject to the same limitations. Common-law and same-sex couples who meet certain criteria are treated the same as spouses for purposes of calculating child care expenses (as well as for all other tax purposes—see 2.2.1).

Single parents who are full-time students and two-parent families where both parents are full-time students can also deduct their child care expenses. A reduced child care expense deduction is available to part-time students.

You can claim child care expenses for your child or your spouse's child. You can also claim them for a child who was dependent on you or your spouse and whose net income in 2004 is less than $8,012.

Child care expenses include baby-sitting, day nursery services, day camps, boarding schools and camps.

For child care expenses to be claimed, they have to have been made to allow you or your spouse to work, carry on business, attend school "full-time" or "part-time" or carry on grant-funded research.

> Working parents and students—claim your child care expenses.

"Full-time" attendance at school for these purposes means that you must be enrolled in a secondary or post-secondary program that is at least three consecutive weeks long and requires you to spend at least 10 hours per week on course work. You are attending school "part-time" if the program lasts at least three consecutive weeks and involves at least 12 hours per month on course work.

Assuming you are a single parent or the lower-income spouse, the deduction for child care expenses is limited to $7,000 times the number of your children who are under seven at the end of the year, plus $4,000 times the number of children seven and over but under 17. It is also limited to two-thirds of your "earned income" (basically salary and business income).

Where a child, at any age, has a severe and prolonged mental or physical impairment for which the disability credit can be claimed (see 2.5.1), special rules allow a maximum deduction of $10,000. If the child is older than 16, but has a less severe mental or physical infirmity that is not eligible for purposes of the disability tax credit, you are entitled to the same $4,000 deduction as that allowed for children aged seven to 16.

In other circumstances, child care expenses are subject to monthly or weekly limits of $175 per child under seven, $100 per child aged seven to 16, and $250 per child eligible for the disability tax credit.

These limits apply to single parents and two-parent families where both parents are attending school. In these cases, child care expenses are deductible against your actual net income up to the applicable child care deduction limit for each week that the single parent or both parents are attending school full-time.

For part-time students, the child care expense deduction is limited to the same amounts for each month for which the part-time education credit (see 2.4) is claimed. If you have a working spouse, the deduction is also limited to two-thirds of his or her earned income.

The deduction is based on when the services are provided rather than when the amounts are paid, so prepaying in December does not give you the deduction a year earlier.

Payments to a boarding school or camp are subject to the same limits for each week that the child attends the school or camp.

> Mary and Adam are married and have two children under seven. Mary earns $120,000 and Adam earns $28,000. They pay $12,000 in 2004 to a nanny to take care of their children while they are working.
>
> Adam must be the one to claim the expenses, since he is the lower-income spouse. His deduction is the least of: (a) the amount paid—$12,000; (b) $7,000 per child—$14,000; and (c) two-thirds of his earned income—$18,667. He can therefore claim $12,000 as a deduction against his $28,000 of employment income. This will reduce his tax bill by about $2,880.
>
> If Mary was a single parent, she could claim the same amount as a deduction against her own income of $120,000 and reduce her tax bill by about $5,400.

There are special circumstances where the lower-income spouse is not expected to care for the children. These are: where the spouse is disabled; in prison or hospital; confined to bed or a wheelchair, for at least two weeks; attending full-time high school or post-secondary school; or where the spouses have separated. In such cases, the higher-income spouse can claim the deduction up to the above limits for each week that the condition continues.

The tax treatment of child care expenses for Québec purposes is discussed at 17.2.2.

2.4 Students

Tuition fees qualify for a 16% federal credit if you pay them for yourself. Tuition fees paid for your child or other person cannot be claimed by you, subject to the transfer rules discussed below.

To be eligible for a credit, the fees must be paid to a Canadian university, college or other post-secondary educational institution, or to an institution certified by the Ministry of Human Resources Development. Fees paid to post-secondary institutions in other countries may qualify as well. Any fees you claim must total more than $100 per institution.

Along with admission fees, eligible tuition fees include library and lab charges, examination fees, application fees, mandatory computer service fees, charges for certificates and diplomas, and the cost of books included in the fees for a correspondence course. Also eligible are mandatory ancillary fees for health services, athletics and various other services (but not student association fees, fees covering goods of value that you retain, or ancillary fees at institutions sanctioned by the Ministry of Human Resources Development).

Fees paid to private schools for grade-school or high-school education will not entitle you to a federal tax credit. However, religious private schools may be able to provide a tax receipt for some of your tuition fees, treating that amount as a charitable donation (see 8.1) made toward the school's religious instruction.

As a separate credit from the tuition fees, you are entitled to a further federal education tax credit of $64 (federal) for each month you are in full-time attendance at a post-secondary educational institution.

For part-time post-secondary students, the education amount is about $19 per month that you attend an eligible program at least three consecutive weeks long and involving at least 12 hours of course work per month. Students with disabilities may qualify for the full $64 per month amount even if they attend the institution only part-time.

For 2004 and later years, you can claim the education tax credit if you pursue post-secondary education that is related to your employment, as long as you are not reimbursed by your employer for any of the costs of the education.

If you are not able to use your tuition and education credits (because you have no tax to pay), up to $800 in federal credits for the two combined may normally be transferred to your spouse or to a parent or grandparent. Alternatively, you can carry forward any unused and untransferred tuition and education amounts and claim them against your taxable income in any later year. Note, however, that such amounts carried forward cannot be transferred—only the student can claim them in a later year.

Students and former students can claim a 16% non-refundable federal tax credit on their interest paid on student loans under the *Canada Student Loans Act*, the *Canada Student Financial Assistance Act*, or equivalent provincial programs. The credit is available for interest paid in the year or any of the five preceding years. Although the credit is not transferable, it can be carried forward for up to five years.

> Take advantage of the tax credit for interest paid on student loans.

Full-time students who are single parents, or who are married and both parents attend school, and part-time students may be able to deduct child care expenses paid to attend school; if you are the working spouse of a full-time student, you may be able to deduct them on your own return (see 2.3.2). In certain cases, students may also be able to deduct their moving expenses (see 13.1.2)

Students can also withdraw funds from their RRSPs (within limits) to help finance their education—see 3.3.7.

If you are a student who lives in Québec, see 17.2.4.

2.5 People with disabilities

2.5.1 Disability credit

If you suffer from a severe and prolonged mental or physical impairment, you get an additional federal credit of $1,038. Depending on the nature of the impairment, your status must be certified by a medical doctor, an optometrist, an audiologist, an occupational therapist or a psychologist.

To qualify as having a severe and prolonged impairment, your ability to perform a "basic activity of daily living" must be "markedly restricted", and the impairment must have lasted or be expected to last for at least a year. People who must undergo therapy (e.g., dialysis) at least three times a week for an average of 14 or more hours of therapy in order to sustain their vital functions are also eligible for the credit.

The *Income Tax Act* has specific definitions to determine whether you qualify. The rules can be found on the CRA's disability credit certificate, Form T2201. If you have a disability and reside in Québec, see also 17.2.11.

> If the CRA challenges your disability claim, consider objecting.

It is often difficult to determine whether one qualifies or not, and the Tax Court of Canada has issued a slew of decisions interpreting these rules. In some cases, the Court has found the CRA's view to be incorrect. Therefore, if you believe you fit within the Income Tax Act's definition of disabled, you should consider pursuing your claim if it is denied.

If you have a dependent relative who qualifies for the disability credit but does not earn enough income to be able to use all of it, the dependant's unused credit can be transferred to your return. For this purpose, eligible dependants include your spouse, child, grandchild, parent, grandparent, sibling, aunt, uncle, niece or nephew.

Additional assistance is available for families caring for children with severe disabilities in the form of a supplementary credit of up to $605. This amount is reduced by child care expenses (see 2.3.2) and attendant care expenses (see 2.5.4) over $2,216 claimed for the child.

Low and moderate income families caring for children eligible for the disability tax credit may also qualify to receive payments under the Child Disability Benefit program (see 2.3.1).

If you support a dependent child age 18 or over who has a disability, you can claim an additional federal credit of $605. This credit is reduced by 16% of your infirm dependant's income over $5,368 and is thus reduced to zero if the dependant's income is more than $9,152.

You may also be able to claim a portion of your medical expenses for the medical expense credit (see 2.7.1) and for the refundable medical expense supplement (see 2.7.1).

2.5.2 Disability supports deduction

If you have a disability, you can deduct some or all of the costs of disability supports needed to allow you to earn employment income or pursue your education, unless the costs have been reimbursed by a non-taxable payment (such as an insurance payment). New for 2004 and later years, the disability supports deduction replaces the more narrowly targetted deduction for attendant care expenses that was allowed in earlier years.

The disability supports deduction is limited to your "earned income" (basically salary and business income), plus, if you attend school, the lesser of your income from other sources (to a maximum of $15,000) and $375 per week of school attendance.

Eligible disability supports expenses include amounts paid for sign-language interpretation services, real-time captioning services, and teletypewriters that allow deaf or mute people to use telephones, speech synthesizers and equipment that allows blind people to use computers or read print. Certain other expenses are eligible for the deduction, but only if the need for the items or services is certified by a medical practitioner. These expenses include the costs of note-taking services, tutoring services, talking textbooks and attendant care services provided in Canada.

> Persons with disabilities — weigh the benefits of deducting disability supports expenses or claiming the costs for purposes of the medical expense credit.

As an alternative, disability supports expenses can generally be claimed for purposes of the medical expense credit (see 2.7.1), whether or not you are earning income or attending school. In some cases, it may be more beneficial to claim these costs as medical expenses on your own or your spouse's tax return. To determine which option generates greater tax savings, calculate and compare the net tax results of claiming these costs through the disability supports deduction versus the medical expense credit.

2.5.3 RRSP withdrawals under the Home Buyers' Plan

Under the Home Buyers' Plan (see 3.3.6), you can withdraw up to $20,000 as a loan from your RRSP to buy or build a home and not pay tax on the amount as long as you repay it over 15 years beginning in the second year following the year of withdrawal. Since the Plan was originally intended to help first-time home buyers, you are generally ineligible if you owned a home in any of the five calendar years up to and including the current calendar year.

However, the five-year qualifying period under the Home Buyers' Plan does not apply to persons with disabilities and their relatives if the new home is more accessible to or better suited to the personal needs and care of a person with a disability who will reside there.

See 3.3.6 for a more detailed discussion of the pros and cons of participating in the Home Buyers' Plan.

2.5.4 Caregivers credit

A tax credit of up to $605 is available for caregivers who provide in-home care for elderly or infirm relatives who live with them in the same self-contained home. The credit is reduced if the infirm relative's income is between $12,921 and $16,705 and is not available if the relative's income exceeds $16,705. You cannot claim the caregiver credit if you claim the eligible dependant or other dependant tax credits (see 2.2.1) in respect of the care recipient.

2.6 Marital breakdown — Child and spousal support payments

While marriage breakdown is often an occasion for bitter disputes, you and your spouse (through your lawyers, if necessary) should co-operate to minimize your joint tax bill and share the resulting savings.

If you're separating, co-operate to minimize your joint tax bill.

A new system for taxing child support payments took effect for federal and Québec tax purposes was introduced in May 1997. Although the new system was designed to address the widespread perception that the former system was unfair to custodial parents, many divorced or separated couples with child support arrangements may be worse off under the new system than they would have been under the old system.

Under the current rules, child support paid under orders or agreements made or varied after April 30, 1997 is not taxed as income to the recipient, or deducted from income by the paying parent.

Spousal support payments are deductible to the payer and taxable to the recipient if they meet a number of well-defined and strict criteria.

Child support paid under arrangements reached before May 1, 1997 are treated the same way as spousal support payments. If you are a party in a separation or divorce agreement entered into before May 1, 1997, you should aim to preserve your ability to use the former system for child support payments where practical. The new system generally does not apply to court orders made before May 1, 1997 unless a new court order or agreement made after that date changes the amount of child support payable (or unless you and your spouse jointly elect to have the new rules apply).

> Aim to preserve pre-May 1, 1997 child support arrangements where practical.

To be deductible, the spousal support payments and child support paid under pre May-1997 arrangements must be an *allowance*, which has been established in advance as a recurring payment. The amounts payable must be predetermined. (Amounts that are required to be adjusted for inflation can still be considered predetermined.)

The further requirements are:

- the allowance must be paid under a written agreement or under a decree, order or judgment of a competent tribunal; and
- it must be payable on a periodic basis for the maintenance of the recipient (your spouse or ex-spouse) and/or the children of the marriage; and
- you must be living apart from your spouse or ex-spouse, because of the breakdown of your marriage, at the time the payment is made.

Payments to former common-law spouses may be deducted on the same basis, where the recipient is an individual who cohabited with you "in a conjugal relationship" or you are the natural parent of that person's child.

Note that the "periodic basis" requirement excludes one-time payments and transfers of property in settlement of rights of the marriage.

Payments made directly to third parties, rather than to your spouse or ex-spouse, are allowed in limited circumstances. Such payments can include medical bills, tuition fees and mortgage payments for your spouse or ex-spouse's home. Among other requirements, the court order or written separation agreement must specifically provide for the payments and must specifically provide that the relevant tax rules will apply, to make the payments deductible to you and taxable to your spouse or ex-spouse.

In general, you may deduct payments made before obtaining a court order or signing a written separation agreement, provided the order or agreement is signed by the end of the year following the year in which the payment is made, and that it specifically provides that the amounts paid earlier are to be considered as paid and received pursuant to the agreement.

You may also deduct legal costs to establish or enforce a right to child or spousal support, or to obtain an increase in child or spousal support amounts.

Spousal or child support paid to a non-resident of Canada is deductible if the above criteria are met.

If you receive a lump-sum spousal or child support payment over $3,000 relating to prior years, you may ask the CRA to determine whether it is more advantageous to you to recalculate the tax on that income as if you received it in those prior years. This measure is intended to relieve the higher tax liability that may result if the entire lump-sum is taxed in the year of receipt, rather than year by year as the right to receive the payments arose. (Certain employment-related payments also qualify for this relief—see 3.4.1.)

2.7   Other commonly available credits

2.7.1   Medical expenses

Medical expenses over a certain threshold entitle you to a tax credit. The threshold is 3% of your net income, or, if your net income exceeds $60,464, a flat $1,813. All qualifying medical expenses above this amount give rise to a 16% federal credit (if you live in Québec, see also 17.2.10).

> **Example**
> Alison's net income is $30,000. She spends $1,500 on qualifying medical expenses in 2004. Given that 3% of Alison's net income is $900, the remaining $600 qualifies for the medical expense credit. The federal credit is 16% of that, or $96.

Low-income workers with higher than average eligible medical expenses and earned income of at least $2,809 can also claim the "medical expense supplement". This refundable tax credit is equal to the lesser of $562 and 25% of the amount eligible for the credit. The supplement is reduced by 5% of family net income over $21,301.

Claiming the supplement will not affect your ability to claim the medical expense credit.

You can claim expenses for yourself, your spouse and any close relative who is dependent on you for support, including your child, grandchild, parent, grandparent, brother, sister, uncle, aunt, niece or nephew; or any of those relatives of your spouse (including a qualifying common-law spouse as outlined in 2.2.1). Except for your or your spouse's child or grandchild, the person must be resident in Canada.

Starting in 2004, medical expense claims made on behalf of dependent minor children are pooled with those of you and your spouse for purposes of the medical expense threshold of 3% of your net income and $1,813, whichever is less.

For amounts paid on behalf of any other close relative dependent on you for support, the medical expenses you can claim for 2004 and later years is the amount that exceeds the lesser of 3% of the dependant's net income and $1,813. The maximum amount you can claim on behalf of dependent relatives (other than minor children) is $5,000.

The list of qualifying medical expenses is very long, and you should refer to the CRA's Interpretation Bulletin IT-519R2 (see 2.10) if you need specific details. The list includes:

- payments to medical practitioners, dentists and registered nurses, hospital fees not covered by public health insurance, and diagnostic procedures
- prescription drugs
- institutional care (e.g., nursing home)
- the care and supervision of persons with severe and prolonged disabilities living in a group home
- guide dogs (both purchase cost and upkeep cost)
- eyeglasses, hearing aids and dentures
- costs of moving to accessible housing, home renovations and driveway alterations required for someone with a mobility impairment
- cost of training courses related to the care of the disabled relative
- sign language interpreter fee
- cost of disability supports not claimed for purposes of the disability supports deduction (see 2.5.2)
- a long list of specific devices, ranging from crutches to insulin needles, wheelchair lifts, speech synthesizers, visual fire alarm indicators and TDD devices for the deaf.

Since self-employed individuals are allowed to deduct premiums to a drug or dental plan (see 11.2.11), these premiums are not eligible for the medical expense credit.

Combine your family's medical expenses on one return.

Because of the threshold of 3% of net income, you should combine all of the family's medical expenses on one return. It is normally better for the lower-income spouse to make the claim, provided that spouse has enough tax to pay to use up the credit, since the 3% threshold will be smaller. On the other hand, the credit might be slightly more valuable to a high-income spouse because it will reduce the application of high-income provincial surtaxes levied in some provinces (see 2.1.3).

Choose your own 12-month period for medical expense claims.

When claiming medical expenses, you can pick any 12-month period ending in the year. If, for example, you made no claim for 2003, and you have large medical expense bills in February 2003, January 2004, and November 2004, you might be better off to use January 2004 as the end of your 12-month period, claim the February 2003 and January 2004 expenses for 2004, and leave the November 2004 expenses to be claimed on your 2005 return.

Plan for the timing of your family's medical expense payments.

You can also plan for the timing of medical expenses, since they are based on when they are *paid*. If you are using a December end for the 12-month period, and you have pending expenses (perhaps for medical equipment purchases or large dental bills) that are due early in the new year, consider prepaying them so that you can claim them one year earlier.

2.7.2 Political contributions

If you are interested in the greatest "bang for your buck", consider a contribution to your favourite federal political party or election candidate. Contributions to federal political parties and to candidates in federal election campaigns entitle you to a credit, which is federal only. A donation of $400 will cost you only $100.

Take advantage of Canada's generous tax break for political contributions.

To encourage small political donations by many people, the federal credit is most generous at the lowest levels. For 2004 and later years, the credit is 75% for the first $400 of donation; 50% for the next $350; and 33.33% for the next $525. There is no additional credit for donations beyond $1,275.

Example
Jacquelin contributes $500 to a federal political party in 2004. Jacquelin's political contribution credit for 2004 will be 75% on the first $400 ($350) plus 50% on the next $100 ($50), for a total of $450. There is no reduction in provincial tax resulting from this credit.

In addition, many of the provinces have their own credits for contributions to provincial parties and candidates. The Québec credit for political donations is discussed at 17.2.12.

Note that contributions to a candidate in a federal leadership campaign are not eligible for the credit. However, political parties sometimes set up funds that allow you to contribute to the party itself and direct that your contribution be used to support a particular leadership candidate.

2.7.3 Other credits

There are a number of other credits with a provincial equivalent available when computing "basic federal tax" (and also reducing provincial taxes and surtaxes, as discussed in 2.1.2). These include the credit for donations to registered charities (see 8.1), pension income (see 20.3.5) and age credits (see 20.3.4) and the dividend tax credit (see 7.1.2).

Other federal-only credits include the investment tax credit, which is an incentive for those carrying on business to invest in particular regions or sectors of the economy (see 11.2.14) and the foreign tax credit (also available in Québec), which offsets the impact of foreign tax paid on one's income from a foreign source, to reduce double taxation.

2.8 Other commonly available deductions

2.8.1 Legal fees

Whether or not you can deduct legal fees you have paid depends on why you paid them.

Legal fees are generally deductible if they are paid for the purpose of earning income from business or property. Legal fees to acquire or preserve a capital asset are normally not deductible, though there are a number of exceptions.

Legal fees associated with an objection or appeal of your income tax assessment (see 9.5) are deductible. This includes the costs of negotiations with CRA officials prior to filing a formal Notice of Objection. The fees are also deductible if you are appealing a Québec income tax assessment or an income tax assessment of a foreign government, or an Employment Insurance or Canada/Québec Pension Plan decision.

Legal fees to collect unpaid salary or wages owed to you by your employer or former employer are deductible.

Legal fees generally can be deducted where they are incurred to obtain a "retiring allowance" (including severance pay) or a pension benefit (see 10.9.5), but only up to a limit of your income from those sources (in the current year or past years).

Finally, you may deduct legal costs to establish or enforce a right to child or spousal support, to obtain an increase in child or spousal support amounts, or to make child support non-taxable. (See 2.6; see also 17.2.8 if you live in Québec.)

2.8.2 Northern residents

If you live in northern Canada for not less than six consecutive months beginning or ending in a year, a special deduction is available to help offset the higher costs of living and the hardship and isolation relative to the more populated parts of the country. The deduction is limited to the lesser of 20% of your net income and, if you live in the "prescribed northern zone", up to $15 per day ($5,475 per year). If you live somewhat further south, in the "prescribed intermediate zone", you can only claim half as much. As well, if your employer pays the cost of travel for you and your family (e.g., an annual trip to southern Canada), a deduction is available to offset part or all of the taxable benefit that is thereby included in your income — see 10.9.8. A similar deduction is available for Québec tax purposes if you live in northern Québec.

2.8.3 Other deductions

Some other common deductions are covered in other chapters. See, for example, 3.1.3 (contributions to RRSPs), 6.2.3 (allowable business investment losses), 6.3 (capital gains deduction), 7.2.3 (interest paid), 10.9 (deductions available to employees) and 13.1 (moving expenses). Some of the deductions relating to self-employment (carrying on business) are discussed in Chapter 11.

2.9 Canada/Québec Pension Plan Contributions, Employment Insurance and GST

2.9.1 CPP/QPP contributions and EI premiums

A federal credit of 16% of all Canada (or Québec) Pension Plan (CPP/QPP) contributions and Employment Insurance (EI) premiums is available, effectively giving you back about 24% of these amounts when the equivalent provincial credit is factored in. If you are employed, these amounts are normally taken off your pay cheque at source by your employer.

If you are self-employed, you will normally have to calculate and remit both the employer and employee portions of CPP/QPP (but not Employment Insurance) contributions on your net self-employment income. Self-employed individuals may deduct the employer's portion — see 11.2.3.

2.9.2 EI clawback

If you receive Employment Insurance benefits and your net income exceeds a certain threshold, a portion of your benefits received during the year will be taxed back through a special tax, commonly called a "clawback", paid through your income tax return.

The clawback applies if your net income exceeds $48,750. You must repay $30 for each $100 of net income over your threshold, up to a maximum of 100% of the benefits received. Benefits that are not clawed back are taxed as regular income.

The clawback does not apply if you are receiving EI benefits for the first time in the last 10 years or if you are receiving only maternity, parental, or sickness benefits.

2.9.3 GST credit

The GST credit is aimed at low-income individuals and families. It is designed to offset the GST paid by consumers on most goods and services. As of July 2004, the credit is $224 per adult and $118 per child in the family annually, reduced by 5 cents for each dollar that family net income exceeds $29,123. The credit is generally prepaid in quarterly instalments to qualifying families, based on their previous year's income. If your GST credit is less than $100, you should receive it in one lump-sum payment in July.

An extra GST credit supplement of up to $118 is available if you are single, including a single parent, separated, widowed or divorced. The GST credit supplement is the lesser of $118 or 2% of net income over $7,253. The total of the GST credit and the supplement are reduced by 5 cents for each dollar of income over $29,123.

Many provinces also have sales tax credits for low-income taxpayers. For the Québec credit, which parallels the GST credit, see 17.2.13.

2.9.4 GST rebates

In addition to the GST credit described in 2.9.3, certain employees and members of partnerships can claim a GST rebate on their income tax returns. The rebate is available to employees who claim income tax deductions relating to their employment expenses, and partners who claim deductions on expenses they incur outside the partnership to earn partnership income. (See 10.10, 11.2.4 and 11.3.7 for more details; see also 17.2.13 if you live in Québec.)

Non-residents are eligible for a full refund of the 7% GST and the 15% Harmonized Sales Tax (HST—see 11.2.5) paid on most goods they take back with them (but not alcohol and tobacco), as well as hotel or other short-term accommodation while in Canada. The rebate can only be claimed on a minimum of $200 in taxable purchases of goods and accommodation.

Your visitors should keep receipts and apply for a refund directly from the CRA. They can also claim their refunds at duty-free stores at many land border points (all the airport duty-free shops have opted out of the refund program, not being able to handle the volume). Telephone 1-800-668-4748 (within Canada) or (902) 432-5608 (outside Canada) for information on this Visitors' Rebate Program.

To claim a refund of tax paid on eligible goods, proof of export is required. Receipts for eligible goods must be validated by Canada Customs officers or participating land-border duty-free staff.

The refund does not apply to purchases of services consumed in Canada, such as restaurant meals, gas or haircuts.

Many provinces also provide a refund of provincial sales tax on goods taken out of the province.

2.10 References

The following publications can be obtained (in person or by telephone request) from your nearest CRA Tax Services Office. Some of the CRA's guides, brochures and forms are also available from the CRA's Internet site at *www.cra-arc.gc.ca*.

Interpretation Bulletin IT-91R4, "Employment at Special Work Sites or Remote Work Locations"
Interpretation Bulletin IT-99R5, "Legal and accounting fees"
Interpretation Bulletin IT-495R2, "Child care expenses"
Interpretation Bulletin IT-513R, "Personal tax credits"
Interpretation Bulletin IT-515R2, "Education tax credit"
Interpretation Bulletin IT-516R2, "Tuition tax credit"
Interpretation Bulletin IT-519R2, "Medical expense and disability tax credits and attendant care expense deduction"
Interpretation Bulletin IT-523, "Order of provisions applicable in computing an individual's taxable income and tax payable"
Interpretation Bulletin IT-530R, "Support Payments"
Information Circular 75-2R7, "Contributions to a registered party, a registered association or to a candidate at a federal election"
Guide, "GST/HST Credit"
Guide, "Northern residents deductions — Places in prescribed zones"
Guide, "Students and Income Tax"
Guide, "Support Payments"
Guide, "Tax Refund for Visitors to Canada"
Guide, "Information Concerning People with Disabilities"
Guide, "Your Canada Child Tax Benefit"
Form GST 176, "Application for Visitor Tax Refund"
Form T778, "Child care expenses deduction for 20___"
Form T929, "Attendant care expenses"
Form T1157, "Election for child support payments"

Form T1158, "Registration of family support payments"

Form T1198, "Statement of qualifying retroactive lump-sum payment"

Form T2201, "Disability tax credit certificate"

Form T2202, "Education amount certificate"

Form T2202A, "Tuition and education amounts certificate"

Form T2222, "Northern residents deductions"

RRSPs and other tax deferral plans

- Consider a self-directed RRSP for greater flexibility (3.1.6)
- Think about transferring shares that you already own to your self-directed RRSP (3.1.6)
- Think about using your RRSP to shelter future gains on high-growth private company shares (3.1.6)
- Think about holding your own mortgage through your RRSP (3.1.6)
- Think about boosting your self-directed RRSP's foreign content (3.1.7)
- Contribute as much as you can to an RRSP (3.1.9)
- Contribute early in the year instead of the following February (3.1.9)
- Think twice before borrowing funds to contribute to your RRSP (3.1.9)
- Withdraw funds from your RRSP in low-income years (3.2.1)
- Contribute to your spouse's (or common-law spouse's) RRSP if your spouse's projected income on retirement will be lower (3.3.1)
- Make spousal RRSP contributions in December instead of the following February (3.3.1)
- Transfer pension commuted value, retiring allowances or severance pay to your RRSP (3.3.2)
- Top up your RRSP with a non-deductible $2,000 overcontribution (3.3.4)
- Consider shares of a labour-sponsored venture capital corporation for your RRSP (3.3.5)
- Consider Home Buyers' Plan withdrawals to buy or build your first home (but be sure to weigh the loss of RRSP growth) (3.3.6)
- Consider withdrawing RRSP funds under the Lifelong Learning Plan to help pay for training or post-secondary education programs (3.3.7)
- Ask the CRA to recalculate your prior-year tax liability on retroactive lump-sum pension and other payments (3.4.1)
- Consider contributing to your RRSP instead of a money-purchase RPP (3.4.1)
- Find out about the vesting of your pension benefits, especially before making a career change (3.4.1)
- Weigh the advantages of establishing an "individual pension plan" (3.4.2)

Deferred income plans, particularly RRSPs and registered pension plans, are the most widely-used tax shelters in Canada. Put simply, almost everyone should have one.

The concept of deferred income plans is quite simple, although the particular rules can get rather complex. In this chapter, we'll take you through the basic rules, so you understand the system in general. We also discuss the options you have and steps you can take for tax planning.

The rules are essentially the same for Québec tax purposes.

3.1   Registered retirement savings plans—RRSPs

3.1.1   What is an RRSP?

You hear a lot about RRSPs every February, when the annual contribution deadline approaches. Although the acronym stands for "registered retirement savings plan," an RRSP does not necessarily have anything to do with retirement. It can be used simply as a tax deferral tool.

The concept behind an RRSP is quite simple. If you agree to put some of your salary or self-employment income away and not have immediate access to it, the tax system will tax that income—along with all the interest and other income it earns—when it is *received* rather than when it is *earned*.

> **Example**
>
> If you earn $60,000, you pay tax on $60,000.
>
> Suppose you earn $60,000 but you put $2,000 of that into an RRSP. You will be taxed on only $58,000—the amount you have *received*.
>
> If, some years later, the $2,000 you put away has grown (in a tax-free environment) to $3,000, you can take the $3,000 out of your RRSP, and it will be taxed (added to your income) at that point. Again, the original $2,000, now grown to $3,000, is being taxed in the year it is *received* rather than when it was *earned*.

The rules governing RRSPs are more complex than the above example indicates, of course. The amount you can contribute to an RRSP is limited in various ways.

3.1.2   How do you set up an RRSP?

An RRSP can be set up easily at almost any bank or trust company or through a stockbroker, life insurance agent, mutual fund company or mutual fund distributor. Basically, you just fill out a form and contribute money to the plan. Some institutions will give you your official tax receipt immediately; others will mail it to you later, in time for you to file it with your tax return.

3.1.3 How much can you contribute?

Contributions to an RRSP are deductible for any given year if they are contributed in *the year* or *within 60 days after the end of the year*. So if you contribute by March 1, 2005, you can get a deduction for your 2004 tax return (and any resulting refund will come sometime in the spring of 2005 after you have filed your return).

There are three factors that limit the amount you can contribute to an RRSP: a dollar limit, which is $15,500 for 2004; a percentage (18%) of the previous year's "earned income"; and your "pension adjustment". We'll look at each of these in turn.

Dollar limit

The RRSP contribution limit rose to $15,500 in 2004 (from $14,500). The limit is scheduled to rise to $16,500 for 2005 and $18,000 for 2006, after which the limit will be indexed.

Percentage of previous year's earned income

The annual deduction (subject to the $15,500 dollar limit and pension adjustment) is limited to 18% of the *previous* year's earned income. That is, 18% of your 2003 earned income will be used to determine your 2004 contribution (made by March 1, 2005).

"Earned income" for most employees is the same as "salary"—the gross amount of salary, before deductions for income tax, EI, CPP, etc., which are withheld at source. "Earned income" includes business income, if you are self-employed or are an active partner in a business (see 16.2.4). It also includes:

- research grants, net of deductible related expenses
- royalties from works or inventions that you wrote or invented
- taxable spousal and child support received (see 2.6)
- net rental income from real estate
- disability pension income received under the CPP/QPP.

Earned income is *reduced* by:

- deductible alimony, maintenance and child support you pay
- most deductible employment-related expenses, such as union dues and travelling expenses (but not pension plan contributions)
- rental losses.

Earned income does not include most investment income, such as interest or dividends, or capital gains. Nor does it include pension benefits, retiring allowances, severance pay, death benefits or amounts received from an RRSP, RRIF or deferred profit-sharing plan.

If your 2003 earned income was more than $86,111, your 2004 contribution will be limited to $15,500 (minus the pension adjustment as discussed below). Otherwise, you will be limited by the 18% factor.

Pension adjustment

Once you have calculated your maximum contribution limit as 18% of your previous year's earned income, subject to the dollar limits discussed above, you must subtract your pension adjustment, if any. This figure represents the deemed value of your pension earned for the previous year. In other words, the more that has been put aside (by you and your employer combined) towards your retirement pension, the less the *Income Tax Act* allows you to contribute to an RRSP.

If you are *not* a member of an employer's pension plan or deferred profit-sharing plan, your pension adjustment is zero, and you can contribute the full 18% of your previous year's earned income (subject to the annual $15,500 dollar limit).

Otherwise, your pension adjustment for 2004 should have appeared on your 2003 T4 slip, as well as on your Notice of Assessment received in the spring of 2004 following the filing of your 2003 return.

For "money-purchase" pension plans (see 3.4.1), the pension adjustment is the total contributions made to your pension by you and your employer combined. The same applies to deferred profit-sharing plans (see 3.5), except that the contributions are made only by your employer. For "defined benefit" pension plans, the pension adjustment is based on a calculation that takes into account the benefit you may receive on retirement based on the past year's employment.

In some situations, the calculation of your RRSP limit may also be reduced by a past service pension adjustment (PSPA). In general terms, a PSPA can arise when your pension benefits under a defined benefit pension plan are improved on a retroactive basis.

Example

Melanie is a chemical engineer who belongs to her employer's pension plan. Her 2003 earned income was $60,000. Her pension adjustment for 2004, as reported to her on her 2003 T4 slip and her 2003 assessment received from the CRA in mid-2004, is $3,200.

Before accounting for her pension adjustment, Melanie's contribution limit for 2004 is 18% of her 2003 earned income, to a maximum of $15,500. For 2003, 18% of her earned income is $10,800. From this amount she must deduct her pension adjustment of $3,200. Melanie may therefore contribute up to $7,600 to an RRSP by March 1, 2005 for a deduction on her 2004 tax return.

If you terminate your employment before retirement, you may be entitled to a pension adjustment reversal (PAR). The PAR is designed to give you back some of the RRSP contribution room lost due to pension adjustments (PA) while you were a member of a company pension plan.

If you were a member of a defined contribution plan or deferred profit-sharing plan, your PAR will be the total of all PAs reported by your employer since 1990 that have not yet "vested" (see 3.4.1). If you were a member of a defined benefit plan and you have not reported any PSPAs, your PAR will be equal to your total PAs since 1990 less the post-1989 portion of any lump sums paid to you or transferred to an RRSP or money-purchase pension plan (if you have reported any PSPAs, your PAR calculation will be more complex but, whatever your plan, your employer's pension plan administrator will figure it out for you). You will not be entitled to a PAR if you maintain any entitlement to periodic pension payments from the plan.

PARs increase RRSP room for the year of termination. If you have ended or will be ending company pension plan membership in 2004, you may want to encourage your employer to report your PAR shortly after your termination so you can make use of the related extra RRSP room as soon as possible. Your employer must report your PAR for your year of termination within 60 days of the end of the quarter in which termination occurred (or by January 31 of the following year if termination occurs in the fourth quarter).

Carry forward of unused deduction room and undeducted contributions

If in any year you contribute less than the maximum to an RRSP, you can "carry forward" the extra deduction room and make that much more contribution in any following year. You can also carry forward unused RRSP room created by a PAR. If you contribute an amount for a year but choose not to deduct the amount for that year, you can claim the deduction in any subsequent year (provided you still have contribution room).

> **Example**
>
> Melanie, from the example above, has $7,600 of contribution room for 2004. She chooses to contribute only $5,000 to an RRSP for the year.
>
> Melanie has unused RRSP contribution room of $2,600 to carry forward. As a result, she may increase her contribution by that amount in any following year. If Melanie's contribution limit for 2005 is again $7,600, she can contribute up to $10,200 for deduction in 2005.

You should carefully review your assessment from the CRA to make sure the contribution limit reported is correct, before relying on it. A wrong statement from the CRA will not entitle you to deduct a contribution you would otherwise be entitled to.

In some cases you might contribute more than you can actually deduct. We discuss overcontributions in 3.3.4.

3.1.4 What's your contribution worth?

What is your contribution worth in tax savings? It depends on your marginal tax rate. Tax rates and brackets vary among the provinces (see Appendix II), but they are approximately:

- 24% on income from $8,000 to $35,000
- 34% on income from $35,000 to $70,000
- 41% on income from $70,000 to $113,800
- 45% on income over $113,800

In the example above, if Melanie's taxable income (after other deductions) is between $35,000 and $70,000, her contribution of $5,000 to an RRSP will save her about 34% of that amount, or $1,700, in tax for 2004. For someone whose taxable income stays over $113,800 even after making the RRSP contribution, the same $5,000 contribution would be worth about $2,250. Clearly, RRSPs are more tax-effective to those with higher incomes.

You should keep the value of your deduction in mind and try to take maximum advantage of the carry-forward mechanism in claiming your RRSP deductions. In a low-income year, for example, it may be advantageous to make your maximum RRSP *contribution*, but to defer claiming the *deduction* until a later year when your income is taxed at a higher marginal rate.

3.1.5 What happens to the funds in the RRSP?

While your funds are in the RRSP, they are not subject to tax at all. No matter what amounts of interest, dividends, capital gains—or losses—result, there will be no tax effect until you withdraw the funds. (As we shall see in 20.4, you must close out the RRSP by the end of the year in which you turn 69, but even then the tax effects can be partially deferred.)

The effects of having income compound without tax are quite dramatic. Compare the following two situations: A, where you invest $5,000 of your salary in an RRSP for 10 or 20 years at 6%, and B, where you earn the same 6% but it is subject to tax. (The example assumes a 45% marginal tax rate.)

	2004	2014	2024
A. Invest $5,000 in an RRSP	$5,000	$8,954	$16,036
After withdrawal		$4,925	$8,820
B. Do not put $5,000 in an RRSP, so you are immediately taxed on the $5,000 as salary and taxed on the income it earns	$2,750	$3,805	$5,264

In case A, you pay 45% in tax when you withdraw the funds, but they have grown substantially in the meantime. After 20 years, your $5,000 is worth $8,820 *after* tax. In case B, since the annual 6% interest is taxed, you have only 3.3% to reinvest for compounding purposes. The fact that you can use the $5,264 (after 20 years) directly in case B, without having to pay 45% tax on it as in case A, doesn't come close to making up for the tax-free compounding of interest.

Of course, if you are paying non-deductible interest such as mortgage interest, that interest also effectively compounds on a pre-tax basis, and you might be better off to pay down your mortgage rather than contribute to an RRSP. In such a case, you can generally use all your unused RRSP contribution room by making and deducting a "catch-up" RRSP contribution in a later year, when you have the funds to contribute.

As we mentioned earlier, your RRSP can be invested in a number of different forms. The simplest, and usually lowest-paying, is a deposit account that pays interest monthly or twice a year. Many people invest instead in longer-term Guaranteed Investment Certificates (GICs) and term deposits. Equity mutual funds are popular as a method of indirectly investing RRSP funds in a number of different equity investments, but they can entail a higher level of risk. See 1.1.4 for tips on choosing investments and advice on developing an appropriate investment strategy.

3.1.6   Self-directed RRSPs

If you're a do-it-yourselfer who would like a wider range of investment choices and you're willing to take a little more risk with your funds, you can set up a self-directed RRSP and gain

> Consider a self-directed RRSP for greater flexibilty.

hands-on control over the investment of funds in your RRSP. This is normally done through a financial consultant with a brokerage firm or financial services institution, and is typically subject to an annual fee in the $100 to $150 range (plus normal commissions on any stock trades or mutual funds, where applicable). Some financial institutions offer a low- or no-fee self-directed plan—it pays to shop around to find the plan that's right for you.

With a self-directed plan, you decide what to invest in within your RRSP. There are restrictions—the system tries to ensure that your money, while not necessarily "safe," is at least invested in reasonable places. "Qualified investments" for an RRSP include:

- cash
- government, Crown corporation or municipal bonds
- GICs, term deposits and treasury bills (T-bills)

- certain government-insured mortgages
- shares or bonds of corporations listed on Canadian stock exchanges
- RRSP-eligible mutual funds and segregated funds
- shares listed on certain foreign stock exchanges, bonds of certain foreign governments and mutual funds and segregated funds invested in foreign markets (however, as discussed in 3.1.7, no more than 30% of an RRSP may be directly invested in foreign assets)
- certain small business shares.

The rules governing the details (e.g., which mortgages and small business shares are qualified investments) are extremely complex, and you should consult a professional adviser if you wish to do more with your self-directed RRSP than simply buy, say, T-bills and government bonds (which are generally regarded as good safe investments, incidentally). If you have the time to give it the attention it needs, a self-directed RRSP can prove to be much more rewarding in the long run. The control you will gain over investment decisions will diversify your risk and give you the flexibility to pursue a different range of investment opportunities—including some that are generally only possible through self-directed RRSPs, like strip bonds, mortgage-backed securities, index funds and other less common RRSP investments. If you only plan to invest in mutual funds and GICs, a self-directed RRSP may not be required; in this case, you may be better off using a regular plan to save on annual administration fees.

The broader range of investment options you may acquire with a self-directed RRSP comes with a higher level of risk. The financial markets are volatile, but they tend not to move in step with each other, so you should be able to minimize the level of overall risk in your portfolio through diversification—holding a mix of different types of investments (i.e., cash, fixed income and equities) and ensuring that at least a portion of them have fixed rates of return, such as GICs or strip bonds.

Your investment mix or asset allocation should also be a function of your age, family situation and risk tolerance. When determining your investment mix and allocating your assets, be sure to consider your total portfolio, and not just those investments inside your RRSP. See 1.1.4 for details on developing an appropriate investment strategy.

Consider contributing shares (or interest-bearing investments) that you already own to your self-directed RRSP in lieu of cash contributions. Shares in small businesses can be contributed in limited circumstances (for example, you must not be a controlling shareholder of the corporation). However, most shares and bonds of Canadian public corporations are fair game. If you have shares that you intend to hold for a long time, you can contribute them to your RRSP and get a tax deduction without any cash outlay.

> Think about transferring shares that you already own to your self-directed RRSP.

A transfer of investments to your RRSP can trigger a capital gain (see 6.2.1), since the transfer will be deemed to take place at fair market value. However, you are prohibited from claiming a capital loss (see 6.2.2) on the transfer of investments to your RRSP. Professional advice should be obtained before entering into this type of transaction.

If you have shares that have declined in value, you cannot transfer the shares to your RRSP to trigger a capital loss to use to offset any capital gains you may have realized—the tax law won't let you claim a capital loss on the transfer of investments to your RRSP.

However, you can sell the shares on the open market, contribute the proceeds in cash to your RRSP and, after 30 days, have your RRSP acquire a similar position. This strategy will permit you to trigger the capital loss on the shares, which you can apply against other taxable capital gains, while effectively transferring ownership of the shares to your RRSP so that any future growth will be tax-sheltered.

You can also swap investments owned outside your RRSP with assets inside your plan. Capital gains may still be realized on a swap if an investment held outside the plan has an unrealized capital gain. As noted, claims for capital losses on such transactions will be denied. For assets transferred out of an RRSP under a swap, no capital gains or losses will arise. Assets swapped must be equal in value at the time of the trade. Swaps can be an effective way to rebalance your investment portfolio.

Note that capital gains and dividends are effectively fully-taxed when withdrawn from an RRSP, since you're taxed on the total amount withdrawn. So if you contribute shares (or buy shares inside your RRSP), any capital gains and dividends will eventually be taxed at a higher rate than if you earned them directly (see 6.2.1 and 7.1.2). If you leave the funds in the RRSP for long enough, the deferral of tax and tax-free compounding of interest should more than make up for the tax rate differential, however. Consider holding fixed income investments inside your RRSP and equities outside your RRSP as part of your overall asset mix.

When considering investments within your RRSP, bear in mind the one major drawback of long-term investments such as five-year GICs. If you decide to withdraw the funds sooner for tax purposes (see 3.3.4), or to use the Home Buyers' Plan (see 3.3.6), you may find that you cannot get access to your investment.

Think about using your RRSP to shelter future gains on high-growth private company shares.

If you're a shareholder of a start-up company or a company that has high growth potential, you may want to consider owning part or all of the shares through your RRSP or transferring such shares to your RRSP early in the company's life cycle when the shares have relatively low value. Future gains on the shares will then be sheltered from tax inside the RRSP and you will be able to diversify your investment base by having your RRSP sell the shares and acquire a broader range of investments. (Bear in mind our comments above on capital gains and dividends.)

Think about holding your own mortgage through your RRSP.

It is even possible for you to arrange for your RRSP to hold your own mortgage—in other words, you put funds into your RRSP, receive a tax deduction, and lend the funds to yourself. This is not easy to do, however; the mortgage must be federally insured, and various other restrictions apply.

Investing in your own mortgage may make you feel good, but does not always make sense financially. Since the investment must be at the market rate, you may be no better off depending on the size of the mortgage, once all fees (legal, insurance, appraisal, etc.) are taken into account. As a general rule of thumb, to be a worthwhile investment, the mortgage's principal should be in the $50,000 to $100,000 range with a term of at least five years. Alternatively if you don't have that much cash in your RRSP, some financial institutions offer a program through which the mortgage is "shared" between your RRSP and your institution. You should also consider whether holding a mortgage in your RRSP is consistent with your overall investment strategy.

3.1.7 Self-directed RRSP investments in foreign properties

One advantage of a self-directed RRSP is that it allows you more scope to maximize your RRSP's foreign content. Through a self-directed RRSP, you can invest in shares listed on certain foreign stock exchanges, certain foreign government bonds and other foreign properties, within limits.

Generally, only 30% of the cost amount of all property held by your RRSP can be invested in foreign property. The calculation is performed at the end of each month. Foreign property values over the threshold are subject to a special tax of

> Think about boosting your self-directed RRSP's foreign content.

1% per month payable by the RRSP. The limit is generally based on the property's cost at the time of purchase, not its current market value. Your RRSP's administrator should monitor your RRSP's foreign content holdings and warn you if it is in danger of going off-side.

With the right investment mix, you can boost your self-directed RRSP's foreign content to a maximum of 50% of the cost amount of property held by it. To assist small businesses in obtaining equity financing, a special rule permits you to increase your RRSP's holdings of qualifying foreign property without penalty by $3 for every $1 that you invest in a certain Canadian small business corporation. That means a 6.67% holding of a qualifying small business property will enable you to increase your foreign property holdings by 20%, up to the 50% maximum.

However, if you own more than 10% of the shares of a small business, your RRSP's ability to invest in that business may be restricted or denied. Since these restrictions and the rules governing the types of small businesses that qualify are quite complex, you should consult your tax adviser if you are considering increasing your self-directed RRSP's foreign content through small business investments.

Another indirect way of further increasing your self-directed RRSP's foreign property content is to invest in a qualifying mutual fund trust. As long as the trust meets certain conditions, the mutual fund trust in which you invest can also invest up to 30% of the cost amount of its holdings in foreign property.

You can also boost your RRSP's participation in foreign markets by investing in:

- RRSP-eligible mutual funds and segregated funds that gain exposure to foreign markets through the use of derivatives such as options and futures
- shares of Canadian corporations with significant foreign operations
- shares of Canadian corporations that trade on foreign stock exchanges.

Don't let periodic downturns in foreign markets scare you away from increasing your RRSP's foreign holdings. As long as you plan to invest for the long term, maximizing your RRSP's foreign content will increase the diversity of your investment mix and thus reduce your overall investment risk.

3.1.8 RRSP fees

Administration, trustee and investment management and counselling fees related to your RRSP are not deductible. However, you can use funds already deposited in your RRSP without having to pay tax on the amount as you would if you withdrew the money for another purpose. Alternatively, you can pay these fees from funds outside your RRSP and the amount will not count as part of your contribution for the year.

If you have not used all of your available contribution room and you do not foresee doing so in the future, consider contributing the amount of the fees and paying them with funds inside the plan so you will get a regular RRSP deduction for that amount. On the other hand, if you have or will be maximizing your RRSP contributions, you will be better off paying the fees with other funds so you do not erode the amount of RRSP funds available to grow tax-free.

3.1.9 How to make the most of your RRSP

Contribute as much as you can to an RRSP.

If you have cash in the bank earning interest, even if you are young and not yet concerned about retirement, you should contribute as much as possible to an RRSP. The example we saw in 3.1.5 above shows how valuable it is to have your funds earning tax-free income.

Contribute early in the year instead of the following February.

If possible, you should contribute early, rather than waiting until the deadline. Your 2004 contribution, for example, may be made any time until March 1, 2005 if you intend to deduct it on your 2004 tax return. If you contribute at the beginning of 2004, all of the income earned for that extra year will accumulate tax-free. The effect of early contributions over several years will be dramatic. Do ensure, however, that you have enough contribution room before you commit your contribution for the year, and remember that each year's contribution will be limited to 18% of your previous year's earned income.

You can store up any unused RRSP contribution room if you can't afford to make a contribution now, and make your contribution and claim the deduction in later years.

If you're behind on your RRSP contributions, you might be thinking about taking out an RRSP loan. Generally, this strategy only makes sense if you can repay the borrowed funds within about a year, or if your income for the current year falls into a higher tax bracket than usual. Otherwise, the non-deductible interest that you will pay on the loan may negate the tax benefits of your contribution. Instead, consider making regular catch-up payments later when you have the funds to contribute.

> Think twice before borrowing funds to contribute to your RRSP.

If you have the cash and the contribution room, but do not want to claim a deduction in the current year because you are already in a low tax bracket, make the contribution but delay the deduction. As discussed in 3.1.3, you can claim the deduction in any later year. If you are confident of being in a higher tax bracket within the next year or so, this strategy can maximize the tax-free growth of funds while also maximizing your tax savings.

For cash-flow purposes, you may wish to set up a monthly transfer of a few hundred dollars from your regular bank account to your RRSP account. That will ensure steady contributions to the RRSP over the course of the year.

3.2   How do you get money out of an RRSP?

At any time, you may withdraw cash from your RRSP. The amount will be included in your income for that year and taxed as ordinary income, just as if it were salary, even if some of the value of the RRSP represents capital gains (which outside an RRSP are normally only partially taxed and, in some cases, could be entirely exempt).

A percentage to cover tax will be withheld at source by the financial institution and remitted to the CRA (and Revenu Québec if appropriate) on your behalf. For federal purposes, a withdrawal of up to $5,000 is subject to 10% withholding; over $5,000 and up to $15,000, 20%; and over $15,000, 30%. In Québec, a withdrawal of up to $5,000 is subject to a combined federal and Québec withholding of 21%; over $5,000 and up to $15,000, 30%; and over $15,000, 35%. You will then report the income and amount of tax withheld on your annual income tax return and either receive a refund or, if not enough tax was withheld, pay the difference.

The government will allow you to make tax-free RRSP withdrawals (within limits) if you use the funds for certain purposes, such as buying a new home (see 3.3.6) or financing training or post-secondary education for you or your spouse (see 3.3.7). Generally, you must repay the amount withdrawn under these plans over a certain amount of time or it will become taxable.

You must wind up your RRSP by the end of the year in which you turn 69. At any time before then, you can transfer your RRSP funds tax-free to an annuity, a registered retirement income fund or a life income fund. Your various options for maturing your RRSP are discussed in 20.4.

3.2.1 Early withdrawals—your RRSP as a tax averaging tool

As discussed in 3.1.5, the funds in your RRSP are not taxed until the year in which you withdraw the funds. As a result, RRSPs can be used as a tax averaging tool rather than just a mechanism for retirement saving. If you are still fairly young and not too worried about retirement income, you can withdraw funds from your RRSP whenever there is a tax advantage to doing so.

> Withdraw funds from your RRSP in low-income years.

Suppose you plan to take some time off to care for your young children, for example, or to go on an extended vacation or take up some other activity. During such years, where your employment income will be low, you can withdraw funds from your RRSP and perhaps pay tax at the low tax rate of about 24% (depending on your province) instead of the middle or high rates. The advantage of low-rate taxation will have to be balanced against the advantage of tax-free growth available by leaving the funds in the RRSP.

In an anticipated low-income year following a high-income year, you can even consider contributing in February, claiming a deduction (say at the middle rate of about 34%) for the previous year, and withdrawing the funds, to be taxed at the low (24%) rate.

You will need to plan around the withholding tax on RRSP withdrawals discussed in 3.2, however. You may be able to arrange withdrawals so that they incur the least possible withholding tax, leaving you with the use of the funds until you file your tax return the following April. Bear in mind, however, that you may have a tax liability to settle up on April 30 to the extent that your tax rate on the income exceeds the withholding tax rate.

3.3 Special RRSP rules

A number of rules deal with special situations with respect to RRSPs. We will refer to them only briefly; you should consult your professional adviser if you are in these situations.

3.3.1   Spousal plans

The RRSP rules allow you to contribute to an RRSP for your spouse, and claim the deduction yourself. Your total contributions (to your own and your spouse's plans) are still subject to your normal limits (18% of your previous year's earned income or $15,500 for 2004, minus any pension adjustment). The advantage is that your spouse will ultimately be the one who reports the income for tax purposes, when the funds are withdrawn on retirement or otherwise. If your spouse has less income than you either on retirement or at some earlier time (including, for example, due to expected maternity leave), this can result in significantly less tax on the income.

> Contribute to your spouse's (or common-law spouse's) RRSP if your spouse's projected income on retirement will be lower.

To prevent spousal RRSPs from being used for "income splitting" (see Chapter 5), the amount you contribute will be taxed back to you (rather than your spouse) to the extent any amount is withdrawn by your spouse in the year in which you contribute or *in the next two calendar years*. See 5.3.9.

> Make spousal RRSP contributions in December instead of the following February.

> **Example**
>
> Jon and Nancy are married. Jon contributes $5,000 to Nancy's RRSP in February 2005, and claims the deduction on his 2004 tax return.
>
> If Nancy withdraws the funds at any time up to the end of 2007, $5,000 of the amount withdrawn will be treated as Jon's income, not Nancy's. (If, however, Jon's contribution had been made in December 2004, this would only be the case until the end of 2006.)

This rule does not apply if the spouses are separated or divorced. We explore this rule in more detail at 5.3.9, in the chapter on Income Splitting.

If you are over 69 (the age at which you must mature your RRSP; see 20.4) and have "earned income" in the previous year, this will create new RRSP room for you in the current year. As long as your spouse is 69 or younger, you can still claim a deduction for a spousal RRSP contribution.

In general, there will be little effect on the real ownership of the funds under provincial law if you and your spouse separate or divorce. The rule in most provinces is that such funds will be pooled and shared between the spouses. There are rules in place to allow a tax-free division of RRSP funds in such situations.

3.3.2 Transfers to and from RRSPs

RRSPs can generally be transferred, with no tax consequences, to other RRSPs, registered retirement income funds (RRIF) or annuities, by simply filling out a form.

> Transfer pension commuted value, retiring allowances or severance pay to your RRSP.

Under pension legislation you may be prevented from immediately withdrawing pension benefits (known as the "commuted value") from your employer's plan on your departure from the company. This legislation is commonly referred to as "locking-in" legislation. Pension benefits subject to these rules may be transferred to a locked-in RRSP, also known as a "locked-in retirement account" (LIRA).

Locked-in RRSPs are essentially subject to the same restrictions on withdrawal of funds as the original pension plan. For example, depending on the applicable pension legislation, you cannot usually access the locked-in plan funds until you are within 10 years of the retirement date set out in the plan documents and, even then, you can only use the plan funds to purchase an annuity or a special RRIF that will provide a lifetime income, called a "life income fund" (LIF) or in some provinces, a "life retirement income fund" (LRIF) (see 20.4.5). With a LIF or an LRIF, you have more flexibility in deciding how to invest the funds.

Where the pension legislation permits a transfer from a registered pension plan to a locked-in RRSP, LIF or LRIF, there are generally no tax consequences to such transfers, though the tax rules may restrict the amounts that can be transferred from a "defined-benefit" pension plan.

Special rules allow a "retiring allowance" (which, as defined for tax purposes, includes severance pay and amounts received for wrongful dismissal as well as unused sick leave credits) to be transferred tax-free to an RRSP, rather than taxed as income when received. The amount that can be transferred is normally limited to $2,000 for each calendar year (or part year) of employment before 1996, plus $1,500 for years of employment before 1989 for which employer pension contributions or deferred profit sharing plan contributions have not vested.

3.3.3 Death

On death, a taxpayer is normally taxed on the entire amount of any RRSPs or RRIFs, except where the funds are left to the taxpayer's spouse or financially-dependent child, in which case they are included in the spouse's or child's income. See 22.4 for details.

3.3.4   Overcontributions

The RRSP contribution limits were discussed in 3.1.3. What happens if you contribute more than the maximum?

First, bear in mind that your financial institution will not prevent you from overcontributing. Your financial institution is not obliged to tell you how much you can or cannot contribute.

Second, any contributions over the maximum are non-deductible. However, once the funds are in your RRSP, they are taxable when withdrawn (whether on retirement or earlier), just like the funds that were deductible when you contributed them. Therefore, there is double taxation—once when you earn the income (and receive no deduction despite putting the funds into the RRSP), and once when you withdraw the funds from the RRSP.

Third, in certain rare circumstances, overcontributing might be valuable despite the double taxation, because of the beneficial effect of tax-free compounding (as illustrated in the table in 3.1.5). Also, you can often deduct an overcontribution in a later year as new contribution room is created.

There is a rule preventing excessive overcontributions. At any one time up to $2,000 can be overcontributed without penalty. Above the $2,000 level, the excess is subject to a penalty tax of 1% per month until the excess is withdrawn. If you are not generating new contribution room from year to year (e.g., because you have no earned income in the prior year), your overcontributions should be withdrawn within two to three years of making the contribution in order to avoid tax on the withdrawal.

The $2,000 figure is designed to catch those cases where you might have miscalculated your pension adjustment (see 3.1.3) and contributed a little too much. However, as long as you are certain about your pension adjustment, you can use the $2,000 deliberately if you wish. So if you are already contributing your maximum for 2004, consider making an additional contribution of up to $2,000 to further benefit from the compounding of tax-free growth.

> Top up your RRSP with a non-deductible $2,000 overcontribution.

3.3.5   Labour-sponsored venture capital corporation shares

In most provinces, a combined federal/provincial credit of 30% to 35% (depending on the province) is available for an investment of up to $5,000 per year in shares of a "labour-sponsored venture capital corporation", or LSVCC. In Newfoundland and Alberta, only the 15% federal credit is available.

Consider shares of a labour-sponsored venture capital corporation for your RRSP.

You can buy shares in a labour-sponsored venture capital corporation and contribute them to your RRSP. You can also generally have the shares bought directly by your self-directed RRSP (see 3.1.6), provided the RRSP uses "new" or previous contribution funds (but not earnings). Either way, you claim the credit on your personal income tax return.

When combined with the deduction for the RRSP contribution, a $5,000 investment in an LSVCC may cost you as little as $1,000 after tax (assuming a 15% provincial credit). Particularly if you are not otherwise making the maximum possible RRSP contribution, an investment in an LSVCC for your RRSP may be worth considering. Before taking the plunge and investing in an LSVCC, make sure you evaluate the relative merits from an investment perspective, as they are generally a higher risk and probably illiquid investment.

3.3.6 The Home Buyers' Plan

Under the Home Buyers' Plan, if you qualify, you are allowed to withdraw up to $20,000 as a loan from your RRSP to buy or build a home, without counting the withdrawal as income. You must then repay the loan, without interest, over 15 years starting in the second year after the year of the withdrawal.

Who may use the Home Buyers' Plan?

The Plan may only be used by what the government calls a "first-time buyer". You are not a "first-time buyer" if you have owned and lived in a home as a principal place of residence at any time during the five calendar years up to and including the current year. (For the current year, you can use the Plan up to 30 days after you acquire a home.) If your spouse has owned and lived in a home during that period, and you have inhabited that home during the marriage, you also do not qualify. (Remember that "spouse" includes a common-law spouse as outlined in 2.2.1.)

Past participation will not prevent you from participating in the Plan again, as long as you have fully repaid to your RRSP the amounts previously withdrawn and you have not owned a home in the past five calendar years (including the current year).

As noted in 2.5.3, the five-year qualification test is waived for disabled persons and their relatives for purchases of new homes that are more accessible to or better suited to the personal needs and care of a disabled person who will reside there.

How does the Plan work?

You can borrow (withdraw) up to $20,000 from your RRSP under the Plan. If you and your spouse each have RRSPs, you can thus borrow up to $40,000 between the two of you if you are taking joint ownership in the property. A qualifying home must be acquired before October 1 of the year following the year of the withdrawal. You must also begin or intend, not later than one year after its acquisition, to use the home as a principal place of residence. No tax will apply to the withdrawal.

When you withdraw the funds, you fill out Form T1036 (TP-935.1-V for Québec purposes), certifying that you have entered into a written agreement to purchase a home, and stating its address. Once you have done this, the financial institution will not withhold tax when it pays the funds to you.

Note that the Home Buyers' Plan does not give you any right to withdraw funds from your RRSP if you didn't already have that right. If your RRSP funds are invested in term deposits or other long-term obligations, you will still need to negotiate with the financial institution to have the funds released as cash. Similarly, if your RRSP funds are in your employer's group RRSP or a LIRA ("locked-in RRSP"), you may not be able to get them out.

Once you borrow the funds, you must normally complete the purchase by September 30 of the *following* year. (A one-year extension may be available if the deal falls through and you buy a replacement property.) If you withdraw less than the $20,000 maximum, you can in many cases withdraw a further amount up to the following January 31 and treat the total as one withdrawal.

The requirement to repay the funds begins in the second year following the withdrawal. You can opt to make any year's repayment up to 60 days after the end of the year.

Example

Olivia has $30,000 in her RRSP. She signs an agreement in September 2004 to purchase a new home. In November 2004 she completes Form T1036 and withdraws $15,000 from her RRSP. The purchase closes in January 2005.

No tax will be withheld from the $15,000 that Olivia withdraws, so she can use the full amount towards the home purchase. Since she withdrew the funds in 2004, Olivia must repay $1,000 (1/15 of the total) to her RRSP during 2006 or by March 1, 2007. If she repays only $600, she will have to include $400 in income for 2006 and pay tax on that amount.

If Olivia repays no more than $1,000 in 2006 (or by March 1, 2007), she will be required to repay 1/14 of the balance, another $1,000, in 2007 (or by March 1, 2008). Suppose she repays $8,000 in 2006, leaving a balance owing of $7,000. For 2007, she will still be required to repay 1/14 of the balance, or $500. The fact she has prepaid more than required will reduce but not eliminate her obligation to continue paying the balance in later years.

If you do not make repayments as required, you must include the shortfall in income for tax purposes. In effect, it's treated as a permanent withdrawal from your RRSP and you're taxed on it.

Contributions in the year you use the Plan

> **Consider Home Buyers' Plan withdrawals to buy or build your first home (but be sure to weigh the loss of RRSP growth.)**

If you contribute to an RRSP and withdraw the same funds within 90 days under the Home Buyers' Plan, you cannot deduct your contribution. For purposes of this rule, any balance that was already in your RRSP can be considered as withdrawn first. Thus, it is only to the extent the amount of your new contribution is needed for the withdrawal (within the 90-day period) that a deduction will be disallowed.

Some special situations

The Home Buyers' Plan may be used for building a new home on an existing lot that you own. Instead of an agreement to purchase the home, you must have an agreement in place to construct it.

If you withdraw the funds but your home purchase does not close, you can generally cancel your participation in the Plan and return the funds to your RRSP with no adverse tax consequences. Alternatively, if you buy another qualifying home as a replacement, you can remain in the Plan.

If you have contributed to a spousal RRSP, your spouse must normally wait two to three years before withdrawing the funds or they will be taxed back to you (see 3.3.1). However, with the Home Buyers' Plan, your spouse can borrow the funds to purchase a qualifying home, and to the extent they are not repaid over the 15-year repayment period, it is your spouse that must include the difference in income, not you. (Note, however, that if your spouse withdraws the funds and does not purchase a qualifying home, so that the full amount withdrawn is taxed in the current year, the attribution rule *will* apply and you, not your spouse, will be taxed on the withdrawal.)

If you become a non-resident of Canada, you must repay the entire outstanding balance to the RRSP within 60 days of leaving Canada. Otherwise, the balance will be included in your income for the year that you became non-resident.

If you should die while you have an outstanding balance to repay, that balance will be included in your income for the year of death and tax will be payable by your estate (see 22.2.1). However, if you leave a surviving spouse, your executor and your spouse may make a special election to have your spouse take over the obligation to repay the funds over the remainder of the repayment period, and the balance will not be included in your income for the year of death.

Should you use the Home Buyers' Plan?

At first glance, the Plan seems attractive, since it gives you ready access to a potentially large chunk of cash. However, there are three costs to consider.

First, you lose the tax-free compounding in your RRSP (see the example in 3.1.5). Balanced against this is the fact that you have probably reduced the mortgage interest expense you would otherwise have to pay out of after-tax dollars. Nevertheless, the value of the RRSP may be significantly less, at your retirement, than it otherwise would have been. If you are depending on your RRSP for your retirement income, you will want to forecast the reduction in income that will result from withdrawing a large chunk of the funds now and repaying it to the RRSP over 15 years starting in the second year after the year of withdrawal.

Second, you have to be able to sustain the cash flow to repay the RRSP; if you cannot, you will end up being taxed on the funds you have withdrawn. When figuring out the cash you need to handle your mortgage and property tax payments, don't forget the 1/15 minimum repayment to the RRSP in each year beginning with the second year after the withdrawal (due by 60 days after the end of the year). Of course, since you are repaying borrowed funds and not contributing new money to the RRSP, no deduction is available for the amounts you repay.

Third, you might not be able to make a contribution to your RRSP for the current year. This will depend on the balance in your RRSP. If your withdrawal does not exceed the value you had in the RRSP 90 days before the withdrawal, you have no problem. Otherwise, you may have to postpone the current year's contribution, and save it for a later year. The result would be one less year for those funds to have earned tax-free interest, and higher tax to pay in the current year since you will not have a contribution to deduct.

Nevertheless, if you need the funds to help you purchase your first home, the Home Buyers' Plan may be a significant help.

Planning for the Home Buyers' Plan

If you're thinking about tapping your RRSP to purchase your first home but your RRSP is not yet at $20,000 and you intend to use the Home Buyers' Plan to its fullest, make your contribution early enough so that it can sit in the RRSP for 90 days before you withdraw the funds. Then the amount you contributed can be withdrawn as well without affecting your deduction for the contribution.

If you are planning to buy a new home and you are close to the four-year cutoff that will re-qualify you as a "first-time buyer", consider waiting and making your purchase at a time when you can use the Home Buyers' Plan. For example, if you sold your last home in 2000, you can use the Plan as of January 1, 2005.

If you are about to be married and your future spouse owns a home that you will be living in, consider borrowing funds under the Home Buyers' Plan before your wedding. Once you are married, you will not be able to do so. However, you are not restricted by a previous home owned by your spouse, as long as you do not live in it while married. Therefore, if you plan on buying a new home after your wedding, you should not (romantic considerations aside) move into your spouse's current home until you have made your withdrawal under the Plan.

The same applies if you have been living in a common-law relationship (and have not had a child together) or a same-sex relationship for less than 12 months . Once you reach 12 months of living together, you are considered "married" for income tax purposes (see 2.2.1). If your partner owns your present home, but you are planning on "moving up" to a larger home, you should consider withdrawing funds under the Home Buyers' Plan before you have lived together for 12 months. However, you will have to take ownership (or at least part ownership) of the new home in your own name.

3.3.7 The Lifelong Learning Plan—RRSP withdrawals for education

> Consider withdrawing RRSP funds under the Lifelong Learning Plan to help pay for training or post-secondary education programs.

You can tap your registered retirement savings plan to help finance your own or your spouse's education. Under the Lifelong Learning Plan, students in full-time training or post-secondary education and their spouses are allowed to withdraw up to $10,000 per year from their RRSPs over a four-year period, as long as the total amount does not exceed $20,000.

Withdrawn amounts must be repaid to an RRSP in equal instalments over 10 years or they will be included in the income of the person who made the withdrawal. The first repayment will be due 60 days after the fifth year following the first withdrawal (or earlier in certain circumstances such as failure to complete courses). If you die or emigrate from Canada, outstanding amounts will be included in your income in the year of death or emigration. In the case of emigration, you can avoid the income inclusion by repaying the outstanding amount within 60 days of emigration. In the case of death, your surviving spouse and your executor can make a special election to take over the obligation to make the repayments over the remainder of the 15-year period and the balance will not be included in your income in the year of death.

3.4 Registered pension plans—RPPs

3.4.1 Ordinary RPPs

A registered pension plan (RPP) is set up by an employer for its employees. Virtually all large companies, and many smaller ones, have such plans. These are quite different from the Canada Pension Plan (or, in Québec, the Québec Pension Plan), to which all employed and self-employed taxpayers must contribute.

The employer contributes (and deducts for tax purposes) an annual amount on behalf of each employee. Unlike most other employment benefits, these amounts are not taxed as benefits from employment in the year they are contributed. Instead, employees are taxed on the income from the pension when they *receive* it, which is normally after retirement.

In some cases, employees may be required or permitted to make additional contributions to the plan, which they can deduct for tax purposes in the year contributed.

There are two general kinds of pension plans: money-purchase and defined benefit. Money-purchase plans are analogous to RRSPs, in the sense that the amount of the pension payments is determined by the contributions and the investment income they earn. Many large and public employers provide defined benefit plans. With such plans, you know from the beginning how much your pension will be, usually based on a percentage of your actual salary over a specified number of years. It is up to the employer to contribute enough, and to the pension fund management to invest wisely, to make sure that the plan remains sufficiently well funded to make those payments.

> Consider contributing to your RRSP instead of a money-purchase RPP.

Once an employee retires and starts receiving pension income, the pension income is taxed as regular income as it is received. Up to $1,000 per year may effectively be exempted through the pension income tax credit (see 20.3.5).

If you receive a lump-sum pension payment relating to prior years, you may ask the CRA to determine whether it is more advantageous to you to recalculate the tax on that income as if you received it in those prior years. This measure is intended to relieve the higher tax liability that may result if the entire lump-sum is taxed in the year of receipt, rather than year by year as your right to receive the income arose. Eligible payments must total at least $3,000 in the year and include superannuation or pension benefits (other than non-periodic benefits), wrongful dismissal and other employment-related payments arising from a court order or similar judgment, and certain other amounts. (This rule applies to qualifying lump-sum payments received after 1994.)

> Ask the CRA to recalculate your prior-year tax liability on retroactive lump-sum pension and other payments.

If you have terminated your employment but are not yet eligible to receive pension income, you are allowed to transfer lump-sum amounts from the RPP to a "locked-in" RRSP or a "locked-in" RRIF (see 20.4.5). Generally, locked-in funds cannot be withdrawn in a lump sum; they must be used to provide a lifetime income. (In some provinces, if the amount of pension is below a certain threshold, it may be paid as a taxable lump sum. Other circumstances such as shortened life expectancy or financial hardship can also give rise to commutation of a pension.)

The amount you can transfer from a defined benefit RPP to an RRSP or an RRIF is limited to the amount of annual pension given up under the RPP multiplied by a factor based on your age at the date of the transfer. The factor is 9.0 if you are under 50, gradually rising to 12.4 at ages 64 and 65. Generally, any amount over this limit must be paid to you in cash and will be taxed as income in the year received.

If you are a member of a money purchase RPP, as of 2004, the plan may allow payouts in the form of the same income stream currently permitted under a RRIF. If the relevant pension legislation and the plan allow it, you would have to withdraw from your money purchase account a minimum amount each year (corresponding to the existing RRIF rules—see 20.4.4), beginning no later than the year in which you turn age 70.

This rule allows members of money purchase RPPs to benefit from the same advantages as RRIF-holders without taking on greater investment management responsibilities or higher investment management fees. If you are a former member of a money purchase RPP who previously transferred your money purchase account to an RRSP or RRIF, you will be able to transfer the funds back into the RPP if you wish. (Note that certain other federal and provincial pension legislation will have to be amended before this change can take effect. Your RPP's administrator will also need to amend your plan to accommodate this change.)

Find out about the vesting of your pension benefits, especially before making a career change.

If you've been making voluntary contributions to your registered pension plan under a money-purchase provision, consider contributing to an RRSP instead. Though the amount you can contribute will normally be the same and your administration and investment management fees may be higher, the RRSP may give you much greater flexibility in terms of your investment choices.

If you are a member of a company pension plan, find out how long it takes for your employer contributions to be "vested". Once they are vested, the pension you have earned becomes yours and, if you change jobs, many plans will permit the transfer of your pension benefit to your new employer's plan. On the other hand, if they are not vested, you get your own contributions back with interest when you leave—but no pension down the road. The vesting of your pension benefits can be a major factor in career change decisions.

3.4.2 Individual pension plans—IPPs

An individual pension plan (IPP) is exactly what the name implies—a defined benefit registered pension plan designed and structured for one individual member. It is possible for owner-managers to meet the qualifications to have this type of pension plan registered with the CRA.

As a defined benefit pension plan, the benefit payable at retirement is specified and IPP contributions are made accordingly. The amount necessary to provide a defined benefit rises at ages closer to retirement since less time is available to accrue investment income in the plan. As such, IPPs are advantageous where the member is close to retirement—the amounts that can be contributed to an IPP are greater than those allowed to an RRSP.

Generally speaking, the IPP concept will be most suitable for you if you are

- a key executive and/or owner-manager of a corporation;
- over 40 years old; and
- earning a base salary of more than about $100,000.

An IPP may also be worth considering if you are already in your employer's group RPP but the benefits from that RPP are not as generous as you would like them to be.

At termination or retirement, any surplus in the IPP can be returned to the member after paying personal tax. The surplus is the excess of IPP assets over the actual cost of the defined benefit pension to be provided under the terms of the plan. Alternatively, the tax sheltering may be allowed to continue if your IPP is able to opt to "self-annuitize" upon your retirement (i.e., rather than purchasing an annuity from a life insurance company, have the IPP pay you, the beneficiary of the plan, a lifetime income). This can have the effect of stretching out the additional tax sheltering represented by any accumulated IPP surplus well into the years beyond retirement and quite possibly until the last of you and your spouse dies. However, some provinces do not allow self-annuitization in a plan with no active members, which will be the case for your IPP after you retire.

Weigh the advantages of establishing an "individual pension plan".

The main advantage of the IPP is that you and your employer usually will be allowed to make higher annual contributions than you would otherwise be entitled to under the RRSP route. In addition to maximizing tax savings, the higher allowable contributions under the IPP concept can be looked on as a form of forced savings. Your employer will be required to top up the funds in the IPP if investment performance is poor and there will be insufficient funds (as determined by an actuary) to pay you the defined benefit pension promised under the plan (which could be a point of concern to your employer). A further advantage is that an IPP is generally creditor-proof, while many RRSPs are not.

Depending on your particular circumstances, an IPP could also provide some scope for making past service pension contributions, which can only be made under defined benefit RPPs. This can further enhance an IPP's tax sheltering value. Keep in mind that the CRA has introduced rules that can limit past service contributions.

There are also significant potential disadvantages of an IPP which you should carefully consider. For example, you may lose the flexibility to split income on retirement, since contributions cannot be made to the IPP for your spouse, as can be done with RRSPs. In contrast to RRSPs, which can be cashed in any time, contributions made to the IPP will be locked in under applicable pension benefits legislation until retirement, at which time they must be used to provide retirement benefits (usually in the form of a life annuity or life income fund). An RRSP, on the other hand, provides a variety of options on termination or retirement (see 20.4). In addition, start-up and ongoing costs of administration of an IPP will be higher than those of your RRSP. This is due to the complex regulatory environment governing pension plans. For example, an actuarial valuation will be required at start-up and every three years thereafter and certain forms must be filed annually.

The rules regarding IPPs are quite complex. You should consult your professional tax adviser for more information.

3.5 Deferred profit-sharing plans—DPSPs

Deferred profit-sharing plans (DPSPs) are less common than registered pension plans. They operate the same way in that contributions are made by the employer and are only taxed in the employee's hands when received, normally on retirement.

Employer contributions to DPSPs are based on current or accrued profits but may have a defined minimum contribution. Such plans may be used, for example, by smaller companies which are not sure of profits and do not wish to commit themselves to large pension contributions, especially if they end up losing money for the year.

Employer contributions to DPSPs are generally limited to the lesser of 18% of your earnings for the year or $8,250 for 2004 ($9,000 for 2005 and later years). Employee contributions to a DPSP are not permitted. Contributions to a DPSP are reported as a pension adjustment on your T4 slip and they therefore reduce the amount you can contribute to an RRSP in the following year (see 3.1.3). Employer contributions vest in an employee after 24 months of plan membership.

DPSPs cannot be set up for employees who are also major shareholders (over 10% of any class of shares) in the employer corporation, or for members of their families. They therefore cannot be used for owner-managers of small businesses.

3.6 References

The following publications can be obtained (in person or by telephone request) from your nearest CRA Tax Services Office. Some of the brochures and forms are also available from the CRA's web site at *www.cra-arc.gc.ca*.

Interpretation Bulletin IT-124R6, "Contributions to registered retirement savings plans"

Interpretation Bulletin IT-307R4, "Spousal or common-law partner registered retirement savings plans"

Interpretation Bulletin IT-320R3, "Qualified Investments—Trusts governed by RRSPs, RESPs and RRIFs"

Interpretation Bulletin IT-337R4, "Retiring allowances"

Interpretation Bulletin IT-528, "Transfers of funds between registered plans"

Information Circular 72-22R9, "Registered retirement savings plans"

Information Circular 77-1R4, "Deferred profit sharing plans"

Information Circular 78-18R6, "Registered retirement income funds"

Guide, "Lifelong Learning Plan"

Guide, "RRSPs and Other Registered Plans for Retirement"

Guide, "Registered Education Savings Plans"

Brochure, "Home Buyers' Plan"

Form RC96, "Lifelong Learning Plan (LLP)—Request to withdraw funds from an RRSP"

Form T1036, "Home Buyers' Plan (HBP)—Request to withdraw funds from an RRSP"

Form T2205, "Calculation of amounts from a spousal RRSP or RRIF to be included in income for 20___"

Registered Education Savings Plans — RESPs

- Consider an RESP for education cost planning, tax deferral and income splitting with the plan's beneficiary (4.1)

- Think about establishing a self-directed RESP to increase your investment options (4.1.2)

- Contribute up to $2,000 annually to an RESP and earn a 20% government grant (4.2)

- If your child does not pursue higher education, consider transferring up to $50,000 to your own or your spouse's RRSP (4.3.2)

RESPs are tax-assisted savings vehicles similar to RRSPs and the other deferred income plans discussed in Chapter 3—but the rules governing contributions to and payments from RESPs are quite different. In the past, restrictions on the use of RESP investment income sometimes outweighed the potential benefits of tax-deferred growth. However, changes to the RESP system over the past few years have made these plans more attractive as education investment vehicles.

4.1   What is an RESP?

RESPs can help you build an education fund for your child or grandchild (or a friend's or relative's child) by allowing you to earn investment income in a tax-deferred environment. You can set up an individual plan with organizations such as life insurance companies, mutual fund companies and financial institutions or you can enrol in a group plan offered by a non-profit scholarship or education trust foundation. If the child goes to college or university, the RESP provides funds to help cover the child's expenses.

Unlike RRSPs, contributions to an RESP are *not* tax-deductible to the contributor. However, the income in the plan grows tax-free, so RESPs enjoy the effect of tax-free compounding of investment income, which we illustrated in 3.1.5. When the child withdraws the funds, the income portion will be taxable to the child. As a student, the beneficiary will probably not have much other income and will be eligible for the tuition and education tax credits (see 2.4), so he or she will likely pay little or no tax. The investment income payments from an RESP are all taxable as regular income, even if the investment income was earned as dividends or capital gains, which are normally taxed at a lower rate.

> Consider an RESP for education cost planning, tax deferral and income splitting with the plan's beneficiary.

4.1.1 How much can you contribute to an RESP?

The maximum contribution to an RESP for any one beneficiary by all contributors is limited to $4,000 per year. There is an overall lifetime contribution limit of $42,000 per beneficiary. Unlike RRSPs, if you contribute less than $4,000 in a particular year, you cannot catch up by contributing more than $4,000 in a later year. Overcontributions are taxed at a rate of 1% for each month that they remain in the plan. Even if overcontributions are withdrawn from the plan, they still count towards the beneficiary's $42,000 lifetime contribution limit, creating a double penalty for overcontributing.

Income generated in an RESP may be sheltered from tax for a maximum of 25 years. You can make contributions to the plan for up to 21 years. The plan can exist and earn tax-sheltered income for four more years, after which the plan must be wound up. You may want to wait until your child is about age five to set up a plan, so it will still be available if your child wants to pursue post-graduate studies. Keep in mind that waiting to set up an RESP means that the funds will have less time to grow.

If an RESP contributor dies, his or her estate can continue to contribute to the plan. However, a trust cannot contribute to an RESP. If you've already established and funded a formal trust for your child, you will have to find other sources of funding for an RESP.

If you wish, you can withdraw your own contributions to an RESP without any tax consequences since you did not get a tax deduction when you contributed the funds. However, you can't withdraw the income earned by the RESP tax-free. You may also be required to pay some or all of any Canada Education Savings Grants upon a RESP withdrawal for non-education purposes—see 4.2.

4.1.2 Choosing the right type of RESP—Group and individual plans

> Think about establishing a self-directed RESP to increase your investment options.

If you choose to set up an individual plan rather than enrol in a group plan, the investments can be self-directed and tailored to your circumstances. The types of investments that may be held in an RESP are the same as those that may be held by an RRSP—see 3.1.6. However, unlike RRSPs, no foreign content limit applies to RESPs.

You can also choose between a single-beneficiary and a multi-beneficiary plan. Under a single-beneficiary plan, the beneficiary does not have to be related to you — he or she can be anyone you choose. You can also set up a single-beneficiary RESP for yourself if you're planning to pursue post-secondary education in the future.

If you're saving for the education of more than one person, you may want to consider a multi-beneficiary or family plan. The beneficiaries under a multi-beneficiary plan may only include your children, brothers, sisters, grandchildren or great-grandchildren. You cannot contribute to the plan for a beneficiary after he or she reaches age 21. Although you can usually change the beneficiaries after you set up either a single or multi-beneficiary plan if you wish, certain plans may have conditions restricting changing beneficiaries. Understanding the terms of any plan contract you consider is critical.

Group plans tend to be more restrictive in terms of required scheduled contributions and the contributor usually has no say in how the contributed funds are invested.

Group plans may require that children be enrolled in the plan before they reach a certain age. They generally allow only one beneficiary to be named and may not allow you to change the beneficiary after he or she reaches a certain age. Again, make sure you understand the terms of the plan before entering into an RESP contract.

4.2   Canada Education Savings Grant

Under the Canada Education Savings Grant (CESG) program, the federal government will provide a direct grant to the RESP of 20% of the first $2,000 of annual contributions made to the RESP in a year. The grant will be worth up to $400 per year for each year the beneficiary is under 18, to a maximum of $7,200 per beneficiary. The grant amount will not be included in the annual and lifetime contribution limits for the beneficiary.

If the $2,000 maximum contribution is not made in a year, entitlement to the grant can be carried forward to a later year (within restrictions). The total CESG per beneficiary per year is capped at

> Contribute up to $2,000 annually to an RESP and earn a 20% government grant.

$800 (20% of the maximum annual $4,000 RESP contribution) or 20% of the unused CESG room, whichever is less.

> **Example**
>
> Robin contributes $1,000 in 2004 to an RESP for her newborn son. This contribution earns a CESG of $200 (20% of $1,000), leaving $1,000 in CESG contribution room available for carryforward in future years.
>
> In 2005, Robin contributes $3,500 to the plan. In this year, the CESG will be limited to the $2,000 of new contribution arising in the year, plus the $1,000 carried forward. As such, the CESG will be 20% of $3,000, or $600.

Note that only unused CESG contribution room can be carried forward; in our example, the extra $500 of contribution could not be carried forward and claimed for CESG purposes in later years. If you expect your annual contributions will vary, consider deferring your "excess" contributions to the next year to secure maximum grants.

CESG contribution room accumulates at the rate of $2,000 for each year for 1998 and after, whether or not the child is currently an RESP beneficiary. So even if you do not start making CESG-eligible RESP contributions in your child's first year, you can make catch-up payments eligible for the grant in later years (subject to the annual limit per beneficiary of $800 or 20% of the unused CESG room).

Example

Nancy's son William was born in 1997 and Nancy sets up an RESP for him in 2004. Since no RESP contributions have been made on William's behalf before 2004, William's unused CESG contribution room carried forward is $2,000 for each year from 1998 – 2002, or $12,000.

Because William's total CESG for 2004 is capped at 20% of the lesser of $4,000 or his unused contribution room of $12,000, the maximum CESG-eligible amount that Nancy (together with other benefactors) can contribute in 2004 is $2,000 for the current year plus $2,000 of the amount carried forward. If the maximum contribution of $4,000 is made, William will earn a CESG of $800 and he will have $10,000 of unused CESG contribution room available for use in 2005 and later years.

Starting in 2005, the CESG rate will rise to 40 per cent for families with income under $35,000 and to 30 per cent for families with income between $35,000 and $70,000. The maximum contribution eligible for the CESG will remain at $2,000, while the maximum CESG payable for a year will be increased from $400 for low and middle income families to accommodate the enhanced CESG rates, as will the lifetime contribution limit. For example, a lower income family that contributes $2,000 in a year could receive a CESG totalling $500 — that is, 40 per cent on the first $500 ($200) and 20 per cent on the remaining $1,500 ($300). Unused access to the enhanced CESG rates cannot be carried forward to future years.

To qualify for the CESG, the RESP beneficiary must be a resident of Canada under age 18 and must have a Social Insurance Number (SIN). You can apply for a SIN for your child by contacting Human Resources and Skills Development Canada. Bear in mind that SIN processing may take several weeks (see 4.4).

If you have already set up an RESP, you should confirm that it qualifies for CESG purposes. If you want to receive a CESG for 2005 but you do not have a plan, you'll need to set one up and make a contribution before December 31, 2004. The contributions must be new — money cannot be withdrawn from existing RESPs and recontributed to a new plan to qualify for the grant. If you change the plan's beneficiary, the grant funds can stay in the RESP if both the old and new beneficiaries are under 21 years old and are related to you.

There are special rules for beneficiaries in the years they become 16 or 17. RESPs for beneficiaries aged 16 and 17 will be eligible for CESGs only if:

- Contributions to all RESPs for the child totalled at least $2,000 before the year in which the child turned 16, or
- If there were contributions for the child of at least $100 per year in any four years before the year in which the child turned 16.

If your child chooses not to pursue post-secondary education, you will have to repay the CESG funds received but you will only have to pay back the principal amount of the grant. You do not have to pay back the income earned on the grant funds; however, the income will be taxed when it is withdrawn from the RESP (see 4.3.2).

4.3 Payments from an RESP

4.3.1 If the beneficiary pursues higher education

Your RESP can begin making educational assistance payments to the plan's beneficiary once he or she enrolls as a full-time student in a qualifying educational program at a qualifying post-secondary institution. Students with disabilities can receive educational assistance payments for part-time study. Payments from the plan can be used to cover the student's living expenses and educational expenses such as tuition fees and books, although certain plans may restrict which expenses payments can cover. A beneficiary cannot receive more than $5,000 during the first three months of his or her post-secondary education. After the first three months, there is no limit on the amount that can be paid, as long as the student continues to qualify.

You can decide whether to let the student use the principal amount contributed to the plan or only the income accumulated in the plan. You can also decide how much is paid out of the plan and when the payments are made, subject to what the plan you choose allows. You may want to spread the payments over the duration of the student's program to minimize taxes. If your RESP received CESGs, in most cases, a part of each income payment will be attributed to the CESG funds received by the plan.

If you contributed to a group RESP, the principal you contributed to the plan will be the first year's payment to the student. The plan administrators will determine the student's share of the income from the pooled funds in the plan and start making those payments in the student's second year of post-secondary education.

For an educational program to qualify, generally it must be at least three weeks long, require at least 10 hours per week of instruction, be at a designated educational institution and not be taken while the student is employed as part of the duties of that employment. Correspondence courses and other distanced education courses may also qualify, as well as universities outside Canada if the student is enrolled in a course of at least 13 weeks leading to a degree.

Some group RESP plans may have other restrictions, such as prohibiting the beneficiary from changing schools or requiring the beneficiary to meet a minimum academic standard.

4.3.2 If the beneficiary does not pursue further education

> If your child does not pursue higher education, consider transferring up to $50,000 to your own or your spouse's RRSP.

What happens to the RESP funds if the intended beneficiaries decide not to enrol in college or university? In the past, if none of the intended beneficiaries went on to higher education, the family would only get back the original amounts contributed to the RESP, while the income earned over the years would be forfeited. However, these rules have been eased in cases where none of the RESP's intended beneficiaries are post-secondary students by age 21 and the plan has been running for at least 10 years. (If a beneficiary is mentally impaired, these conditions may be waived.) Under the current rules, you may transfer up to $50,000 of RESP income to your RRSP (or your spouse's) during your lifetime to the extent you have available RRSP contribution room. This allows the RRSP deduction to offset the inclusion of the RESP funds in your taxable income.

If you do not want to contribute the income to an RRSP or you do not have enough RRSP contribution room to do so, you will be subject to an extra tax of 20% of the excess RESP income, on top of your regular taxes on the amount (the extra tax is designed to make up for the taxes deferred while the funds were in the plan). You must wind up the RESP by March 1 of the year following the year in which you first withdrew income from the RESP.

Family plans are subject to the same contribution limits per beneficiary as single-beneficiary plans but, if one of your children decides against post-secondary school, the funds you have contributed for this child and the income earned on those contributions can be re-directed to benefit your other children who do pursue post-secondary education. If your plan received CESGs, the remaining beneficiaries can use up to $7,200 of CESGs funds each.

Group RESPs will return your contributions, but the income earned will remain in the plan to be distributed to the plan's beneficiaries who go on to post-secondary education.

4.4 References

The following publications can be obtained (in person or by telephone request) from your nearest CRA Tax Services Office. Some of the brochures and forms are also available from the CRA's web site at *www.cra-arc.gc.ca.*

Information Circular 93-3R, "Registered Education Savings Plans"

Guide, "Registered Education Savings Plans"

Form TIE-OVP, "Individual's income tax return for RESP overcontributions"

Form T1171, "Tax withholding waiver on accumulated income payments from RESPs"

Form T1172, "Additional tax on accumulated income payments from RESPs"

Information on Canada Education Savings Grants is available from Human Resources and Skills Development Canada's web site at *www.hrsdc.gc.ca.* Information on how to apply for a Social Insurance Number is available from Social Development Canada's web site at *www.sdc.gc.ca.*

CHAPTER 5

Reducing your family's tax bill through income splitting

- Watch out for the income splitting tax on certain income received by minor children (5.2.4)
- Beware of the "general anti-avoidance rule" (5.2.6)
- The higher-income spouse should pay household expenses (5.3.1)
- Pay your spouse's tax bills with your own funds (5.3.1)
- Pay the interest on your spouse's third party investment loans (5.3.1)
- Pay a salary or consulting fee to your spouse and/or children (5.3.2)
- Think about loaning business assets to your spouse or child (5.3.3)
- Consider making spousal investment loans when interest rates are rising (5.3.4)
- Have your spouse or child earn income on income from lent or transferred funds (5.3.5)
- Shelter future gains by transferring property at fair market value (5.3.6)
- Shelter future gains by transferring capital assets to your children (5.3.7)
- Transfer shares that will pay capital dividends (5.3.8)
- Contribute to your spouse's RRSP (5.3.9)
- Make spousal RRSP contributions by December 31 (5.3.9)
- In the year your children turn 17, give them funds they can invest (5.3.10)
- Let your children invest their own earnings (5.3.11)
- Claim baby-sitting wages paid to your adult children as child care expenses (5.3.13)

"Income splitting" is a term used to describe strategies to save taxes by shifting income from the hands of a family member in a higher tax bracket to the hands of a second family member in a lower tax bracket so that the same income is taxed at a lower rate of tax—or not at all if the second family member's income is low enough. In this chapter, we discuss the tax rules that are in place to prevent many forms of income splitting and point out some of the income splitting opportunities that remain available.

5.1 Why income splitting?

The Canadian tax system uses progressive tax rates, whereby the marginal rate of tax (tax on additional income) increases as taxable income increases.

Marginal rates of tax, tax brackets and surtaxes vary widely from province to province, but are *approximately*:

- 24% on income from $8,000 to $35,000
- 34% on income from $35,000 to $70,000
- 41% on income from $70,000 to $113,800
- 45% on income over $113,800.

As you can see, the tax payable on two $70,000 incomes will be significantly less than that on one $140,000 income—about $11,370 less, in fact. Taxpayers, therefore, have an incentive to "split" income between, for example, a high-income earner and a non-working spouse or children.

The federal *Income Tax Act* contains a number of measures to prevent the most obvious kinds of income splitting (similar rules apply for Québec purposes). However, some opportunities are available. We'll review the rules, so you understand the context in which to plan, together with a discussion of the planning opportunities that remain.

Note that most of this chapter will be irrelevant to you if you do not have funds invested and earning income that is subject to tax. One of the best tax planning techniques is to channel extra cash into paying off any non-deductible interest such as your mortgage or credit card balances.

5.2 Rules that prevent income splitting

5.2.1 Indirect payments

The *Income Tax Act* provides that a payment or transfer made "pursuant to the direction of, or with the concurrence of" a taxpayer to some other person is to be included in the taxpayer's income to the extent it would have been if paid to the taxpayer. So, for example, if you arrange for your employer to pay part of your salary to your spouse, the income will still be taxed in your hands and you will not have accomplished anything.

5.2.2 Attribution between spouses

Suppose you earn $120,000 per year and your spouse earns $15,000. Your marginal tax rate (tax on any additional income) is 45% and your spouse's is 24%. Assume you have $10,000 in bonds that generate $1,000 per year in interest and decide to give, or lend, the bonds to your spouse. As a result you hope to pay only $240 tax on the income instead of $450.

This is the kind of transaction that the attribution rules cover. These rules attribute income from property (in our example, the $1,000 of investment income each year) back to the person who transferred or loaned the property.

The attribution rules with respect to spouses provide that where property (including money) is *transferred or loaned, directly or indirectly* by you to your spouse (or a person who has since become your spouse), then all *income or loss from the property*, and any *capital gain or loss* on the disposition of the property will be *attributed back* to you. So, in our example, the $1,000 income on the $10,000 investment that you gave to your spouse must be reported on your tax return, not your spouse's—and so will be subject to tax of about $450 rather than about $240. This will be true year after year—as long as you and your spouse remain together, any income from the bonds will be taxed in your hands. If you transfer shares, for example, and your spouse sells the shares at some later time, any capital gain or capital loss relative *to your* original cost must be reported as your capital gain or loss, subject to the usual rules for capital gains (see Chapter 6).

Note that common-law and same-sex couples who meet the criteria outlined in 2.2.1 are considered spouses for tax purposes, and are therefore subject to these attribution rules as well.

There is an exception to these attribution rules; an exception that also applies to the rules we will see later. If you transfer for fair market value consideration (for example, sell the bonds to your spouse for $10,000 cash) and report the resulting gain, the rule will not apply. (If you realize a loss on the transfer, a special rule deems the loss to be zero. However the denied loss can be added to your spouse's cost for tax purposes.) If the consideration includes indebtedness (for example, you sell the bonds for a $10,000 promissory note), or if you simply lend funds or property to your spouse, then to avoid the attribution rule you must charge and report interest on the loan. The interest rate must be at least equal to the CRA's prescribed interest rate at that time (see 9.3) or a commercial rate of interest. For this exception to apply, the interest must actually be *paid* in each year, or by the following January 30. If the January 30 deadline ever passes without the interest being paid, that year's income and *all* future income from the loaned property will be attributed back to the lender.

Example

On January 1, 2004, you lend $10,000 cash to your spouse, who puts the money in the bank and earns $600 interest over the course of the year.

If you do not charge interest, then the $600 will be attributed back to you and taxed in your hands. Suppose you do wish to charge interest. The minimum rate would have to be either:

- the rate that would apply between two arm's length parties (assume 5% for this example); or
- the CRA's rate at the time the loan was granted (3% — see 9.3).

If your spouse is required to pay interest on the anniversary date of the loan and actually pays you at least $300 in interest by January 30, 2005, then the $600 interest will not be attributed back to you. Your spouse can deduct the interest paid to you and the amount will be taxable to you as interest income.

The CRA's (and Revenu Québec's) prescribed rate, which is set quarterly, is 4% lower for this purpose than the rate that applies to late payments of tax (see 9.3).

5.2.3 Attribution between parents and children

Suppose you lend $10,000 in bonds to your daughter, who is in high school and can earn $1,000 in interest without paying any tax at all.

Where property is transferred or loaned to a child, there will be attribution of income (or loss), but not of capital gains or losses. The attribution rules apply only for years in which the child is still under 18 *at the end* of the year (though the attribution rules discussed in 5.2.5 will apply once your child turns 18).

Not all children under 18 are caught by the rule. It depends on the child's relationship with the taxpayer who transfers or lends the property. Attribution applies where the taxpayer and the child "do not deal at arm's length", a phrase that is defined to include all persons who are "related" as defined in the *Income Tax Act*. Generally, this covers one's child, grandchild, great-grandchild (including one's spouse's child, one's child's spouse, etc., where "spouse" includes a common-law or same-sex spouse as outlined in 2.2.1) or brother or sister (including brother-in-[common]-law and sister-in-[common]-law). This rule also specifically applies to nieces and nephews. For other relationships, it is a "question of fact" whether two taxpayers deal at arm's length.

Although the attribution rule with respect to minors does not apply to capital gains and losses, the transfer of the property to the minor itself will generally be deemed to take place at fair market value. So any capital gain or loss accruing up to the time of the transfer will be triggered immediately in the transferor's hands, and it is only the gain or loss accruing *after* the transfer that when realized will be taxed in the child's hands.

The exceptions that we saw in 5.2.2, where the transferred property is acquired for fair market value or where interest is paid on any indebtedness or loan, also apply to this attribution rule.

5.2.4 Income splitting tax on certain income received by minor children

Some income splitting arrangements with minor children attract a special "income splitting tax" (sometimes called the "kiddie tax"). The tax neutralizes the benefits of certain arrangements, including some plans involving the use of family trusts (see 21.5.4), by subjecting certain types of dividend, partnership or trust income received by, or used for the benefit of, minor children to tax at the top marginal tax rate, instead of the lower rate that would usually apply on income received by a minor child.

The types of income subject to the tax include:

- taxable dividends and other shareholder benefits on private Canadian and foreign company shares (received directly by the minor or through a trust or partnership)
- income from a partnership or trust derived by the partnership or trust from the business of providing property or services to a business carried on by a relative of the minor or a business in which the relative participates

Trust or partnership income derived from property, such as interest and rental income, used to be exempt from the tax, but a recent tax law change extended the tax to such income for tax years and fiscal periods starting after December 20, 2002. Income splitting arrangements in place on or before that date, including family trust arrangements involving interest-bearing loans, should be reviewed in light of the change.

Parents are jointly and severally liable for the tax if they were active in the business from which the income was derived. The only deductions allowed against income subject to the tax are the dividend tax credit and foreign tax credit.

The tax does not apply to income earned by minors from property acquired on the death of their parent or income earned by minors who have no parent resident in Canada for tax purposes in the year.

Bear in mind that the new rules do not apply if a trust's beneficiary is your spouse or child age 18 at the end of the year or older, so income splitting can still be accomplished by allocating the above types of income to older family members.

> Watch out for the income splitting tax on certain income received by minor children.

5.2.5 Attribution on loans to adult family members

One further rule applies to loans (but not transfers) of property to other persons with whom the taxpayer does not deal at arm's length—such as, for example, one's children who are over 18, or one's in-laws or grandparents. If one of the main reasons for the loan was to achieve income splitting and thereby reduce taxes, the income will be attributed back to the lender. So if you lend $20,000 to your adult son who is in university, and the purpose is to allow him to earn the $1,200 interest and pay little or no tax on it (rather than, say, to allow him to use the $20,000 to pay for his tuition), the $1,200 of interest will be attributed back to you. The exception where interest is charged and paid, as outlined in 5.2.2, applies in this case.

5.2.6 Special anti-avoidance rules

If you are creative and devious enough, you may have thought of some possible ways around the rules we have just described. Don't bother. The federal and Québec tax laws contain special rules designed to thwart the loopholes that creative tax planners exploited in years past. We will summarize them only briefly; basically, anything you can think of has probably been thought of before.

Substituted property. If property is substituted for transferred or loaned property, the attribution rules will apply to income or capital gains from the substituted property, and so on *ad infinitum* (to the extent that attribution would have applied to income from the original property). So if you give $10,000 in bonds to your spouse, who then sells them and buys $10,000 in stocks, any dividends and capital gains on the stocks will be attributed back to you.

Transfers to a trust or corporation. In general, transfers to a trust will result in the same application of the attribution rules as if the transfers were made directly to the beneficiaries of the trust. Transfers to a corporation which result in a benefit to a "designated person" (spouse or related minor children, using the same definition we saw in 5.2.3) are also caught in most cases. So, for example, if you and your spouse each own half the shares in a corporation, and you give $10,000 to the corporation so that your spouse will benefit, you will be taxed as though you had received interest from the corporation. This attribution rule does not apply where the corporation is a "small business corporation" (see 6.2.3).

Back-to-back loans and transfers. If you lend or transfer property to a third party, who then lends or transfers it to a "designated person" (your spouse or related minor children), it will be treated as though you had lent or transferred the property directly.

Guarantees. If you arrange for a third party (e.g., a bank) to lend funds to a "designated person" on the strength of your guarantee, it will be treated as though you had lent the funds directly.

Repayment of existing loan. If you lend funds to a "designated person", and they use the funds to pay off another loan that they used to buy property, your loan will effectively be treated as if it had been used to buy that property. (This is the flip side of the "substituted property" case covered above.) So, for example, if your spouse borrows $10,000 to invest in bonds, and you then lend your spouse $10,000 which is used to pay off that loan, the interest from the bonds will be attributed back to you.

Reverse attribution. The attribution rules can be ignored if you try to use them to turn the tables on CRA and have them apply in the opposite direction from that intended.

General anti-avoidance rule. The Act provides a general anti-avoidance rule (GAAR), applicable to all transactions. If you come up with a way of avoiding the attribution rules that is not caught by the existing rules but is a misuse or abuse of the *Income Tax Act*, it may be caught by GAAR.

> Beware of the "general anti-avoidance rule".

5.3 Income splitting opportunities

In this section we discuss the planning opportunities available to achieve income splitting. For many of these to work, you need to keep careful documentation. Separate bank accounts for spouses will allow you to trace each one's funds properly. (Under provincial family law, this will not normally affect either spouse's rights to the family's funds on marriage breakdown.)

5.3.1 Increasing the lower-income spouse's investment base

The simplest technique is to make sure that daily living expenses (such as groceries, mortgage or rent payments, and credit card bills) are paid by the higher-income spouse. This will allow the lower-income spouse to maintain a larger investment base for earning future income that is taxed at a low rate.

> The higher-income spouse should pay household expenses.

Another way to effectively transfer funds is for you to directly pay your spouse's income tax liability—both in April and any instalments that are due during the year. Simply make sure that the cheque paying your spouse's taxes is drawn on your own account. Since the amount you pay goes directly to the government and is not invested by your spouse, there is no property from which income can be attributed. The result is that any funds your spouse would otherwise use to pay income taxes can be invested without the income being attributed back to you.

> Pay your spouse's tax bills with your own funds.

If your spouse has taken out an investment loan from a third party, consider providing him or her with the funds to pay the interest. There will be no attribution provided you do not pay any principal on account of the spousal loan. (Since the amount you pay is not actually invested by your spouse, there is no property from which income can be attributed.) The interest payment will be deductible on your spouse's tax return. This technique will preserve your spouse's assets and thereby increase his or her investment income.

> Pay the interest on your spouse's third party investment loans.

5.3.2 Employing your spouse and children

If you carry on a business, either personally or through a corporation, consider paying a salary to your spouse and/or children. The salary must be "reasonable" in light of the services they perform for the business. Such services might include bookkeeping, filing, other administrative work, business development planning and acting as a director of the corporation. The CRA and Revenu Québec auditors are usually fairly flexible in interpreting what constitutes a "reasonable" salary, provided services are genuinely being provided.

> Pay a salary or consulting fee to your spouse and/or children.

The cost of payroll taxes, Canada Pension Plan contributions and Employment Insurance premiums should be weighed against any potential tax savings expected from implementing this strategy.

Consider also whether your spouse can provide services on a contract (consulting) basis rather than as an employee. This would allow your spouse the advantages of self-employment income (see Chapter 11), including writing off expenses. This is an aggressive tactic and should only be implemented with appropriate professional advice.

Another possibility is to bring your spouse into partnership with you. Taxation of partnerships is discussed in 11.3 and 16.2.

5.3.3 Transfers of business assets

> Think about loaning business assets to your spouse or child.

The attribution rules, as we have noted, apply to income from *property*—such as interest, dividends, rent and royalties. They do not, however, apply to income earned from a *business*. So if you can transfer or lend business assets in such a way that your spouse or child carries on business on a regular and continuous basis to earn income from business rather than from property, there will be no attribution. Such a step should only be undertaken with proper professional advice, to ensure that the legal steps required to effect the transfer are properly completed and that the possibility of the general anti-avoidance rule applying is minimized.

Note that this generally cannot be done for a passive interest in a partnership (including an interest in a limited partnership). Income from the partnership's business is technically business income, but it is deemed to be property income for purposes of the attribution rules unless the taxpayer is actively engaged in the partnership's business or is carrying on a similar business.

5.3.4 Spousal loans

As we saw in 5.2.2, the attribution rules do not apply where property or funds are loaned and interest is charged at a minimum rate, provided the interest is actually paid. Where assets are expected to produce a return that is well in excess of the minimum rate (the lower of a reasonable commercial rate and the CRA prescribed rate), it may make sense to lend the funds or assets and charge a rate of interest sufficient to avoid triggering the attribution rules. The excess yield from the assets over the amount of interest charged will then effectively be transferred to the lower-income taxpayer and not attributed back to the lender.

If interest rates are rising, the current CRA prescribed rate may be relatively low, since there is a time lag before it is set each quarter. Where such an opportunity arises, consider making a loan to your spouse on which interest is charged, "locking in" at the low prescribed rate, and having your spouse use the funds to invest at current market rates.

> Consider making spousal investment loans when interest rates are rising.

5.3.5 Reinvesting attributed income

We have seen that attribution applies to the income from property that is transferred or loaned. But what about the income from that income (secondary income)? Suppose you give $20,000 to your spouse, who earns $1,200 in interest in the first year, and the $1,200 is attributed back to you. In the second year, your spouse invests the $1,200 as well as the $20,000, and the $1,200 generates a further $72 in interest.

This "secondary income" is not attributed back to you, as it is not income from the property that was transferred. It is thus taxed in your spouse's hands. Over time, a significant stream of such secondary income can be built up. However, accurate records must be maintained. You may wish to have your spouse keep two bank accounts, one for the income that is attributed back to you and one into which all income from the first account is deposited. Only the income from the first account would be reported on your return.

> Have your spouse or child earn income on income from lent or transferred funds.

5.3.6 Transfers for fair market value

As we have seen, the attribution rules also do not apply where property is transferred in exchange for consideration equal to the property's fair market value. (Where the consideration includes indebtedness, such as a promissory note, interest must be charged as outlined above.) A transfer at fair market value may be beneficial where the assets are expected to produce a high yield or to increase in value in the future. (Bear in mind, however, that the transfer may trigger a capital gain or loss subject to the rules discussed in 5.2.2.)

> Shelter future gains by transferring property at fair market value.

5.3.7 Transferring capital property to children

As we saw in 5.2.3, the attribution rules with respect to minor children do not apply to capital gains. If you have assets that are expected to increase substantially in value (such as shares of a corporation), consider transferring them to your children or to a trust for your children. Any dividends will be attributed back

> Shelter future gains by transferring capital assets to your children.

to you as long as your children are under 18 at the end of the year in which the dividend is paid, but capital gains on sale of the assets will not be.

For example, suppose you own shares in your private business corporation. You invested $10,000 originally, and they are now worth $20,000. But you expect the corporation to do well over the coming years. If you give the shares to your children, you will be deemed to have disposed of them at $20,000, but the capital gain may be shielded by the $500,000 capital gains exemption (see 6.3.1). If, a few years later, your children sell the shares for $100,000, the $80,000 capital gain will be taxed in their hands, not yours, and possibly taxed at a lower marginal rate (or not taxed if the capital gains exemption is used).

Other assets that might be appropriate for transfer to children are those which will normally generate capital gains but not income. Examples include jewellery, art and shares in speculative public companies. Transfers to children should be done with proper professional advice. In some provinces there is a question as to whether minors can legally own property such as shares. You may need to set up a trust for this purpose.

5.3.8 Payment of capital dividends

Normally, dividends that are paid on shares you transfer to your spouse or minor children will be attributed back to you. However, the tax system provides for "capital dividends", which are always tax-free. Such dividends include a distribution of the untaxed half of a corporation's capital gains. (For an example, see 14.2.4.)

Transfer shares that will pay capital dividends.

If you transfer shares of a corporation, and the shares subsequently pay capital dividends, there will be no attribution of the income because it is not taxed in anyone's hands in the first place. As well, any income earned from reinvesting the dividends will not be attributed. This technique can work well for shares of private holding companies, but must be undertaken with proper professional advice to minimize the application of various anti-avoidance rules which could turn the dividends into taxable dividends.

5.3.9 Spousal RRSP

A contribution to your spouse's RRSP, as we saw in 3.3.1, is specifically allowed for federal and Québec tax purposes. When the funds are turned into an annuity or RRIF on retirement, there will be no attribution of the income back to you as long as your spouse withdraws no more than the minimum amount from the RRIF in the year of the RRSP contribution or the next two years.

A further technique can be used at any time before retirement. Contributions to your spouse's RRSP, if withdrawn by your spouse, are taxed back in your hands to the extent you have made

> Contribute to your spouse's RRSP.

any spousal contributions in the year of withdrawal or in the two previous years. This means that you can split income, provided you can wait 24 to 36 months and not make spousal contributions in the meantime. It also means foregoing the benefits of leaving the funds to grow tax-free in the RRSP (see 3.1.5).

> **Example**
>
> On December 31, 2004, you contribute $15,500 to an RRSP for your spouse.
>
> This entitles you to a deduction of $15,500 for 2004 (assuming you have adequate contribution room—see 3.1.3—and have made no contributions to your own RRSP for 2004). Any withdrawals of up to $15,500 from your spouse's RRSPs in 2005 or 2006 will be attributed back to you; but on January 1, 2007, your spouse can withdraw the full $15,500, which will be taxed to your spouse as the recipient provided you make no further spousal RRSP contributions in 2005, 2006 or 2007.

Of course, when you contribute to a spousal RRSP you lose your own RRSP contribution room, so the tax advantages of this technique are somewhat limited, but it does achieve income splitting over the long term. You must also consider, however, whether your spouse having a higher income at retirement will affect eligibility for the age credit (see 19.3.4) and will trigger the Old Age Security clawback (see 19.3.2).

Note also that in this example, if you contributed for 2004 on January 1, 2005 rather than December 31, 2004, your spouse would have to wait until January 1, 2008 to withdraw the funds without

> Make spousal RRSP contributions by December 31.

attribution back to you. Contributions to spousal plans should thus not be put off to January or February, as is often done with one's own contributions.

5.3.10 When your children turn 17

Consider giving your children funds that they can invest. If your child turns 17 in the year you make the gift, the funds can be invested in a one-year (or longer) term deposit or certificate, with

> In the year your children turn 17, give them funds they can invest.

the first interest payment being made in the year in which the child turns 18, and no attribution will result. (If the investment is for more than one year with compounding interest, the interest earned must still be reported annually—see 7.2.1.) Do not simply loan the funds without considering the special attribution rule discussed in 5.2.5.

You might also consider a gift of enough funds so that the income earned on the funds will cover the child's university tuition and residence over four (or more) years. Of course, you must be prepared to lose the funds, since they will legally belong to your child and not to you. Consider the use of a trust (with proper legal advice) if this is a concern.

5.3.11 Your children's employment income

Let your children invest their own earnings.

Consider lending your child, interest-free, an amount equal to what he or she earns over the summer and would otherwise spend. This will allow the child to earn investment income on his or her own earnings, and the investment income will not be attributed back to you.

Suppose you have a daughter who attends university and who earns $20,000 over the summer, and your normal arrangement with her is that she uses her income to pay for her tuition and basic expenses. If you lend her $20,000 interest-free, she can use the funds you lend her to pay her tuition and living expenses, and invest her summer earnings. Since the $20,000 invested represents her own funds, the income earned on that amount will not be attributed back to you and will be taxed at her marginal rate (or not taxed at all if her income is low enough). You could then repeat this process through several years of university, and have your daughter pay back the entire amount of the loan when she graduates, using the funds she has invested from her own earnings. Alternatively, you could lend her less money each year, as she will have her investment income available as an additional source of funds.

5.3.12 Assignment of CPP/QPP benefit payments

You may be able to split income by directing that up to 50% of your Canada or Québec Pension Plan (CPP/QPP) benefits be paid to your spouse, provided both of you are over 60. If either of you does this, a portion of the other spouse's CPP/QPP is assigned automatically back to the first spouse and the attribution rules will not apply. See 20.3.1 for details.

5.3.13 Paying children over 18 for child care

Claim baby-sitting wages paid to your adult children as child care expenses.

The deduction for child care expenses was discussed in 2.3.2. No deduction is allowed for payments you make to a person related to you who is under 18. Once your older children turn 18, if you are the lower-income spouse you can claim amounts paid to them for child care or baby-sitting services that permit you to earn employment or business income. Your adult child will need to give you a receipt and report the income for tax purposes.

5.4 References

The following publications can be obtained (in person or by telephone request) from your nearest CRA Tax Services Office. Forms and brochures may also be available from the CRA's Internet site at *www.cra-arc.gc.ca*.

Interpretation Bulletin IT-295R4, "Taxable dividends received after 1987 by a spouse"

Interpretation Bulletin IT-307R4, "Spousal or common-law partner registered retirement savings plans"

Interpretation Bulletin IT-335R2, "Indirect payments"

Interpretation Bulletin IT-369R, "Attribution of trust income to settler"

Interpretation Bulletin IT-510, "Transfer and loans of property made after May 22, 1985 to a related minor"

Interpretation Bulletin IT-511R, "Interspousal and certain other transfers and loans of property"

Form T1206, "Tax on split income"

Form T2205, "Calculation of amounts from a spousal RRSP or RRIF to be included in income for___"

Capital gains and losses

- Classify your gains as capital gains and your losses as business losses, where possible (6.1)

- Make the Canadian securities election to ensure capital treatment for gains on your stock market trades (6.1)

- Consider delaying the sale of all or part of an asset until after year-end to defer capital gains tax (6.2.1)

- If you have unused net capital losses, carry them back or forward to offset taxable capital gains (6.2.2)

- Carry over unused "allowable business investment losses" to reduce taxable income (6.2.3)

- "Purify" your corporation to create qualified small business corporation shares eligible for the $500,000 exemption (6.4.1)

- Plan around your CNIL balance when using the capital gains exemption (6.4.3)

- If you've sold an asset but not received all of the proceeds, claim a capital gains reserve (6.5.1)

- Consider changing principal residence ownership to shelter gains on recreation properties (6.5.2)

- Make the election to treat rented-out property as your principal residence (6.5.2)

- Look into the tax deferral benefits for capital gains on investments in eligible small businesses (6.5.3)

Capital gains and losses are given special treatment in the federal income tax system. Capital gains are effectively taxed at a lower rate than regular income; and individuals are entitled to an exemption for capital gains on certain kinds of property.

The rules are substantially the same for Québec purposes. In this chapter we'll describe the rules in general and take a look at some of the planning opportunities that are available.

6.1 What is capital?

Before we get into the rules that apply to capital gains and losses, it helps to understand what we mean by "capital". Capital property is property that, if sold, will lead to a capital gain (or capital loss). The alternative is property that, when sold, leads to full income inclusion of any gain as income from business. For example, if you speculate on real estate, and you buy and sell a number of properties, your gains on the sales will probably be business income rather than capital gains.

There are no clear rules defining capital property. The *Income Tax Act*'s only comment is to define a "business" as including "an adventure or concern in the nature of trade". The courts have developed guidelines over the years, from which a general picture emerges. If you buy property with the intention of reselling it, and particularly if you sell it quickly and engage in many such transactions, your profit is likely to be considered income from business. If you buy property with the intention of earning income (e.g., rent or dividends) from it, and particularly if this is an isolated transaction and you hold the property for a long time, any gain on a sale is likely to be a capital gain.

Classify your gains as capital gains and your losses as business losses, where possible.

As we'll see in 6.2.1, most capital gains are only one-half taxed and gains on certain small business shares and farm property are eligible for the $500,000 capital gains exemption (see 6.3). So it is much better to have capital gains than regular income. On the other hand, capital losses are of limited use since they can only be used to offset capital gains (see 6.2.2), while business losses can be deducted against other income.

To the extent possible within the law, you should try to classify your gains as capital gains and your losses as business losses. For example, if you buy and sell a commodity on the stock market, how you classify the transaction may depend on whether you have a gain or a loss. Where you are near the borderline between income and capital, you have some leeway to classify the transaction as either. Of course, you should be consistent; you could not take two essentially identical trades and call one a capital gain and the other a business loss.

For example, if you are buying and selling real estate and doing well at it, try to gather data for your files that will support your claim to be engaging in capital transactions. You will want to show that you are purchasing properties purely for their investment value as rental properties, and that any sales were not originally planned but were required by a change in circumstances.

If you are audited, the CRA may reassess you on your classifications. At that point you would have to decide whether to fight the assessment via a Notice of Objection (see 9.4.1), or to accept it and pay the tax that you would have paid in the first place, plus interest. If you are unsure as to whether property you own is capital property or not, you should consult your professional advisers.

If you wish to ensure that your trades on the stock market will always result in capital gains rather than business income, you may file an "Election on Disposition of Canadian Securities" (federal Form T123 or Québec Form TP-250.1-V) with any year's tax return. This will prevent the CRA or Revenu Québec from claiming that you are buying securities for the purpose of selling them and therefore earning business income rather than capital gains.

Once you do so, all "Canadian securities" you ever own will be considered to be capital property for the rest of your life. This includes, generally, shares in Canadian corporations, investments in mutual funds, and bonds, debentures or other debt issued by individuals or corporations resident in Canada (except a corporation related to you). Certain taxpayers, such as traders and dealers, are not allowed to make this election.

> Make the Canadian securities election to ensure capital treatment for gains on your stock market trades.

The downside of making the election is that you will never be able to claim losses on Canadian securities as business losses in the future. Since this is generally hard to do in respect of shares anyway, this may not be a problem for you. You should consider your entire financial position and possibly obtain professional advice to determine the likely effects of the election.

6.2 Capital gains and losses

6.2.1 Ordinary capital gains

Capital gains occur only when property is sold (or is deemed to be disposed of under special rules, which we'll see in 6.4.4 and 6.4.5). So if you own, say, a rental property that has increased in value tenfold, you do not pay any tax on the increase until you actually sell the property. The capital gain is taxed only in the year of the sale.

The basic calculation of a capital gain is easy to understand: proceeds of disposition (normally the sale price), minus any selling expenses (e.g., real estate commissions), minus the "adjusted cost base", equals the capital gain. In most cases the adjusted cost base is simply your cost of the property, but this figure is "adjusted" in various ways. (For the adjusted cost base of an interest in a partnership, see 11.3.5.) Where you have used the election to trigger part of your capital gains exemption (see 6.3), your adjusted cost base will be higher than the actual cost.

Capital gains are, in effect, taxed at a lower rate than regular income. This is done by including in income only the taxable portion of the capital gain, which is one-half of the capital gain for dispositions after October 17, 2000.

> **Example**
>
> Alison paid $5,000 (including commission) for shares of the TD Bank in 1999. On March 1, 2005, she sells the shares for $6,100, of which her broker keeps $100 as commission.
>
> For 2005, Alison has a capital gain of $1,000. The taxable capital gain is one-half, or $500, and this amount is included in her income for tax purposes.

We have mentioned in earlier chapters the marginal tax rates on ordinary income. With one-half taxation of capital gains, the effective tax rates are approximately:

Income level	Salary income	Capital gains (1/2)
$8,000 – $35,000	24%	12%
$35,000 – $70,000	34%	17%
$70,000 – $113,800	41%	20.5%
$113,800 and up	45%	22.5%

The exact tax rates and brackets vary by province.

If you have very large capital gains, minimum tax may apply—see 7.6.

> Consider delaying the sale of all or part of an asset until after year-end to defer capital gains tax.

If you sell an asset after the end of the year, any tax on the capital gain will be payable one year later, giving you the use of the funds for an extra year, except to the extent you are required to make quarterly tax instalments (see 9.1.2). A sale on December 31, 2004 will require tax to be paid by April 30, 2005; a sale on January 1, 2005 will require tax to be paid by April 30, 2006.

Note that most stock and bond market transactions normally settle three business days after the trade is entered. (This is standard practice in the brokerage industry and is recognized by the CRA.) Because weekends and public holidays may affect the determination of "business days", if you intend to do any last-minute 2004 trades, consider completing all trades before Christmas and be sure to check the settlement date with your broker.

In some circumstances, you may wish to sell half of an asset at the end of December and the other half at the beginning of January. Doing this will split your capital gain across the two years. This can be beneficial for two reasons. First, you may be able to reduce the marginal rate that applies in both years by keeping your total taxable income below about

$113,800 for each year. Second, you may be able to avoid minimum tax, due to the $40,000 minimum tax exemption available for each year.

6.2.2 Ordinary capital losses

A capital loss occurs when the capital gain calculation produces a negative amount; that is, the adjusted cost base is greater than the proceeds of disposition minus the selling expenses. Just as capital gains are less heavily taxed than regular income, capital losses are less useful to you than regular (business) losses.

An allowable capital loss is *one-half* of a capital loss. This amount can be offset against taxable capital gains. In normal circumstances, if you have no taxable capital gains, the loss *cannot* be used against other income.

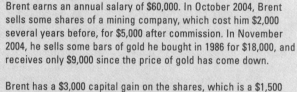

Example

Brent earns an annual salary of $60,000. In October 2004, Brent sells some shares of a mining company, which cost him $2,000 several years before, for $5,000 after commission. In November 2004, he sells some bars of gold he bought in 1986 for $18,000, and receives only $9,000 since the price of gold has come down.

Brent has a $3,000 capital gain on the shares, which is a $1,500 taxable capital gain. He also has a $9,000 capital loss on the gold, which is a $4,500 allowable capital loss. This completely wipes out the taxable capital gain, but the extra $3,000 of allowable capital loss cannot be used to reduce his salary income of $60,000. It can only be used against taxable capital gains of other years, as outlined below.

Allowable capital losses that cannot be used in any given year, as in this example, can be carried back and applied against taxable capital gains of any of the previous three years, subject to whether the capital gains exemption was used in that prior year.

> If you have unused net capital losses, carry them back or forward to offset taxable capital gains.

They can also be carried forward indefinitely; this balance is known as "net capital losses" and can be used against taxable capital gains in any future year. The inclusion rate for loss carryovers (e.g., for losses occurring before October 20, 2000, when the inclusion rate was higher) is adjusted to match the inclusion rate of the taxation year in which they are used.

If you have any net capital losses that cannot be used in the current year, look into whether you can carry them back to any of your three prior years' returns. The CRA and Revenu Québec are required to reopen and reassess your return when you make such a claim. Make sure as well that you keep track of any such losses that you can't carry back, and carry them forward to use in future years.

6.2.3 Allowable business investment losses

There is an exception to the general rule that allowable capital losses cannot be used against ordinary income. The exception applies to allowable business investment losses, which arise when there is a loss on shares of, or debt owing by, a small business corporation.

The term "small business corporation" has a very specific meaning in the *Income Tax Act*. It need not, in fact, be small. The corporation must meet a number of tests, such that it be resident in Canada, a private corporation, not controlled in any manner by non-residents or public corporations, not listed on a Canadian or any of about 25 foreign stock exchanges, and, most importantly, that substantially all (taken by the CRA to mean 90% or more of the value) of its assets be used in an active business carried on primarily in Canada. Shares and debts in such small business corporations can qualify as such assets.

A capital loss on the shares or debt of a small business corporation (including, in some cases, simply determining that the debt has gone bad and will not be repaid) is called a "business investment loss". One-half of this amount is the "allowable business investment loss" (ABIL), which can be deducted against any other income such as employment income or investment income. However, the amount of the ABIL that can be deducted against other income must be reduced by any capital gains exemption claimed in prior years. The amount of this reduction is treated as an allowable capital loss, which you can use to offset any taxable capital gains. In addition, if an ABIL is deducted against other income, you must realize an equal amount of taxable capital gains in later years before you can use the capital gains exemption again. The availability of an ABIL is an extra incentive to investment in private Canadian businesses.

> **Example**
>
> Janet carries on business as the proprietor of a clothing store, from which she nets $50,000 per year in business income. In 1991, Janet invests $12,000 in shares in XYZ Jewellery Inc., a corporation run by her brother which meets the definition of "small business corporation". In December 2004, the corporation goes bankrupt and Janet's shares become worthless.
>
> Janet has a $12,000 business investment loss in 2004, resulting in a $6,000 allowable business investment loss. She can use this against her $50,000 business income, and so will be taxed in 2004 as if she had earned only $44,000.

Allowable business investment losses that cannot be fully used (because you have already wiped out all of your income) are given the same treatment as business losses (see 11.4.1). That is, they can

> Carry over unused ABILs to reduce taxable income.

be carried back and used to offset income in any of the three previous years (even though you have already filed returns and paid tax for those years), or, for tax years ending after March 22, 2004, they can be carried forward and used to offset income in any of the next ten years (seven years for earlier tax years). Any unused balance remaining after the tenth year is reclassified as an allowable capital loss.

6.3 The capital gains exemption

Every individual (but not a trust or corporation) is entitled to a lifetime $500,000 "capital gains exemption" on certain small business shares and farm property.

A general $100,000 capital gains exemption, which applied to all kinds of property, was eliminated as of February 22, 1994. An election was available to use up your exemption for gains accrued to that date. If you made the election for holdings in flow-through entities, your election created an "exempt capital gains balance"—see 6.3.4.

Technically, under the *Income Tax Act* and on the CRA's forms, the exemption is called the capital gains *deduction*. Where it applies, the taxable capital gain is still included in income for tax purposes (see 6.2.1), but an offsetting deduction from net income is allowed when computing "taxable income", the last step on the tax return before calculating tax and tax credits (see 2.1.1).

Note that your $500,000 exemption is limited to the *total* gains on both small business shares and family farms (plus any other exemption claimed up to February 22, 1994) over your lifetime. If, for example, you have already claimed an exemption in respect of, say, $420,000 of gain on small business shares, the maximum exemption available to you for farm property would be $80,000.

6.3.1 Qualified small business corporation shares

Up to $500,000 of capital gains on "qualified small business corporation shares" can be exempt.

The meaning of "small business corporation" was discussed in 6.2.3. The definition of "qualified small business corporation share" is very complex. In very general terms:

- substantially all (considered by the CRA to mean 90% or more of the value) of the business' assets must be used for carrying on an active business in Canada or be shares and debt in other small business corporations (or any combination thereof);

- nobody but you or a person "related" to you can have owned the shares for the two years before you sell them; and
- throughout the two-year period, more than 50% of the corporation's assets must have been used principally in an active business carried on in Canada or invested in other small business corporations (or any combination thereof).

Consult your tax adviser for the specific details as they apply to any shares you own.

Example

Arnold has not used any of his capital gains exemption in the past. He owns all the shares of a corporation. The shares, which are "qualified small business corporation shares", originally cost him $20,000. On March 1, 2004, Arnold sells the shares for $200,000.

Arnold's capital gain is $180,000. One-half of the gain, or $90,000, is included in Arnold's income for 2004, but an offsetting capital gains deduction of $90,000 is allowed in computing his "taxable income"—so he pays no extra tax, except possibly for minimum tax (see 7.6). Of his $500,000, Arnold still has $320,000 of capital gains ($160,000 of taxable capital gains) that can be exempt in the future.

As you can see from the example, it doesn't matter whether you think of the exemption as covering $500,000 (in the example, $180,000 plus $320,000) of capital gains, or $250,000 ($90,000 plus $160,000) of taxable capital gains. It comes to the same thing.

Note that the capital gains inclusion rate will vary for purposes of the exemption, depending on when the gain arose—see 6.2.2.

"Purify" your corporation to create qualified small business corporation shares eligible for the $500,000 exemption.

If you own shares in a small business, and are considering selling them, or transferring them to your children, you should investigate whether the corporation's shares qualify for the $500,000 capital gains exemption. There may be steps you can take to "purify" the corporation so that it meets the criteria discussed above.

It is also possible to transfer the assets of a business that you carry on personally (as a proprietor) into a corporation on a tax-free basis in order to take advantage of the $500,000 exemption. This procedure, known as a "section 85 rollover", requires professional advice, as do other mechanisms for "crystallizing" the exemption (see 14.1).

There is also a special election that lets you take advantage of the exemption for qualified small business corporation shares if the corporation goes public, without having to actually sell the shares. (Once the corporation becomes a public corporation, the shares will no longer qualify for the exemption.)

6.3.2 Qualified farm property

The $500,000 exemption generally applies to family farms and farm quotas that meet certain conditions. In general terms, the property will qualify if you have owned the property for at least two years before you sell it, have used the property in the business of farming on a regular and continuous basis, and have earned more gross income from farming than from other sources. (If you acquired the property before June 18, 1987, it will be qualified farm property if it was used in the business of farming by you or a family member either in the year you sell it or in any five previous years.) Similar rules allow the exemption to be claimed for gains realized on the sale of shares of a family farm corporation or an interest in a family farm partnership.

If you own farm property that you are considering selling, you should obtain professional advice to determine whether you are eligible for the $500,000 exemption.

6.3.3 Restrictions on use of the exemption

The *Income Tax Act* provides rules to prevent people from taking what is considered unfair advantage of the capital gains exemption. The exemption is supposed to exempt capital gains from being taxed. If, however, you are able to use the system of capital gains taxation to claim capital-related losses against other income, the rules prevent you from getting the exemption as well. We'll look at the details in this section.

Allowable business investment losses

If you have allowable business investment losses (see 6.2.3), you will lose your capital gains exemption to the extent that the losses are or can be written off against your ordinary income. The idea is that such losses should effectively be netted against your taxable capital gains first. In other words, you cannot both have a gain that is sheltered by the capital gains exemption, and also use allowable business investment losses against your other income.

Cumulative net investment loss (CNIL)

As discussed in 7.2.3, interest paid on a loan is deductible if you use the loan to invest in shares. Even though your real reason for buying the shares may be to obtain capital gains, the fact that the shares *could* pay dividends (which are income from property) is generally considered enough to make the interest on the loan deductible as interest on funds borrowed to earn income from property.

Tax policy-makers consider it unfair for people to be able to take out large loans, write off the interest, and use the funds to buy shares which would increase in value, giving them a capital gain that is tax-free due to the capital gains exemption. This kind of "double-dipping" is not allowed.

Your capital gains deduction (normally taken, as we have seen, when calculating your "taxable income") is therefore *reduced* by the amount of your cumulative net investment loss, or CNIL (pronounced "see-nile"). The basic idea is that if you borrow money, buy an investment and the investment goes up in value, you should not be able to get both the capital gains exemption and your interest expense write-off.

The actual calculation is rather more complicated. Your CNIL is the total of your investment expenses minus all your investment income, cumulative since January 1, 1988. "Investment expenses" include interest you have deducted, investment counsel fees, partnership losses (except where you are an active partner), losses from rental property, and most tax shelter write-offs. Investment income includes interest, dividends ("grossed-up" by one-quarter as explained in 7.1.2), rental income and income from a partnership where you are not an active partner.

Example

Arnold has not used any of his capital gains exemption in the past, but has claimed a total of $10,000 in net investment expenses since 1991, so his CNIL balance is $10,000. He owns all the shares of a corporation. The shares, which are "qualified small business corporation shares", originally cost him $20,000. On March 1, 2004, Arnold sells the shares for $200,000.

Arnold's capital gain is $180,000. One half of the gain, or $90,000, is included in Arnold's income for 2004. Because of his $10,000 CNIL balance, the offsetting capital gains deduction is only $80,000, not $90,000.

In effect, Arnold must "eat through" his CNIL balance and pay tax on the $10,000 before he can start to use his capital gains exemption.

Note that the CNIL limitation applies even though the investment expenses and the capital gain are unrelated. However, taxable capital gains that are actually taxed, because you cannot or do not offset them with your capital gains exemption, effectively reduce the impact of the CNIL balance.

Note also that the calculation of the exemption (and CNIL) is done at the end of the year. It is therefore possible to realize a capital gain that you think is exempt, but for which you cannot claim the exemption because you create a CNIL balance later on in the same year. So if you have a CNIL balance, consider reducing or eliminating it before the end of the year. This can be done by increasing your investment income. For example, if you are the owner-manager of an incorporated business (see Chapter 14), you may be able to reduce your salary and increase your dividends from the corporation to use up your CNIL balance. There may also be situations where you can advance interest receipts to before the end of the year, or defer deductible interest payments until after December 31, to reduce your CNIL.

> Plan around your CNIL balance when using the capital gains exemption.

6.3.4 The $100,000 exemption and exempt capital gains balance

Until 1994, a general $100,000 exemption was available for capital gains on most property. The federal budget eliminated the regular exemption for gains after that date. An election was available for gains accrued to February 22, 1994. To the extent you would otherwise have been able to claim the exemption, you could have *elected* to treat any property as if you had sold it on February 22, 1994 at a particular price (up to the property's fair market value) and immediately bought it back at the same price. (The exemption was also eliminated for Québec tax purposes and a virtually identical election was introduced.)

Flow-through entities—mutual funds and others

Certain investments can have capital gains calculated at the investment level and then flowed through to you so that you report the capital gain on your personal income tax return. These are called "flow-through entities". They include mutual funds (see 7.3.1), segregated funds (similar to mutual funds, but offered through life insurers), partnerships (see 11.3.3), investment corporations, mortgage investment corporations, employee profit sharing plans and certain other special trusts.

You can have capital gains on flow-through entities in two ways. First, gains incurred in the entity are flowed through to you. Second, you can sell your interest in the entity.

If you made the election in 1994 to trigger your capital gains exemption in respect of holdings in flow-through entities, the effect is very different than for other property. Rather than increasing your cost base in the investment, your election created an "exempt capital gains balance" that you can use until 2004 to reduce any capital gain resulting from either the sale of the property or capital gains flowed through to you. Thus, you can shield "flow-through" gains in future years, even though you may not have sold the investment.

Note that you will have to track the "exempt capital gains balance" for each mutual fund or other investment on which you make the election. You cannot use the balance from one fund to shield capital gains distributions from another fund.

If you sell all of the units of a property, any remaining exempt capital gains balance is added to the adjusted cost base of the last units of the flow-through entity to be sold, which will enable you to realize a capital loss at that time. If you still own the units of the flow-through entity at the end of 2004, any remaining exempt capital gains balance is added to the cost base of the units.

6.4 Special cases

6.4.1 Reserves

If you sell a property for a capital gain but do not receive all of the proceeds right away, you may be able to claim a reserve, to defer recognition of the gain for tax purposes.

> If you've sold an asset but not received all of the proceeds, claim a capital gains reserve.

Suppose, for example, you sell a house you have been renting out. The house cost you $100,000 and you sell it for $300,000. But you take back a mortgage for $150,000. You can normally claim a reserve on the capital gain, reflecting the fraction of the purchase price that you haven't yet received. In this case, since you haven't received half of the purchase price, you would only have to recognize half of the gain in the year of sale.

Under the reserve rules, you must recognize at least 1/5 of the gain each year (cumulatively), so that the entire capital gain must be accounted for by the fourth year after the year of sale.

Claiming a reserve might not be beneficial where you may be in a higher tax bracket in later years.

6.4.2 Principal residence

A gain on selling your home is normally completely exempt from taxation. The exemption is based on the definition of "principal residence". This term includes, among other things, a house, a condominium and a share in a co-operative housing corporation. It also includes the land around the house, but normally only up to 1/2 hectare (about 1.2 acres).

You, or your spouse or child, must have "ordinarily inhabited" the residence for it to qualify, so you can't use the exemption on property you rent out without ever having lived in it, or for vacant land. However, it need not have been your "principal" residence in a literal sense. It can be a cottage, for example.

Since 1982, each family unit is limited to one "principal residence" at a time. For this purpose, the family unit means you, your spouse (including a common-law or same-sex spouse as outlined in 2.2.1), and any unmarried children under 18. So if you designate your house as your principal residence for a period of several years, your spouse cannot also designate your cottage as a principal residence over the same period. (The designation is only made when you file your tax return for the year in which you sell the property, so you can decide at that point which property to claim the exemption on.)

Before 1982, each taxpayer was entitled to a principal residence exemption. So if you and your spouse or another member of your family unit have owned two residences (such as a regular home and a summer cottage) since before 1982, it may be possible to structure your holdings so that the pre-1982 portion of the capital gain on the second residence will be exempt. Consult a professional adviser on this matter.

> Consider changing principal residence ownership to shelter gains on recreation properties.

If you have adult children, consider giving them the ownership of a second residence. If you own your house and your 19-year-old son owns the cottage, he can designate it as his principal residence when he sells it. However, at the time you transfer it to him you will have to recognize any increase in value since you purchased it (subject to a reduction if you made an election to use your capital gains exemption on it). You should also be sure you are satisfied with the *legal* effect of what you are doing—giving away your cottage—before you embark on such a transaction for tax purposes.

An exemption is also available in some cases where you rent the property out, either before or after you use it as your own residence. If you move out of your home and rent it out, you can continue to designate it as your residence for up to four years (provided you do not claim any other property as your principal residence and you file a special election with your tax return for the year in which you begin to rent the property). If you move due to relocation of your or your spouse's employment, the four-year period can normally be extended indefinitely, provided you move back to the home upon leaving that employment.

> Make the election to treat rented-out property as your principal residence.

If you acquire property and rent it out, and then move in at some later date, you can file a special election with your tax return for the year in which you move in to defer the capital gain that would normally apply when you change the property from income-earning to personal-use. If you do this, you may be able to get an exemption for four years during which you rented the property.

6.4.3 Capital gains rollover for investments in eligible small businesses

Look into the tax deferral benefits for capital gains on investments in eligible small businesses.

Under a tax incentive to encourage investments in small business corporations, individual investors may defer capital gains on a small business investment where the proceeds from the investment are used to make other small business investments.

The deferral is available for capital gains arising after February 27, 2000 on small business investments. The deferred gain reduces the tax cost of the new investment, which may be subject to tax when it is disposed of later.

> **Example**
>
> On March 31, 2004, Will sells an eligible share investment in Bio Ventures Inc. for $100,000. Since Will had initially invested $40,000 in the company, he realizes a capital gain of $60,000. If only $90,000 of the total proceeds is reinvested in shares of the replacement investment, Agri Tek Inc., then 90% of the gain can be deferred, or $54,000. Will's net capital gain, one-half of which will be subject to tax, is equal to the portion that cannot be deferred, or $6,000. The deferred gain of $54,000 reduces the cost of the Bio Ventures Inc. shares to $36,000, resulting in a potentially larger gain when the shares are sold in the future.

For reinvestments after February 18, 2003, there are no limits on the total amount that can be reinvested. For reinvestments on or before that date, no more than $2 million reinvested in shares of any particular company or related group would qualify for the deferral. You do not have to deal at arm's length with the corporation you are investing in.

To qualify for the rollover treatment, an investment must be ordinary common shares issued from the treasury of an eligible "small business corporation" (see 6.2.3). At the time of the share issue, the total carrying value of the corporation's assets and the assets of any related corporations cannot exceed $50 million. Throughout the period the investor holds the shares, the issuing corporation must be an eligible "active business corporation" (that is, the company must essentially meet the tests for a small business corporation, except that it does not need to remain a private corporation).

Among other requirements, the eligible investment must be held for more than six months before a gain can be deferred. You must acquire the replacement investment at any time in the year of the disposition or within 120 days after the end of that year. For example, if you sell an investment in 2004, you must acquire another by April 29, 2005 to qualify for the deferral.

6.4.4 Other rules

Death—When you die, you are generally deemed for tax purposes to have sold your capital property for its current fair market value, thus triggering a capital gain on all of the increase in value that has accrued since you purchased it. The treatment of capital gains on death is discussed in detail in 22.2.3.

Non-arm's length transfers—When you give or sell property to a member of your family, you are normally deemed to have received fair market value for it, triggering recognition of any accrued capital gain (or loss) for tax purposes. However, if you transfer property to your spouse, it is normally deemed to have been sold at your cost unless you elect to realize a gain. This rule also applies to common-law spouses and same-sex spouses who meet the criteria outlined in 2.2.1.

Personal-use property—No capital loss is available on personal-use property, except for "listed personal property" (jewellery, works of art, stamps, coins and rare books) losses that can be used only against listed personal property gains.

As well, the adjusted cost base and proceeds of disposition of personal use property are deemed to be $1,000, which essentially means that capital gains on personal-use property only apply to the extent the sales price exceeds $1,000. The $1,000 deemed adjusted cost base and deemed proceeds of disposition do not apply if the property is acquired after February 27, 2000 as part of an arrangement in which the property is donated as a charitable gift.

If you change a property from personal use to income-earning use, you are normally deemed to have sold it at its fair market value, requiring you to recognize for tax purposes any accrued capital gain.

Options—Special rules apply to determine capital gains where you purchase or grant options (e.g., on the stock market).

Superficial loss—If you sell property (e.g., shares) to trigger a capital loss, and you or your spouse or a corporation controlled by either of you acquire identical property within 30 days before or after your sale, the capital loss will be called a "superficial loss" and ignored for tax purposes. The denied loss will be added to the cost of the identical property.

Insurance or expropriation proceeds—If property of yours is lost or destroyed, or expropriated, any insurance settlement or expropriation payment is considered to be proceeds of disposition, for purposes of the calculation described in 6.2.1.

Pre-1972 property—If you have property that you have owned since before 1972, when capital gains were not taxed at all, only the gain accruing since the end of 1971 will be taxed. For publicly-traded shares, valuation is easy; for real estate and shares in private businesses, valuation as of December 31, 1971 may be difficult to accomplish. When you report such a gain, you will need to estimate the value of the property on that date, and use that as the cost of the property (assuming it is higher than your actual cost).

6.5   References

The following publications can be obtained (in person or by telephone request) from your nearest CRA Tax Services Office. Forms and brochures may also be available from the CRA's Internet site at *www.cra-arc.gc.ca*.

Interpretation Bulletin IT-120R6, "Principal residence"

Interpretation Bulletin IT-133, "Stock exchange transactions—Date of disposition of shares"

Interpretation Bulletin IT-170R, "Sale of property—When included in income computation"

Interpretation Bulletin IT-218R, "Profits, capital gains and losses from the sale of real estate, including farm land and inherited land and conversion of real estate from capital property to inventory and vice versa"

Interpretation Bulletin IT-232R3, "Losses—Their deductibility in the loss year or in other years"

Interpretation Bulletin IT-387R2, "Meaning of identical properties"

Interpretation Bulletin IT-456R, "Capital property—Some adjustments to cost base"

Interpretation Bulletin IT-459, "Adventure or concern in the nature of trade"

Interpretation Bulletin IT-479R, "Transactions in securities"

Interpretation Bulletin IT-484R2, "Business investment losses"

"Capital Gains Tax Guide"

Form T1A, "Request for loss carryback"

Form T123, "Election on disposition of Canadian securities"

Form T657, "Calculation of capital gains deduction for 20___ on all capital property"

Form T936, "Calculation of cumulative net investment loss to December 31, 20___ "

Form T2091 (IND), "Designation of a property as principal residence by an individual (other than a personal trust)"

Form T2091 (IND)-WS, "Principal residence worksheet for 20___"

Investments

- Consider acquiring preferred shares to enhance after-tax yield (7.1.2)
- If you're the higher-income spouse, consider electing to report your spouse's dividend income on your own return (7.1.6)
- Look into the potential benefits of investing in a dividend reinvestment plan (7.1.7)
- Defer tax by acquiring investments that mature shortly after year-end (7.2.1)
- Structure your investments to make interest deductible (7.2.3)
- Look into the benefits of investing in units of an income fund (7.3.2)
- Consider the merits of acquiring an exempt life insurance contract (7.3.3)
- Consider investing in tax shelters—but don't let tax write-offs drive your decision (7.5)
- Before investing in a tax shelter, obtain its Identification Number (7.5.1)
- Be aware of the possible impact of minimum tax on otherwise tax-free capital gains (7.6.3)
- Limit your "tainted" tax shelter deductions (7.6.3)

In this chapter we look at how investment income is taxed, how interest expense can be written off, and a few types of tax shelters, along with a number of tax planning ideas that you should keep in mind. We also discuss special tax rules that apply to foreign investments. The chapter concludes with a discussion of Canada's alternative minimum tax, which may apply depending on the nature of your investments. For advice on developing an appropriate investment strategy, see 1.1.4.

7.1 Dividends

7.1.1 What is a dividend?

A dividend is a distribution of after-tax profits to the shareholders (owners) of a corporation. A corporation may have many classes of shares. Preferred shares are shares on which dividends must generally be paid first, before dividends can be paid on a corporation's common shares.

Preferred shares typically pay a fixed annual or quarterly dividend. In some ways, they are similar to bonds or other debt, since the return is a fixed percentage. However, in certain situations a corporation may not be *required* to pay dividends on its preferred shares as long as it does not pay dividends on its common shares. If the corporation suffers losses, its board of directors may well decide not to pay dividends on preferred shares.

From a tax point of view, for individuals, preferred shares are identical to common shares (which typically pay dividends that bear some relationship to the corporation's profits).

7.1.2 How is a dividend taxed?

Dividends received by individuals from Canadian corporations are taxed in a rather peculiar manner, designed to reflect the fact that the corporation paying the dividend has already paid tax on its profits. The amount included in the individual's income is "grossed-up" to reflect the total amount of pre-tax income that the corporation is presumed to have earned. The individual then receives a credit to offset the tax the corporation is presumed to have paid (at about 20%). In no case, however, is the *actual* income earned or tax paid by the corporation taken into account.

Canadian dividends received are grossed-up by one-quarter. That is, you add 25% to the amount received, and show the total as income from dividends on your tax return. The offsetting federal dividend tax credit is then two-thirds of the amount of the gross-up—two-thirds of that 25%, or, if you like, 13.33% of the total you report as dividend income. Similar credits are available at the provincial level. In Québec a separate dividend tax credit is available for 10.83% of the grossed-up dividend.

> **Example**
>
> Melissa earns $35,000 per year. She also owns shares in Canadian Inc., which pay her a dividend of $1,000 in 2004.
>
> Melissa's income for 2004 will be $35,000, plus the $1,000 dividend, plus a gross-up of one-quarter of the dividend, or $250. Her tax will be calculated on this income of $36,250. From the tax, she will deduct her regular credits (see Chapter 2) and a federal dividend tax credit of $166.67 (two-thirds of the $250 gross-up). Melissa then calculates her provincial dividend tax credit. The net result is that the dividend is taxed at about 19% instead of 34%.

(See 14.2.1 for more detail on the dividend tax credit from the perspective of the corporation.) On average, the effect of the dividend tax credit is to tax dividends at *approximately* the following rates:

Income level	Salary income	Dividend income
$8,000 – $35,000	24%	7%
$35,000 – $70,000	34%	19%
$70,000 – $113,800	41%	26%
$113,800 and up	45%	31%

The exact numbers vary significantly by province. Remember that these numbers apply only to dividends from Canadian corporations. Dividends from foreign corporations are taxed as ordinary income.

Since preferred shares pay dividends rather than interest (which is taxed like regular income, as we'll see in 7.2), preferred shares may offer a better after-tax rate of return than many interest-earning investments while still coming close to a guaranteed yield. While the yield is never completely guaranteed, many major public companies will continue to meet preferred share dividend expectations even when they suffer losses.

> Consider acquiring preferred shares to enhance after-tax yield.

The yields on preferred shares usually reflect the fact that dividends are less heavily taxed than interest (as well as the fact that dividend payments are not deductible to the corporation). You will have to monitor preferred share prices on the market to find the best yields.

7.1.3 Stock dividends

A corporation will sometimes pay a stock dividend by issuing new shares to pay the dividend rather than giving you cash. In such a case, the gross-up and dividend tax credit still apply, and you must pay tax on the stock dividend even though you have received no cash. The amount of the dividend on which the gross-up is calculated is the increase in the paid-up capital resulting from the issue of new shares.

7.1.4 Capital dividends

You may also receive capital dividends from private corporations. They are completely tax-free (see 5.3.8). A capital dividend is generally a distribution of the untaxed one-half of capital gains. As we saw in 6.2.1, that fraction of the capital gain is not taxed at all. The capital dividend mechanism is used to distribute the untaxed portion without any tax consequences to the shareholder. (For an example, see 14.2.4.)

7.1.5 Dividends received by a corporation

Intercorporate dividends are normally tax-free. The assumption is that once a corporation has paid tax on its income, its profits can be distributed through a chain of holding corporations with no further tax consequences until an individual receives a dividend at the end of the chain. However, a special refundable tax—"Part IV tax"—can apply to intercorporate dividends in some circumstances, including most dividends received on investments in public corporations. The Part IV tax is 33 1/3%.

7.1.6 Election to transfer dividends from spouse

Since the dividend tax credit is a credit against tax owing, it is worthless if there is no tax to pay. If your spouse's income is very low, and you claim a credit for your spouse as a dependant (see 2.2.1), a relatively small amount of dividend income, when grossed-up by 25%, can take your spouse over the $680 income threshold for 2004 and thereby reduce your spousal tax credit. At the same time, since your spouse does not pay any tax, the dividend tax credit is of no use.

> If you're the higher-income spouse, consider electing to report your spouse's dividend income on your own return.

In such a case, you may elect to report all of your spouse's dividend income on your own tax return. While this may result in the income being taxed at a higher rate, it will avoid the erosion of the spousal tax credit. You will have to calculate tax both ways to see which is better. This election is done by including the dividends directly on Schedule 4 (Investment income) on your tax return, not Schedule 2 (Amounts transferred from spouse). If you live in Québec, you do not need to make the similar election for Québec tax purposes. Québec taxpayers are able claim the unused portion of their spouse's non-refundable tax credits, including the dividend tax credit (see 17.2.1).

7.1.7 Dividend reinvestment plans (DRIPs)

> Look into the potential benefits of investing in a dividend reinvestment plan.

Dividend reinvestment plans may offer a cost-effective way of building your investment portfolio. DRIPs give investors the opportunity to automatically reinvest their cash dividends by purchasing additional shares or fractional shares directly from the company on the dividend payment date. The additional shares are usually purchased at a discount from the current share price and without brokerage commissions.

Many of these plans also allow you to periodically purchase more shares of the company with cash at a discount for nominal or no fees. (Depending on the nature of the plan, the discount may trigger a taxable shareholder benefit—check with your broker or the plan's administrator to avoid surprises.)

Bear in mind that you will still be liable for tax on the dividends in the current year. Because the dividend income is reinvested, you will have to pay the tax with other funds. Amounts reinvested will also incrementally increase the cost base of your investment, which will affect the average cost of the shares for capital gains tax purposes when you sell them (see 6.2.1).

7.2 Interest income

Interest income is taxed at the same rates as employment or business income.

7.2.1 Accruing interest

Suppose you acquire a five-year GIC for $1,000 that will return $1,150 after five years. When do you report the $150 in interest?

Each year you must declare the interest accrued to the anniversary date of when you acquired it. Your financial institution should issue you a T5 slip showing the interest accruing on all such long-term investments.

The accrual rules apply to almost all kinds of investments, including stripped bonds (see 7.2.2 below), Canada Savings Bonds, and mortgages or loans to relatives on which interest is allowed to accrue.

> **Example**
>
> In 1999, Christine lent $10,000 to her cousin, who is attending university and needed the funds for tuition and residence. Her cousin agreed in writing to pay 6% annual interest (not compounded) on the loan, but that he will not pay back the loan or the interest until after he has graduated and secures a job.
>
> Christine is required to report and pay tax on $600 of accrued interest income each year beginning in 1999. If in 2004 her cousin pays her $13,000 to cover the loan and all interest, she will only report $600 as income in 2004, since she will have already reported $2,400 over the previous four years.

As a general deferral technique, acquire investments that mature shortly after year-end rather than before. For example, if you are investing in T-bills on July 15, and you can choose

> Defer tax by acquiring investments that mature shortly after year-end.

between maturity dates of December 29 and January 2, then you should choose January 2 if all else is equal. That way you will defer reporting and paying tax on the income by one year. Of course, tax considerations should not override normal investment considerations, such as the available rates of return and the question of when you will need access to the funds.

7.2.2 Strip bonds and clipped coupons

Strip bonds are long-term government or government-backed (e.g., provincial hydro) bonds that pay interest when their coupons are cashed in. A typical bond might have a 20-year term, have a face value of $100,000 and come with coupons paying $2,500 in interest, cashable every six months. At the end of the 20 years one simply redeems the bond for $100,000.

Brokerage firms often acquire such bonds and split up the bond and its coupons, selling them separately. The $100,000 bond maturing in 20 years, in our example, might be sold for $10,000, while the forty $2,500 coupons would be sold at prices reflecting the length of time until their maturity.

For tax purposes, the difference between the discounted price of the bond (or coupon) and the amount you receive when it is redeemed is considered to be interest. Because of the annual accrual rule, such bonds generally are unattractive to many taxpayers—you have to pay tax annually on interest that you will not receive for some time. However, they can be excellent investments for self-directed RRSPs and other tax-deferred plans (see Chapter 3).

One should be cautious when acquiring strip bonds or clipped coupons—or, for that matter, any long-term bond. If you need to sell them before they mature, you will find that their value may fluctuate considerably due to trends in interest rates. If interest rates in general have gone up, the resale value of your bond or coupon will likely have gone down.

7.2.3 Deductibility of interest expense

As a general principle, interest is deductible for tax purposes as long as the loan was used for the purpose of earning income from a business or property. Such expenses are also called carrying charges. Specifically, under draft tax rules released in October 2003 that will take effect as of 2005 (if enacted), you must have a reasonable expectation of cumulative profit over the expected life of the business or property before you can deduct the interest on the borrowed funds—see 10.4.1.

If you borrow money to buy common shares on the stock market, or to invest in a business, the interest you pay is generally deductible. If you borrow to invest in preferred shares, you can deduct your interest expense to the extent of the grossed-up dividend on the shares. For example, if the dividend rate is 4%, being effectively 5% when grossed-up by 25%, and the interest on your borrowed funds is 6%, only the first 5% of interest on the loan can be deducted.

On the other hand, if you buy an investment with a fixed interest rate, you can only deduct interest on your loan if the loan interest is less than the rate that your investment pays (otherwise, no reasonable expectation of profit exists). For example, if you borrow at 5% and use the funds to purchase an investment with a fixed 6% return, the interest you pay is deductible.

Interest is not deductible where the loan was taken out for some purpose other than to earn income subject to tax. Examples include:

- home mortgage, except to the extent you use a home office for business purposes (see 11.2.10)
- car loan, where the car is used solely for personal use
- credit cards, except to the extent the charges are for business expenses
- loan to contribute to an RRSP or RESP
- interest on late income tax or instalment payments.

If you dispose of the property that you borrowed money to acquire, you can continue to deduct the interest in certain cases even though the underlying source of income has been lost. The rules in this respect are complex, and professional advice may be required if you are in this situation.

For Québec purposes, as of March 30, 2004, you may only deduct expenses paid to earn income from property from your investment income earned in the year—see 17.2.22.

Interest on a car loan, where the car is used for your employment or business purposes, is limited to the employment or business portion of $250 or $300 per month, depending on when the car was purchased—see 12.3.

Since interest on consumer loans and home mortgages is normally not deductible, while interest on loans taken out to purchase income-generating investments is generally deductible, you should try to ensure that all loans you take out are for a deductible purpose. For example, if you have funds that you could put towards either a home mortgage or investments and you plan to do both, you will probably be better off to use the funds towards the mortgage and take out a loan to purchase the investments.

> Structure investments to make interest deductible.

The CRA often pays special attention to deductions for interest expense. It is wise to keep on file, along with your tax return, accurate records showing the amount of the loan, the purpose of the loan and the interest paid during the year, along with the relevant financial statements and possibly a confirming letter from your financial institution. It may be appropriate to file this information with your tax return if you have done so in previous years.

For minimum tax purposes, interest expense must be added back to your income if it relates to tax shelters or other "tainted" deductions. See 7.6.2.

7.3 Other tax-effective investments

7.3.1 Mutual funds

Mutual funds are pools of assets that are invested by professional managers, either in general investments or in a particular sector (such as real estate or natural resources). Investors purchase units if the mutual fund is a trust or purchase shares if the fund is a corporation.

Mutual fund trusts and corporations are flow-through entities for tax purposes—taxable income earned inside the entity is treated as if you held the investments directly, instead of through the fund. As such, the income retains its character for tax purposes (e.g., as dividend income, capital gains or interest) when it is distributed to you during the time you own the shares or units, and taxed accordingly.

> Look into the benefits of investing in units of an income fund.

When you redeem or sell the units or shares, you are taxed on the capital gain, if any, according to the regular treatment of capital gains discussed in 6.2.1.

If you owned any mutual fund units or shares as of February 22, 1994, you may have an "exempt capital gains balance"—see 6.4.4.

7.3.2 Income funds

Income funds have risen in popularity during the past few years. Though these vehicles come in a variety of forms, they are generally publicly traded mutual fund trusts that own businesses, such as real estate, resource properties (oil, gas, and mining) and other assets, which typically produce a stable stream of cash flow. Cash flows from the operating business to the income fund, and the fund makes distributions to its investors at regular intervals.

Distributions from the fund to investors are generally a mix of income and capital payments. Amounts paid or payable to an investor as income are taxed according to the regular rules for interest, dividends or capital gains, depending on the payment's nature (provided the fund makes the appropriate designations). But, as we will see in 14.2.5, an amount received as a payment of capital may be treated as a return of funds that the investor initially used to buy the asset, so no tax should apply to the capital payment.

Example

Tom invests $10,000 in units of an income fund in 2004. During that year, he receives $1,000 in distributions from the fund. Of these distributions, $700 is identified as interest income, which Tom must include in his income for the year. The other $300 is identified as a capital payment, so it is not taxable. Instead, it reduces the tax cost of Tom's investment to $9,700 ($10,000 - $300), which will increase the taxable capital gain that will arise when Tom eventually sells the income trust units. In 2004, Tom will only pay tax of about $315 on the $1,000 distribution, instead of the $450 in tax he would have paid had he received the entire amount as interest.

Amounts received as repayments of capital from an income fund reduce the "adjusted cost base" of your investment (see 6.2.1), which will be subtracted from your sales proceeds when you sell the investment to determine your capital gain. Though you will not pay current tax on a portion of investment income received during the year, you will eventually pay tax on a larger capital gain on the investment when you sell your income fund units.

As with any investment, when deciding whether you should invest in an income fund, you should examine factors beyond its tax implications, including the income fund's stability and the consistency of its record in making distributions. Purchasing an income fund should be considered as a possible choice in implementing your investment strategy (see 1.1.4).

Income fund investors should also be aware of the potential application of the minimum tax (see 7.6).

7.3.3   Exempt life insurance contracts

The life insurance industry has developed attractive and highly sophisticated products that can help you meet two planning objectives at once: having insurance coverage and providing retirement income from tax-sheltered growth.

These policies allow you to pay insurance premiums and make deposits to a tax-sheltered investment account at the same time. You can choose between more conservative investments, such as GICs, or investments that involve more risk, such as equity indices. Unlike RRSP contributions, which are made with before-tax dollars, insurance premiums are not deductible. In both cases, the income earned is tax-sheltered until maturity of the plan or policy. Funds withdrawn from the policy during your lifetime are taxable to the extent the amount withdrawn exceeds its adjusted cost base. On death the entire amount (that is, the original insurance amount plus the accumulated cash value) is received tax-free as a death benefit. Alternatively, funds withdrawn may be treated as a loan against your policy which is repaid from the death benefit.

> Consider the merits of acquiring an exempt life insurance contract.

If you have maximized your RRSP contributions, this type of life insurance policy may provide another opportunity for you to shelter your savings from tax.

There are many issues to look at when considering whether to acquire such a contract, such as the underlying mortality costs and administrative expenses, a guaranteed minimum rate of return compared to a similar return in a non-tax sheltered environment, your required life insurance coverage, your income objectives, the financial reserves and strength of the insurance company and so on. Professional advice is a must when assessing the merits of this type of "investment". They are, however, a potential opportunity for those who cannot otherwise find alternative tax deferral arrangements.

Life insurance is discussed in more detail at 21.7.

7.3.4 Systematic withdrawal plans (SWPs)

Systematic withdrawal plans are tax-effective investment vehicles that rely on the untaxed nature of capital repayments (see 14.2.5). Under a SWP, you invest in, for example, a mutual fund or equity, and then sell a fixed dollar amount of the fund at regular intervals (e.g., monthly or quarterly).

Amounts withdrawn in the early years of your investment will be repayments of capital, which are not taxed in the year received. The opportunity for capital repayments each year will depend on the investment's rate of return and the size of your regular withdrawal.

Over time, the untaxed capital portion of the regular withdrawal will decline while the income portion of the withdrawal will increase. However, this income will still benefit from the preferred tax treatment of capital gains.

7.4 Special rules for investments in foreign property

Over the past few years, new tax rules have been introduced to address the government's perception that many Canadians are avoiding Canadian tax by transferring their assets and income outside of the country. Some of these rules are discussed below.

The tax rules in this area are quite complex and penalties for non-compliance may be quite onerous. If you own investments outside of Canada, you should consult with a tax adviser to make sure your Canadian tax obligations are met.

For a discussion of foreign investments that can be held within a self-directed RRSP, see 3.1.7. If you own assets or other property in the U.S., see Chapter 19. If you contribute to or are a beneficiary of a trust resident outside of Canada, see 7.4.3.

7.4.1 Reporting rules for foreign investment property

You have to file an annual information return with the CRA if you own or have interests in foreign property where the aggregate original cost is more than $100,000. For these reporting purposes, foreign property includes:

- funds in foreign bank accounts
- rental property outside Canada
- Canadian securities held outside Canada

- investments in foreign corporations, trusts, partnerships or other foreign entities.

Excluded from these rules are interests in foreign affiliates (see below), property used in an active business, property held in RPPs, RRSPs and RRIFs, and personal-use property such as a vacation property.

Form T1135, "Foreign Income Verification Statement" is due at the same time as your personal tax return. You must describe each foreign property and disclose its cost and whether any income was earned from the property during the year. (New immigrants to Canada do not have to file this information return in the year in which they become resident.)

Similar reporting rules apply if you own (together with related persons) 10% or more of a foreign corporation, if you transfer or loan property to a non-resident trust (or a corporation controlled by it), and if you receive distributions from, or are indebted to, an offshore trust.

The information required is extensive and the penalties for non-compliance are severe. You should seek help from your tax adviser if you own or have an interest in such foreign property.

7.4.2 Foreign investment entities

If you own certain types of foreign investments, tax rules that took effect for 2003 and later years may greatly increase your tax burden. Generally, these rules are designed to accelerate a Canadian tax liability in the hands of taxpayers owning an interest in a vehicle meeting the definition of a "foreign investment entity" (FIE).

Under these rules, if you have a FIE investment, specific amounts (determined under a complex calculation) will be taxed in Canada as investment income in your hands each year, whether or not you actually received any income from the investment.

The FIE rules apply to most Canadian taxpayers, including individuals, corporations, trusts and partnerships. Only individuals who have been resident in Canada for less than five years and certain non-profit entities are exempt.

A FIE can be any non-resident corporation or trust, or any other entity that is formed and governed outside of Canada, such as an association, fund, organization, joint venture or syndicate. Interests that are potentially affected include, among others, investments in foreign mutual funds, public and private corporations, call options and certain convertible securities.

Some investments are specifically excluded from the rules. For example, if you own foreign public company shares or mutual fund units that are traded on a U.S., U.K., or certain other foreign stock exchanges, or an interest in a U.S. real estate investment trust (REIT) or regulated investment company (RIC), the rules probably will not apply to your investment. A similar exemption from the rules applies if you are an employee who has received stock options in a foreign entity (such as your employer's U.S. parent corporation).

If you have an interest in any form of non-resident entity, you should ask your tax adviser whether the rules could apply to your foreign investments.

7.4.3 Trusts resident outside of Canada

If you are a Canadian resident contributor to a non-resident trust or a Canadian resident beneficiary of a non-resident trust, you may face a substantial tax liability as a result of tax rules regarding the taxation of income earned by non-resident trusts.

These rules generally apply to non-resident trusts that have a Canadian resident contributor, or a Canadian beneficiary and a contributor with a significant connection to Canada.

If the rules apply, the trust will be deemed to be a resident of Canada and will be subject to tax in Canada on its worldwide income and capital gains. At the same time, all Canadian-resident contributors and beneficiaries will be jointly liable for the tax liability of the trust.

If you have an interest in or are involved in any way with a non-resident trust, contact a tax adviser for help in determining the potential impact of these rules. (For a general discussion of the taxation of trusts, see 21.5.)

7.5 Tax shelters

Tax shelters are no longer as important to tax planning as they were some years ago. For a variety of reasons, there are now relatively few publicly-offered vehicles for sheltering your ordinary income from tax.

Contrary to popular perception, tax shelters are generally not "loopholes" in the system. Preferences are given to certain types of investment as a deliberate move by the government to stimulate economic activity in a particular area. Whether it is investment in small business corporations, scientific research or exploration for oil and gas or computer software, the specific write-offs and credits in the *Income Tax Act* are put there to encourage investors to invest funds in a particular area.

One should only invest in a tax shelter if, after taking the tax benefits into account, there is a reasonable expectation of profit from the shelter. The CRA is extremely aggressive in challenging tax shelter-related deductions. The tax benefits alone should rarely control your investment decision.

> Consider investing in tax shelters — but don't let tax write-offs drive your decision.

Strict rules have been enacted over the years that make many tax shelters unattractive. For example, "at-risk" rules prevent you from writing off more than the original cost of your investment (that is, in a limited partnership tax shelter—see 7.5.2). Other rules take aim at certain types of tax shelter investments that have rights to receive future income, such as limited partnership structures involving mutual fund limited partnerships and film production services, curtailing the tax benefits of such investments.

When investing in tax shelters, one must be aware of the possible application of the minimum tax (see 7.6). Finally, you must always be aware of the possible application of the general anti-avoidance rule discussed in 5.2.6.

For details on RRSPs and other tax deferral plans, see Chapter 3.

7.5.1   Tax shelter identification number

Anyone selling an interest in a tax shelter must obtain an identification number from the CRA (and Revenu Québec, in some cases) and provide that number on all documents and financial statements relating to the shelter. *If you do not have the identification number, or if any penalties relating to the identification number are payable by the promoter and have not been paid, you will not be able to claim the benefits of the shelter.*

The identification number does not indicate approval by the CRA or Revenu Québec of the proposed benefits. It merely ensures that the shelter has been registered for administrative purposes, making audit and reassessment easier

> Before investing in a tax shelter, obtain its Identification Number.

for the CRA and Revenu Québec if they eventually decide to disallow some or all of the tax benefits.

7.5.2   Tax shelters involving limited partnerships

Tax law changes over the years have curtailed the benefits of tax shelters involving the purchase of an interest in a limited partnership.

A limited partnership is a partnership, in that you share the profits of the business with the other partners, and report a percentage of the partnership's income (or loss) directly as your income—whether or not you have received any of the profits. This is in contrast to corporate profits, which are reported only when distributed as dividends, as we saw in 7.1.2 above. However, a limited partnership is similar to a corporation in that you have limited liability—you cannot be sued for the partnership's debts. In general, you can only lose your original investment.

Because you can report partnership losses directly on your own tax return, limited partnerships used to be an attractive investment where the partnership business was expected to have losses in its initial years (either real losses due to start-up costs, or tax-created losses due to high write-offs available on certain kinds of investments).

However, you may not write off more than the original cost of your investment. The *Income Tax Act*'s "at-risk" rules provide that you cannot deduct more than the amount you have at risk in a limited partnership. Other rules severely restrict the use of limited partnerships to create losses where there is "non-recourse" debt (i.e., you are required to contribute amounts to the partnership, but cannot be forced to do so from your own funds, only from the profits from your partnership interest).

Further, losses from limited partnerships must be added back into income for minimum tax purposes. See 7.6.2.

7.6 Minimum tax

7.6.1 What is the minimum tax?

The minimum tax was enacted as a political solution to the perception that many high-income taxpayers were paying little tax through the use of tax shelters and other so-called tax preferences. It is relatively narrow in focus, concentrating on specific shelters and credits.

The minimum tax is an alternative tax calculation. You must calculate your tax both normally and under the minimum tax rules, and pay the higher of the two.

In simplest terms, you calculate minimum tax by taking your taxable income, adding back "tainted shelter" deductions (such as resource write-offs and tax shelters) and 60% of the untaxed one-half of capital gains, taking a $40,000 exemption and then calculating federal tax at 16%. Most personal credits, but not the dividend tax credit or investment tax credits, are then allowed as with regular tax. A similar calculation is required at the provincial level, with provincial minimum tax rates ranging from 35% to 62.2% of federal minimum tax (with adjustments for provincial credits). If you live in Québec, see 17.2.23 regarding the Québec minimum tax.

Minimum tax paid can be recovered in the next seven years to the extent your regular tax exceeds your minimum tax (see 7.6.2). Minimum tax does not apply to the year of death.

7.6.2 Calculating the tax

Somewhat simplified, the calculation is as follows:

1. Start with your taxable income (after all deductions allowed for regular tax purposes).

2. Add back the deductions that you are not allowed to claim for minimum tax purposes:

   • losses from any investment that requires a tax shelter identification number (see 7.5.1)
   • losses from a partnership where you are a limited partner or passive partner (see 7.5.2)
   • certain resource-related deductions
   • carrying charges, such as interest expense, relating to any of the above (see 7.2.3)
   • employee home relocation deduction (see 10.3)
   • 60% of amounts claimed under the employee stock option deduction (see 10.4.1 – 10.4.3)

   These are sometimes called "tainted" deductions, since you cannot claim them for minimum tax purposes.

3. **Add 60% of the untaxed one-half of capital gains**, whether the rest of the gain was eligible for the capital gains exemption or not. (The exemption is still allowed for minimum tax purposes.)

4. **Deduct the gross-up on dividends** (see 7.1.2). Since the dividend tax credit will not be allowed for minimum tax purposes, you are only taxed on the actual dividend received, rather than on the grossed-up amount.

5. **Deduct $40,000** as your basic minimum tax exemption.

6. **Calculate federal tax at 16%.**

7. **Deduct personal credits** (see Chapter 2), such as your basic credit, other dependants, old age, disability (for self or spouse only), CPP/QPP contributions, EI premiums, tuition, education, medical and charitable. Do not deduct investment tax credits (10.2.14), political contribution credits (2.7.2), pension tax credits (19.3.5), transfer of unused tax credits from spouse (2.1.3), tuition and education credits transferred from a child (2.4), dividend tax credits (7.1.2) or labour-sponsored venture capital credits (3.3.5).

8. If the resulting tax is higher than your federal tax calculated normally, you must pay the minimum tax.

Provincial minimum tax is then generally calculated by multiplying the federal minimum tax amount by the applicable provincial minimum tax rate.

If you find that you have to pay minimum tax in any given year, the excess of your minimum tax over your regular tax becomes a "minimum tax carryover", which can be used in any of the next seven years.

In a future year, you can use the carryover to the extent your regular tax exceeds your minimum tax.

> **Example**
>
> Riley's 2004 regular federal tax is $30,000. His 2004 minimum tax (federal) is $35,000.
>
> Riley must pay the $35,000 tax and provincial taxes (total about $56,000). However, he has a $5,000 federal minimum tax carryover. If, in 2005 his regular federal tax is $32,000 and his minimum (federal) tax is $22,000, Riley can deduct the carryover from his regular federal tax and pay only $27,000 basic federal tax (before calculating provincial tax).

7.6.3 Tips for minimizing minimum tax

Exempt capital gains

Be aware of the possible impact of minimum tax on otherwise tax-free capital gains.

The minimum tax can have a serious impact on capital gains, particularly where the $500,000 capital gains exemption would otherwise enable you to avoid regular tax entirely.

> **Example**
>
> Max sells the shares of his small business corporation for a $480,000 capital gain, which is fully exempt under the $500,000 capital gains exemption (see 6.4.1). Max has no other income in 2004.
>
> Max will pay no regular tax. For minimum tax purposes, however, his adjusted taxable income will be about $144,000 (one-half of $480,000 x 60%), minus the basic $40,000 exemption. His federal minimum tax will therefore be 16% of $104,000, or $16,640, minus personal credits. The federal minimum tax of $16,640 (net of personal credits) may be carried forward for seven years and applied against regular federal tax payable in those years.

Interest expense and business losses

Two important deductions are not affected by the minimum tax. The first is deductible interest paid (see 7.2.3) on loans not used for tax shelter purposes. The second is business losses and loss carryforwards (see 11.4) other than loss carryforwards that are attributable to "tainted" shelters (see 7.6.1). Where it otherwise makes sense from a business perspective, you can generate such deductions without triggering any minimum tax liability.

Keep in mind, however, that high interest expense may give you a high cumulative net investment loss (see 6.4.3) and thus make the capital gains exemption unavailable to you, to the extent you would otherwise want to use it (see 6.4.1 and 6.4.2).

Tax shelter deductions

Be aware of possible minimum tax implications when planning for large tax shelter claims, particularly on resource funds such as drilling funds and flow-through shares. Resource expenses that exceed your total income from such funds (and are therefore claimed as losses) must be added back for minimum tax purposes.

To the extent you have loss carryforwards from previous years that are attributable to "tainted" shelters, they must also be added back to your taxable income for minimum tax purposes.

> Limit your "tainted" tax shelter deductions.

7.7 References

The following publications can be obtained (in person or by telephone request) from your nearest CRA Tax Services Office. Forms and guides may also be available from the CRA's Internet site at *www.cra-arc.gc.ca.*

Interpretation Bulletin IT-66R6, "Capital dividends"

Interpretation Bulletin IT-67R3, "Taxable dividends from corporations resident in Canada"

Interpretation Bulletin IT-232R3, "Losses—Their deductibility in the loss year or in other years"

Interpretation Bulletin IT-295R4, "Taxable dividends received after 1987 by a spouse"

Interpretation Bulletin IT-396R, "Interest income"

Interpretation Bulletin IT-533, "Interest deductibility and related issues"

Form T691, "Alternative minimum tax"

Form T1134A, "Information return relating to foreign affiliates that are not controlled foreign affiliates"

Form T1134B, "Information return relating to controlled foreign affiliates"

Form T1135, "Foreign income verification statement"

Form T1141, "Information return in respect of transfers or loans to a non-resident trust"

Form T1142, "Information return in respect of distributions from and indebtedness to a non-resident trust"

Charitable donations

- Combine two or more years of charitable donations into one year (8.1)
- If you have a spouse, combine your charitable donations and claim them on the higher-income spouse's return (8.1)
- Consider donating publicly traded securities or other assets to charity (8.1)
- Consider planned charitable gifts and bequests (8.2)
- Think about donating publicly traded securities instead of cash (8.3.3)

Canada's tax system provides generous incentives to encourage Canadians to donate to charities. In this chapter we provide an overview of these incentives and discuss ways of structuring your gifts to make the most of the available tax benefits.

8.1 Tax credit for charitable donations

Charitable donations entitle you to a two-tier credit. The first $200 of donations for the year (total to all charities) gives you a 16% federal tax credit, worth about 25% when provincial tax is taken into account. All donations above that level give you a 29% federal tax credit, worth about 45% when provincial tax is factored in (see 17.2.9 if you live in Québec).

For federal purposes, charitable donations above $200 for the year are therefore given the same treatment as if they were deductible, if you are in the top federal tax bracket ($113,800 and over in taxable income for 2004). If you are in a lower bracket, the credit for large donations is worth far more than a deduction.

To claim charitable donations, you must have official receipts that show the recipient organization's charitable registration number. The CRA's administrative policy allows you to claim receipts made out in either your name or your spouse's.

> Combine two or more years of charitable donations into one year.

The maximum amount of donations you can claim in a year is 75% of your net income. To the extent you have receipts for more than this amount, or if you choose not to claim a donation for any other reason, you can save the receipts and claim the credit in any of the following five years.

The annual limit for donations in the year of death and the year before (including bequests and legacies) is 100% of net income for the year (see 8.2 below for more on making charitable bequests in your will).

If you donate only small amounts over a year, consider combining two or more years of donations into one year to put yourself over the $200 threshold. A $100 donation above the $200 level for the year costs you only about $55 instead of about $76 below that level.

> If you have a spouse, combine your charitable donations and claim them on the higher-income spouse's return.

Once you are over the $200 level, consider making extra contributions in December rather than early in the new year. Your tax saving through the donations credit will come one year earlier.

If you and your spouse donate separately, you should combine your receipts and claim them all on one return (the CRA's administrative practice permits this), to avoid having to get the low-rate credit on $200 twice. If your province levies a high-income surtax (see 2.1.3), the higher-income spouse should claim all the donations.

The CRA's administrative policy also allows a donation made by one spouse to be split between the two spouses in whatever proportion they choose. Further, spouses may be able to claim each other's unused charitable donation carryforwards from a prior year.

> Consider donating publicly traded securities or other assets to charity.

Instead of donating cash, you should also consider the potential benefits of donating property such as publicly traded securities, artwork or real estate. The tax treatment of donations of property—or "gifts in kind"—is more complex but may result in greater tax savings for you and may enhance the value of your gift to the charity. Gifts in kind are discussed in 8.3.2.

8.2 Charitable bequests

> Consider planned charitable gifts and bequests.

Charitable gifts can be made through your will. A bequest in your will is treated as if the gift was made in your final year and is claimed for credit on your final tax return. The charitable donations limit in the year of death and the immediately preceding year is 100% of the deceased's "net income". Any donations not claimed on your final tax return can be carried back and claimed in the year before death.

If you name a charity as the beneficiary of your life insurance (or your RRSP or RRIF) in your will, your estate will be able to claim the amount as a charitable donation on your final tax return or in the preceding year.

It is possible that large bequests in your will (or large donations during your lifetime) may become unusable for tax purposes, if they far exceed the allowable threshold. You may therefore want to consider other options to maximize the tax credits and the funds available to your beneficiaries—both family members and charities.

Proper will planning can help ensure that your bequest will be made as you intend and provide significant tax savings for your estate.

Careful planning together with an informed adviser can ensure your philanthropic goals are met and the tax benefits are available when you need them most.

8.3 Types of charitable gifts

In this section we look at some ways you can structure charitable gifts, both during your life and through your will, to further your philanthropic and estate planning goals and make the most of the available tax credits. The options are much broader than simply donating cash or leaving a sum of money to a charity in your will.

There are many ways in which gifts may be made to charitable organizations—including gifts of property (such as securities, artwork, real estate), life insurance and annuities—with significant tax benefits. These benefits depend on the type of gift, the timing of the donation and the nature of the charitable organization.

A gift made today can provide a current tax saving and, in addition, a charitable gift annuity (see 8.3.6 and 8.3.7) or a gift of a remainder interest in a trust or property (see 8.3.8) will also allow you the continued use of, or income from, the property itself.

8.3.1 Gifts to the Crown

Before 1997, gifts to the federal or a provincial government ("Crown gifts") were not subject to the charitable donations limits. You could claim up to 100% of your net income for Crown gifts. To level the playing field for other charities, the federal limit for claiming Crown donations was reduced to 75% of net income, the same limit that applies to gifts made to other charities.

8.3.2 Gifts in kind

Both during your lifetime and on your death, you can donate property to a charity as an alternative to money. A gift of property is called a gift in kind. Examples include artwork, shares and real estate, as well as some more esoteric gifts we discuss below, such as life insurance or a residual interest in real property. (You cannot "give" services, however—only property.)

A gift in kind is normally valued at its fair market value. For purposes of determining the tax credit for your donation, it will be the same as a gift of cash. Thus, the tax credit will generally be worth about 45% of the value of the property. However, at the time of the donation you are deemed to have disposed of the property at its fair market value—meaning that you must recognize any capital gain or income that would apply had you sold the property for that price.

However, if you have large capital gains in a year from other dispositions, gifts that trigger significant gains could result in a liability for alternative minimum tax (see 7.6). Before you make such a donation, run the numbers to ensure that minimum tax will not result.

For purposes of the tax credit, the 75% net income limit is effectively increased to 100% of net income for:

- gifts of ecologically sensitive lands to municipalities and certain charities (plus a reduced income inclusion for resulting capital gains—see 8.3.4)
- gifts of "certified cultural property" (and capital gains on such property may not be taxable—see 8.3.4).

For donations of capital property resulting in taxable capital gains and donations of depreciable property that trigger recapture of capital cost allowance (see 11.2.7), a mechanism is in place to increase the 75% net income limit so that 100% of the taxable capital gain and recaptured CCA are included in the donation limit.

Individuals and corporations who donate securities listed on prescribed stock exchanges, mutual funds and segregated funds of life insurance companies to charities (other than private foundations) need only include in their taxable incomes one-quarter of the capital gain (instead of the usual one-half) that arises on the securities' disposition. If your corporation makes the donations, its capital dividend account (see 14.2.4) will be increased by the non-taxable portion (or three-quarters) of the capital gain; this amount can then be paid to the corporation's shareholders tax-free. (If you live in Québec, see 17.2.9.)

If you make a gift of capital property, you can file an election with your tax return to use a lower amount than the fair market value, for purposes of determining both your proceeds of disposition of the property and the value of your donation. You can elect any amount between the adjusted cost base (see 6.2.1) and the actual fair market value.

Whether the election is useful depends on a number of factors, including your tax bracket, your other sources of income and deductions, and your prospects for income in future years against which to use up the charitable donation carryforward.

The election described above can also be used by artists for gifts of work they have created (which is inventory rather than capital property).

8.3.3 Cash vs. shares—which should you donate?

Say you want to make a $2,000 donation to a favourite cause and you have publicly traded securities that originally cost you $1,000 and that are now worth $2,000. Should you sell the securities and donate the proceeds or should you simply donate the securities? Assuming your income is taxed at the top marginal rate of about 45% and you have already donated $200 in the year, the tax effects of both choices are as follows:

> Think about donating publicly traded securities instead of cash.

- If you sell the shares and donate the before-tax proceeds, a $1,000 capital gain will arise on the securities' sale. You would then have to pay $225 in tax on the taxable portion of your gain (one-half of $1,000 $\times$ an assumed 45% tax rate). Your $2,000 donation will give you a tax credit of $900 (45% $\times$ $2,000). In the end, the donation will result in net tax savings of $675 ($900 tax credit − $225 capital gains tax).
- If you donate the shares directly, the charity will still get the full $2,000 value of the shares. The taxable portion of the $1,000 capital gain will only be one-quarter, so your tax payable will only be $113 (one-quarter of $1,000 $\times$ 45%). You will also get a tax credit of $900 for the donation (45% $\times$ $2,000). The net tax savings resulting from your donation will be $787 ($900 tax credit − $113 capital gains tax).

As you can see, you will come out ahead if you donate the securities directly. In the above example, you give up property of the same value but your after-tax cost is $112 less than it would be had you sold the securities and donated the proceeds.

8.3.4 Gifts of cultural property and ecologically sensitive land

Gifts of "cultural property" to certain public authorities or institutions (such as museums) also produce tax benefits. If the property being gifted is certified as being of cultural significance to Canada, the donation will be equal to the property's fair market value for purposes of the credit but no taxable capital gain will arise. Any capital loss that may arise may be deductible in some circumstances.

For gifts of ecologically sensitive lands to Canadian federal or provincial governments, municipalities or approved registered charities, the income inclusion for capital gains arising from such gifts is reduced to one-quarter (instead of one-half).

8.3.5 Gifts of life insurance

If you have a "permanent" life insurance policy (see 21.7), such as whole life or universal life, you can donate it to a charity by transferring the ownership of the policy to the charity and having the charity become the beneficiary of the policy. For tax purposes, the value of your donation will be the policy's cash surrender value, plus any accumulated dividends and interest that are also assigned, minus any policy loan outstanding. However, to the extent that value exceeds the tax cost of the policy to you, you must recognize the excess as income, as if you had cashed in the policy.

Once you have donated the policy to the charity, if you continue to pay the premiums on the policy, each such payment will be considered to be an additional charitable donation entitling you to a tax credit.

If you make the charity a beneficiary of a life insurance policy that you continue to own, the payment of the death benefit to the charity is considered a donation made by you before your death. The donation can be claimed on your final tax return or on your return for the prior year.

8.3.6 Purchasing an annuity from a charity

You can purchase an annuity from a charity, whereby you give the charity a sum of money up front and receive a fixed annual payment for the rest of your life. This planning idea is not as tax-effective as it was in the past because the tax rules in this area were changed significantly for annuities issued after December 20, 2002.

For annuities issued before December 21, 2002, you will still be entitled to a charitable donations tax credit if the original sum you gave to the charity is greater than the total payments you expect to receive from the charity during your lifetime. Annual payments received from the charity will be tax-free to you. If the total payments that you expect to receive are more than the amount given to the charity, you will not be entitled to a tax credit and the excess amount will be taxable to you on an annualized basis.

For annuities issued after December 20, 2002, the tax rules are quite different. You will earn a charitable donations tax credit if the amount you give to the charity is greater than the market price you would otherwise pay to buy an annuity offering the same annual income from a life insurance company. A portion of the annual payments received from the charity may be taxable to you. If the total payments that you expect to receive from the charity are greater than the market price, you will have to bring the difference into your taxable income over your projected life expectancy.

8.3.7 Charitable insured annuity

Another strategy is to set up a "charitable insured annuity". You buy an annuity from a life insurance company, and use part of the monthly payments to pay the premiums on a life insurance policy with a charity as the owner and beneficiary. Thus, you receive an income stream over your lifetime (from the annuity), and tax credits for the insurance premiums you pay. On your death, the charity receives the insurance proceeds.

8.3.8 Charitable remainder trusts

If you have property that you would like to donate to a charity, but you need the income from the property during your lifetime, consider donating a "residual" interest in the property—that is, the capital that will remain on your death. One way to do this is to set up a "charitable remainder trust". This is a trust (see 21.5) with the conditions that income be paid to you during your lifetime, while the *capital* will go to the charity on your death. In some cases, you can transfer the residual interest in property (e.g., real estate) directly, without setting up a trust.

The value of a gift of the residual interest in a property is its discounted present value. This value will depend on factors such as the current fair market value of the property, current interest rates and your life expectancy. The gift entitles you to the normal tax credit for charitable donations. If you arrange to receive less income from the trust (or property) than you might otherwise be entitled to, the value of your donation may be higher.

Such a gift has several attractions. First, the charity gets a vested right to the property immediately, and need not worry about whether you will leave the property to it in your will (or whether your will might be contested). Second, you get an immediate tax credit based on the amount of your donation (the residual value). Third, you continue to receive the income from (or use of) the property for the rest of your life.

You will be deemed to have disposed of the property transferred to the trust for its fair market value. This may lead to a capital gain and an income inclusion for tax purposes, with an enhanced tax credit as illustrated in the example in 8.3.2 above. In addition, the trust will have to file an annual tax return (see 21.5.3), though it will normally not pay any tax since all of its income will be paid out to you.

8.4 References

The CRA publishes the following publications, which are available (in person or by telephone request) from your nearest CRA Tax Services Office. Forms and guides may also be available from the CRA's Internet site at *www.cra-arc.gc.ca*.

Interpretation Bulletin 110R3, "Gifts and official donation r
  eceipts"

Interpretation Bulletin IT-226R, "Gift to a charity of a residential interest in real property or an equitable interest in a trust"

Interpretation Bulletin IT-244R3, "Gifts by individuals of life insurance policies as charitable donations"

Interpretation Bulletin IT-288R2, "Gift of capital properties to a charity and others"

Interpretation Bulletin IT-297R2, "Gifts in kind to charity and others"

Dealing with the tax collectors

- File your return on time even if you can't pay your taxes owing (9.1.1)
- Pay your taxes owing by April 30 even if you're filing later (9.1.1)
- NETFILE, EFILE or TELEFILE your return for a quicker refund (9.1.2)
- Consider prepaying instalments to reduce deficient instalment charges (9.2.2)
- Be aware of the CRA's interest rates and compounding of interest (9.3)
- If you know you owe interest on late or deficient instalments, think about paying an estimate with your final payment (9.3)
- Sign a waiver only if necessary (9.4.3)
- File a Notice of Objection to preserve your right to appeal (9.5.1)
- When your return is reopened on reassessment, consider requesting other adjustments (9.5.1)
- Be sure you understand the legal issues when appealing (9.5.2)
- Consider paying the amount owing even if you are filing an objection (9.5.4)

In this chapter we deal with the administrative side of the tax system—how tax is collected, how your return is assessed and what you can do if you disagree with the Canada Revenue Agency or Revenu Québec as to the amount of tax you owe.

9.1 Tax returns

9.1.1 Filing your return

Most individuals are required to file their federal and Québec tax returns by April 30 each year. The deadline for individuals who have business income and their spouses (including common-law and same-sex spouses—see 2.2.1) is June 15. Even though the return may not be due until June 15, any balance of tax owing for the year is due on April 30.

If you have no tax to pay for the year (as distinguished from no balance owing in April), no return is required unless you disposed of capital property or realized a capital gain in the year or unless the CRA or Revenu Québec requests one.

In all provinces except Québec, you file a single return with the CRA to cover both federal and provincial tax. Québec residents and taxpayers with business income from operations in Québec must file a Québec provincial tax return as well (see Chapter 17).

The return must be postmarked (or transmitted electronically) by the due date. If the return is late, an automatic penalty of 5% of any tax still owing applies. This penalty is increased by 1% of the unpaid tax for each full month that the return is late, to a maximum of 12 months. Repeated failures to file a return on time results in higher penalties.

File your return on time even if you can't pay your taxes owing.

To avoid the 5% penalty, you should file your return on time even if you are not able to pay your balance owing. Interest will accrue on the unpaid balance, but the penalty will not apply.

Pay your taxes owing by April 30 even if you're filing later.

Conversely, if you are unable to get your return completed (or your return is not due until June 15), but you do have a rough idea of how much tax you owe, it is a good idea to pay that amount to the CRA or Revenu Québec by April 30. Make sure to have it credited to the correct taxation year (and not as an instalment for the subsequent year, for example).

9.1.2 Electronic filing

The CRA offers three options for most taxpayers to file their returns in electronic form: NETFILE, EFILE and TELEFILE. NETFILE allows you to file returns prepared on your personal computer via the Internet. To use NETFILE, you will need CRA-approved tax preparation software, a web browser that meets the CRA's security standard and an access code, which you should receive with your 2004 income tax forms in the mail.

The EFILE system allows authorized tax return preparers or transmitters to file returns directly to the CRA using tax return preparation and transmission software. Most professional tax return preparers offer this service in addition to preparing the actual tax returns. If you prepare your own return, most EFILE preparers will charge a small fee to transmit it. The Québec government also allows electronic filing for Québec provincial tax returns.

Under the CRA's TELEFILE program, certain employees, students or seniors can file their returns by telephone. If you are eligible, the CRA will send you an invitation to use TELEFILE and an access code in your personalized income tax package. To use TELEFILE, complete your tax return and then use a touch tone phone to call the service and enter the information as prompted.

The main benefit of these electronic filing options to taxpayers is the ability to have the return assessed and a refund paid in as little as two to three weeks, as opposed to a somewhat longer wait using the conventional filing method. If you are expecting a refund, electronic filing will speed up the processing of your return and the delivery of your refund cheque.

Further, you do not need to file paper returns or receipts with the return. (However, receipts and other supporting documentation still must be retained for any subsequent review by the CRA.) This reduces the paper burden on you and the tax authorities.

> NETFILE, EFILE or TELEFILE your return for a quicker refund.

If you are concerned about reassessment of your return down the road, electronic filing will normally get your return assessed sooner and start the three-year reassessment period (see 9.4) earlier.

If you have a balance due, you can use NETFILE, EFILE or TELEFILE before the deadline but you will have until April 30 to mail in your payment. (You may also be able to pay your taxes electronically—see 9.2.3.)

9.2 Payment of tax

9.2.1 Source withholdings

Tax is withheld at source and remitted to the CRA and Revenu Québec by employers and others. Tax withheld from a payment to you is considered to have been paid by you to the tax authorities, even if your employer never remits it. It is also considered to have been paid to you in the sense that it forms part of your income.

Source withholding applies to the following kinds of payments, among others:

- employment income
- pension benefits
- unemployment insurance benefits
- withdrawals from an RRSP
- annuity payments
- Old Age Security benefits
- payments of passive income to non-residents (interest, dividends, rent, royalties, etc.)
- purchase of real estate from a non-resident (unless the non-resident has a certificate from the CRA and Revenu Québec, where applicable).

Note that there is no withholding of tax on interest, dividends, rent or royalties paid to Canadian residents. Self-employment income such as consulting fees (see 11.1) is also paid without source deductions.

9.2.2 Instalments

You must pay instalments if the difference between your tax payable (including provincial tax except Québec tax) and amounts withheld at source is more than $2,000 in both the current year and either of the two preceding years. For Québec residents, since provincial tax is not collected by the CRA, the threshold is $1,200 of federal tax instead of $2,000—see 17.7.24.

Quarterly instalments are due on the 15th of March, June, September and December.

There are three possible ways to calculate your instalment obligations.

The first method is for your total instalments, paid in four equal payments, to equal the tax owing for the year on your sources of income from which tax is not withheld. In other words, your instalments should equal the balance owing at the end of the year.

The second method is for your quarterly instalments to equal the tax owing on your previous year's sources of income for which tax was not withheld. In other words, take the balance you had to pay last year after accounting for source withholdings, and pay that amount over the year in instalments.

The first method requires you to estimate your current year's income. If you guess low, you will end up not paying enough. The second method lets you use the previous year's income, but on March 15, when the first instalment is due, you might not yet have calculated your previous year's total tax. For this reason the third method was introduced.

Under the third method, your March and June instalments are each one-quarter of the *total* tax owing on income from which tax was not withheld for two years ago. Your total instalments for the year must still equal the total amount for one year ago, as with the second method. Therefore, the September and December instalments must be enough to reach this total. The CRA and Revenu Québec will mail you a statement twice a year advising you of your quarterly instalment obligations under the third method.

Example

Alexander is self-employed as a consultant. His 2003 tax payable (combined federal/provincial) was $20,000. His 2004 tax payable was $24,000. He expects his total 2005 tax bill to be $27,000.

Alexander should pay quarterly instalments on March 15, June 15, September 15 and December 15, 2005, totalling $24,000, his tax payable for the previous year. If he wishes, he may pay four instalments of $6,000 each.

The CRA will advise Alexander in February 2005, however, that his March and June payments should be $5,000 each—one-quarter of his 2003 tax payable, since his 2004 figures are not yet available. If he makes these payments, and then pays $7,000 on each of September 15 and December 15, he will have paid the required $24,000 and met his instalment obligations under the "third method".

The $3,000 balance (assuming Alexander's estimate of income for 2005 turns out to be correct) will then be due on April 30, 2006, although his return need not be filed until June 15.

If instalments are made on time and in the correct amount as per any of the three methods, no interest is payable. If instalments are not made when required or are deficient, interest is

> Consider prepaying instalments to reduce deficient instalment charges.

assessed at the CRA's and Revenue Québec's current high "prescribed rate" (see 9.3), compounded daily.

You cannot *earn* interest by paying instalments early, but you can earn "contra-interest" at the same rate as applies to late payments, to offset interest that would otherwise be assessed on late instalments. If you've fallen behind in your instalments, consider making an extra or early payment to offset the (non-deductible) interest that will otherwise be assessed.

Example

Alexander, from the above example, does not make any instalment payments until June 15, 2005. On that day he makes a single payment of $15,000. He then makes a $2,000 payment on September 15, 2005 and a $7,000 payment on December 15, 2005.

Alexander should not owe any interest on instalments, assuming the prescribed interest rate stays constant through 2005. His June 15 payment can be thought of as three parts: $5,000 due in March, paid three months late; $5,000 paid on time; and $5,000 of the $7,000 not due until September, paid three months early. The payment that is early will generate "contra-interest" to offset the interest that Alexander would otherwise have to pay due to his being late with his March payment.

For federal purposes, if the interest owing on late instalments is greater than $1,000, you may be subject to an additional penalty of up to 50% of the interest.

9.2.3 Electronic tax payments and refunds

The federal government offers a "Direct Deposit" service whereby tax refunds, GST credits and Child Tax Benefit payments can be deposited directly into your account at any financial institution in Canada. The service can get tax refunds and other payments into your hands more quickly because it saves the time it takes to print and mail the cheques. It also avoids the problem of cheques lost in the mail.

To take advantage of the service, complete the area "Direct deposit—Start or change" on the back page of the T1 General income tax return. You can also make the request by completing Form T1-DD or, if you are filing electronically, Form T183. For other government payments, such as monthly Old Age Security or Canada Pension Plan payments, contact your financial institution for the appropriate forms.

You may be able to pay your taxes electronically using your financial institution's phone and Internet banking services. Contact your financial institution for information about its electronic payment services.

9.3 Interest

Interest that you owe on late payments of tax and instalments and on refunds is calculated at a prescribed rate, which varies quarterly based on the average yield of Government of Canada 90-day treasury bills. The new rate for each quarter is announced by the CRA in a news release about three weeks before the quarter begins.

> Be aware of the CRA's interest rates and compounding of interest.

There are three different "prescribed" interest rates each quarter. The lowest rate, which is roughly the Bank of Canada rate for the previous quarter, applies for purposes of applying the attribution rules (see 5.2.2) and the employee and shareholder loan rules (see 10.3 and 14.2.6). The middle rate, which is two percentage points higher, applies to refunds paid by the CRA. The highest rate, which is a further two points higher, applies to late payments of tax and instalments owing by taxpayers.

Although the rate is expressed as an annual rate, it is in fact compounded daily, so the effective rate is somewhat higher than shown. A 10% interest rate, for example, is equivalent to a rate of about 10.52% in simple annual interest.

Interest that you owe on late payments runs from when the payment was due. Interest on refunds generally runs from 45 days after the due date for the return, or from the day on which you file your return, whichever is later. However, if you have a June 15 filing deadline because you have self-employment income (see 11.2.1), interest will not be paid until 45 days after April 30 or 45 days after the date that the return is actually filed, whichever is later.

Interest that you are required to pay to the CRA, such as on late payments of tax or instalments, is not deductible.

Interest paid to you on a refund is taxable in the year in which you receive it. Thus, if you file your 2004 return when it is due in April 2005 and receive a refund in August, the interest from June 14 included in that cheque must be reported on your 2005 return.

> If you know you owe interest on late or deficient instalments, think about paying an estimate with your final payment.

If you have tax owing at April 30 and you know interest will be charged because of late or deficient instalment payments, consider paying an estimate of the interest with your April 30 payment to stop any further interest from accruing.

The federal prescribed interest rates for the last few quarters to time of writing are:

Quarter	Low rate	Middle rate	High rate
October – December 2003	3%	5%	7%
January – March 2004	3%	5%	7%
April – June 2004	3%	5%	7%
July – September 2004	2%	4%	6%

As noted, the high rate applies to late tax and instalment payments and the middle rate to refunds. The low rate applies for the purposes of the attribution rules and shareholder and employee loans.

For Québec purposes, the low rate is the same as the federal rate and the middle rate is slightly lower (so less interest is paid to you on refunds). For late taxes, the Québec high rate is the same as the federal rate, but a whopping 10% higher for late Québec tax instalments.

9.4 Assessment, audit and reassessment

9.4.1 "Quick" assessment

When you file a conventional (paper) return, it is processed over a period of typically three to six weeks, after which you receive a "Notice of Assessment" and any refund owing to you. The processing includes a review of the numbers on your return to make sure they are consistent (for example, that your arithmetic is correct and that any numbers that need to be supported by receipts or information slips are consistent with them).

Most EFILE, TELEFILE and NETFILE users can expect their returns to be assessed in two to three weeks.

The assessment is normally not based on any investigation beyond what is on your return. It is sometimes referred to as a "quick assessment". The fact that a particular claim is allowed at this point does not mean that the CRA or Revenu Québec is "letting" you claim it; it merely means that the CRA has not addressed the issue in any detail.

For a partnership, the tax authorities may issue a determination of the partnership's income or loss, which is effectively an assessment of each partner's portion of the income or loss. See 11.3.6.

9.4.2 Audit

Some time after the initial assessment, your return may be selected for audit. Most audits of individual taxpayers (as opposed to corporations) are "desk audits", in which the auditor will ask you to supply supporting material for claims you have made. Some audits are "field audits", in which the auditor will come to your place of business to look at your records.

If you file using one of the electronic options, you will not have to file any receipts with your return. However, the CRA or Revenu Québec may later "spot-check" your return to verify certain claims, such as donations, RRSP contributions or tuition fees. This is normally just a formality, designed to maintain the integrity of the electronic filing systems.

You should be aware of your rights on an audit. The auditor is not entitled to go on a "fishing expedition" through your books. He or she may request specific information, and you may ask why that information is needed. If you anticipate problems, you may wish assistance from your professional advisers in dealing with the auditor.

If you have not engaged in tax evasion, an audit should not normally be cause for concern.

9.4.3 Reassessment

If the audit (or an audit of another taxpayer) turns up an indication that your tax payable should be other than what was initially assessed, the CRA will issue a reassessment. If the reassessment results in more tax payable by you, this will not normally be done without you first being consulted and given an opportunity to explain your position.

A reassessment cannot normally be issued more than three years after the date of the original assessment. However, in cases of fraud, or misrepresentation attributable to "neglect, carelessness or wilful default", the reassessment may be issued at any time.

Sign a waiver only if necessary.

There are several other situations where the three-year limitation does not apply. The most important is where you have filed a waiver. The waiver, which is directed to a specific issue that is in dispute, will allow the CRA to reassess you on that issue at any time. You can revoke a waiver on six months' notice to the CRA. If you are asked by a CRA auditor to sign a waiver, consider the request carefully and obtain professional advice before agreeing.

First, consider the auditor's alternative if you do not sign the waiver. You are under no obligation to file a waiver simply to make the auditor's life easier. If the three-year reassessment period is about to expire, and the auditor does not yet have enough information to justify a reassessment, it may be to your advantage not to sign the waiver. Bear in mind that a reassessment normally takes some time to work its way through the CRA's internal system, although it can be rushed through in a couple of days in extreme cases.

Second, make sure that the waiver is very specific and waives the three-year period only in respect of the specific issues that are under investigation or dispute.

Similar rules apply for Québec tax purposes.

9.4.4 Requests under the "Fairness" rules

What happens if you cannot pay your taxes or make a tax filing on time because of a natural or human-made disaster, serious illness or accident? The *Income Tax Act*'s "Fairness" rules give the CRA the discretion to waive penalties and interest on overdue taxes if you were unable to pay on time because of circumstances beyond your control. (In the case of large natural disasters such as floods, the CRA may extend tax-related deadlines for everyone in the affected area.)

Under the Fairness rules, the CRA may also issue tax refunds even where the return is filed after the late-filing deadline (that is, generally three years from the original due date) and accept late-filed elections, or allow you to amend or revoke an election after the applicable deadline.

Aside from natural disaster or personal misfortune, the Fairness rules can apply if you could not make a tax payment or file an election on time for more mundane reasons such as incorrect information provided in writing by the CRA or service disruptions such as strikes. But if you were simply negligent or unaware of the rules, you will still have to pay the usual penalties and interest on your overdue taxes.

In weighing your Fairness request, the CRA may consider your previous compliance record and your promptness in bringing the matter to the CRA's attention.

Although the provinces generally do not have formal Fairness legislation, this should not stop you from applying for similar relief provincially. Ontario, for example, has internal guidelines for waiving interest and penalties that have not been released to the public.

9.5 Objections and appeals

9.5.1 Notice of Objection

If you cannot come to an understanding with the auditor and a reassessment is issued, or if you disagree with the original assessment, you may file a Notice of Objection. This is done by writing to the Chief of Appeals of your local district taxation office. It begins the formal administrative appeal process. The notice should set out the specific issue(s) that you are objecting to.

When you file a Notice of Objection, your objection is reviewed by an Appeals Officer within the CRA. The Appeals Officer is independent of the Audit Branch, and he or she should conduct the review impartially and objectively.

File a Notice of Objection to preserve your right to appeal.

To be valid, a Notice of Objection must be filed either within 90 days of the date of the assessment or reassessment to which you are objecting, or within one year of the original due date for the return. For example, an objection to an assessment of your 2004 return would have to be filed by April 30, 2005 or 90 days after the (re)assessment you are objecting to, whichever is later. The same deadlines apply for Québec purposes.

Filing your Notice of Objection before the deadline is vital—even if you are in the midst of discussions with the CRA authorities, and even if you have been assured that a reassessment in your favour will be issued. Otherwise your right to appeal vanishes, and any reassessment will be entirely up to the CRA.

Even if the period for objecting has expired, you may request a reassessment of your return. In this case, you have no legal right to force a reassessment, but in many cases the reassessment will be issued anyway. The CRA will allow a reassessment of a return for any year back to 1985, if the request meets the guidelines issued under the government's "Fairness Package". For 2005 and later years, you may only request "Fairness"-based adjustments for the preceding 10 years.

In some cases you can also apply to the CRA or the Tax Court of Canada for extension of the time for filing a Notice of Objection.

When your return is reopened on reassessment, consider requesting other adjustments.

If the CRA issues you a routine reassessment for some reason after your own right to force a reconsideration of your return has expired, bear in mind that the reassessment reopens your return for 90 days. If this happens and there are other issues that you want to contest or change, you can raise them within the 90-day period and file a Notice of Objection to preserve your rights of appeal. However, you cannot do this where the return was reopened for any of a number of special reasons (such as a carryback of losses from a later year).

Similar rules and deadlines apply for Québec tax purposes.

9.5.2 Appeal to the Tax Court

The Appeals Officer is normally your last level of appeal within the CRA. A further appeal is available to the Tax Court of Canada (or the applicable provincial court if provincial taxes are in dispute).

You have a choice between the Court's "informal" and "general" procedures for making an appeal.

Be sure you understand the legal issues when appealing.

The general procedure normally requires you to retain a lawyer. It is similar to higher court proceedings in provincial courts. If the amount of tax in dispute for any one taxation year is more than $12,000 of federal tax (about $19,000 including provincial tax other than Québec tax), you must follow the general procedure. In certain "test cases", the CRA may also force a case below the threshold into the general procedure, in which case the CRA will be required to reimburse you for most or all of your legal fees.

The informal procedure, as its name suggests, is much less complicated. You may appear on your own, or have someone else (such as a lawyer, accountant, consultant or friend) there to assist you. No specific form needs to be filed to launch the appeal. The formal rules of evidence that normally apply to court proceedings will not necessarily apply. Under the informal procedure, your case will normally be heard fairly quickly, and a judgment given within a year of when you first file the appeal. The decision given is not binding as a precedent for future cases, whether yours or another taxpayer's.

If you are taking an appeal to the Tax Court of Canada, make sure you understand the legal issues involved. Even if you wish to represent yourself or be represented by a friend or relative, consult with a qualified tax professional before the appeal. Many issues in tax law have answers on which all the advisers (and the judge!) will agree, yet which will not be obvious to the non-expert.

9.5.3 Appeal beyond the Tax Court

A decision of the Tax Court of Canada under its informal procedure can be appealed, on a question of law only, in the form of a "judicial review" by the Federal Court of Appeal. A decision under the general procedure can be appealed directly to the Federal Court of Appeal. In either case you would need a lawyer for such an appeal, which would typically take about two years from time of filing until judgment is given. Provincial decisions may be appealed to the applicable provincial appeal court.

Once a decision is given by the federal or provincial appeals courts, either you or the tax authority may seek "leave to appeal" from the Supreme Court of Canada. Only if a panel of three justices of the Supreme Court grants the application for leave to appeal can an appeal be made. The Supreme Court rarely grants leave to appeal in tax cases; typically only three or four tax cases a year reach the Supreme Court.

9.5.4 Amounts in dispute—should you pay up?

Suppose you are contesting an amount of $10,000, but you are not sure whether you will win or not. Although you have filed a Notice of Objection or perhaps an appeal, you are receiving notices from the CRA Collections asking you to pay even though the CRA cannot start collection action as long as you have an objection or appeal outstanding.

It may be a good idea to pay the balance anyway. The interest rate charged on late payments (see 9.3) is likely higher than the rate you would otherwise earn with your money, or higher than the rate at which you must borrow from the bank. If you ultimately succeed in your appeal, you will recover all the funds you paid, plus interest (at the middle rate shown in 9.3).

Note also that when you receive a statement from the CRA, you normally have 20 days to pay without further interest charges applying. If you are going to have to pay anyway, you may as well take advantage of this "interest-free" period and pay the balance on the 20th day.

Taxpayers sometimes think they should not pay an amount in dispute because "that would be an admission of guilt", or because the CRA would then have no incentive to settle the case. Such reasoning is misplaced. You cannot prejudice your case by paying the tax. The determination as to your legal rights is not affected by whether or not the tax has been paid.

> Consider paying the amount owing even if you are filing an objection.

The only circumstance where you are better not to have paid your account is where you are applying for a waiver of interest and penalty, at the CRA's discretion, on the grounds of "inability to pay". Once you have paid, it is difficult to argue that you cannot find the money to pay your tax bill and require a waiver of interest to be able to meet the requested payments.

9.6 References

The following publications can be obtained (in person or by telephone request) from your nearest CRA Tax Services Office. Forms, guides and information on the CRA's electronic filing and payment options are available from the CRA's Internet site at *www.cra-arc.gc.ca*.

Information Circular 75-7R3, "Reassessment of a return of income"
Information Circular 92-1, "Guidelines for accepting late, amended or revoked elections"
Information Circular 92-2, "Guidelines for cancellation and waiver of interest and penalties"

Information Circular 92-3, "Guidelines for refunds beyond the normal three-year period"

Form T1, "General individual income tax return"

Form T1-DD, "Direct deposit request form for individuals"

Form T183, "Information return for electronic filing of an individual's income tax and benefit return"

Form T400A, "Notice of objection"

Form T1013, "Authorizing or cancelling a representative"

Form T1033-WS, "Worksheet for calculating 20__ instalments"

Form T2029, "Waiver in respect of the normal reassessment period"

Guide, "Canada Customs and Revenue Agency: Our Programs and Services"

Guide, "Paying Your Tax by Instalments"

Guide, "Your Rights in Your Dealings with the Canada Customs and Revenue Agency"

If you are employed

- Arrange to get non-taxable benefits (10.1.1)
- Ask to have your source withholdings reduced where possible (10.2)
- Pay interest owing on loan from employer by January 30 of the following year (10.3)
- Consider employees' profit-sharing plans for cash flow purposes (10.5.2)
- Transfer retiring allowances to an RRSP (10.6)
- Claim rebate for GST paid on expenses deductible from your employment income (10.9)

As a general principle, all income (including tips) and benefits from or related to your employment are taxed, except where the federal or Québec rules specifically provide otherwise. Also as a general principle, you cannot claim any deductions against employment income, except for those that are specifically allowed by the system. There are, however, many special rules, and we examine some of them in this chapter.

10.1 Employment benefits

10.1.1 Non-taxable employment benefits

Certain employment benefits are not taxable, even though many of them are deductible expenses to the employer. The government is thus offering an incentive to employers to provide these benefits, since the after-tax returns are greater than straight salary. Non-taxable benefits include:

- Contributions to a registered pension plan (the pension is taxable when received—see 3.4.1).
- Contributions to a group sickness or accident insurance plan.
- Contributions to a "private health services plan", such as those covering drugs, medical expenses and hospital charges not covered by public health insurance, and dental fees (except for Québec purposes—see 17.2.16).
- All or a portion of the cost of free or subsidized school services for your children (for example, if the services are provided in a remote area).
- Contributions to a supplementary unemployment benefit plan.
- Contributions to a deferred profit-sharing plan.
- Non-accountable moving allowance of up to $650 (see 13.1.3).

- Reimbursement of certain moving expenses on work-related relocation (see 13.1.3; however, any reimbursement or compensation to help finance the new residence is excluded—see 13.1.4).
- Payment of club dues if your membership in the club may potentially benefit the employer's business (however, these dues are normally not deductible to the employer).
- Employee discounts, where such discounts are commonly available to other employees (but not below the employer's cost).
- Two non-cash gifts of up to $500 annually (combined for both gifts) intended to mark holidays, birthdays and other special occasions.
- Non-cash awards of up to $500 annually intended to mark special achievements such as length of service or meeting safety records.
- Home computer, as long as it primarily benefits your employer and such computers are made available to all employees (or employees within the same class).
- Tuition fees for courses taken to maintain or improve your skills in an area related to your current or future employment responsibilities.
- Costs of other business-related courses such as stress management, employment equity and language skills.
- Counselling services related to mental or physical health, employment termination, or retirement.
- Subsidized meals, where you are required to pay a reasonable charge covering the cost of the food.
- Uniforms or special clothing you need for your job.
- Transportation to the job, if provided directly by the employer.
- Board and lodging at, and transportation to, a "special work site" where you work temporarily or a "remote work site" that is remote from any established community.
- Use of your employer's recreational facilities.
- Transportation passes given to bus, rail and airline employees, except for airline employees travelling on a space-confirmed basis.
- Transportation and parking costs, whether paid directly by the employer or reimbursed to you, if you are blind or are disabled due to a mobility impairment.
- The cost of an attendant to assist you at work if you are disabled.

Note that where your employer deducts its contributions to a sickness or accident insurance plan, a disability insurance plan or an income maintenance insurance plan, any benefits you receive from the insurance will be taxable (but reduced by your own premium payments to the plan).

Ask your employer to make use of the non-taxable benefits outlined above as much as possible. If you have an employment benefit

> **Arrange to get non-taxable benefits.**

package where you and the employer share the costs, try to have the cost-sharing reallocated so your employer pays for all the non-taxable benefits and you pay for the benefits that are taxable if your employer pays them. In many cases, without changing the cost to your employer, you can reduce your tax burden this way.

One non-taxable benefit that is often overlooked is that of board and lodging at a "special work site". Unlike a "remote work location", a special work site need not be far from an established community; as long as the duties you perform at that location are of a temporary nature, and you maintain another residence, the food and lodging paid by your employer are a non-taxable benefit. This could apply, for example, if you spend several months in another city working on a project for your employer.

10.1.2 Taxable employment benefits

In general, employment benefits other than those listed above are taxed as though you had received an equivalent amount of income. Examples include:

- Tips (gratuities) that you receive from customers.
- Board, lodging, and rent-free or low-rent housing (with some exceptions for remote or special work sites).
- Travelling expenses for personal travel, including expenses for your spouse to travel on a business trip of yours, unless your spouse was engaged primarily in business activities on behalf of the employer during the trip.
- Personal use of employer's automobile (see 12.2).
- Gifts, except for two non-cash gifts with a combined cost under $500 per year as noted above (if the total cost of the gifts is more than $500, the whole amount is taxable, not just the amount over $500; however, for Québec purposes, only the amount over $500 is taxable).
- Allowing you and/or your family to use a vacation property.
- Holiday trips, prizes and incentive awards.
- Use of frequent-flyer credits that you earn through employer-paid trips used for personal trips.
- Cost of employer-paid courses for personal interest or technical skills not related to your employer's business.
- Payment of provincial (public) health insurance premiums (note that most provinces no longer charge such premiums).
- Life insurance premiums.
- Reimbursement for the cost of tools used in employment duties.
- Loans to employees (see 10.3 below).

- Tax equalization payments to relocated employees to offset higher taxes in their new work location.
- Stock option plans (see 10.4.1 below).
- Income tax return preparation and financial counselling (but not retirement or re-employment counselling).

In general, where the employer pays sales tax on goods or services, and then provides those goods or services to you as a taxable benefit, the calculation of the taxable benefit will require an additional 7% to account for the GST. This applies, for example, to automobiles. If you live in Nova Scotia, New Brunswick or Newfoundland, the 15% HST rate will apply (see 11.2.5); for Québec, the benefit is increased by the 7% GST and 7.5% QST.

10.2 Reductions of source withholdings

As we saw in 9.2.1, your employer and others are required to withhold tax at source and remit it to the CRA. The same rules generally apply for Québec purposes.

Ask to have your source withholdings reduced where possible.

In any situation where you expect to receive a refund after filing your return (e.g., due to personal tax credits, RRSP contributions, medical expenses or charitable donations, alimony and maintenance payments), you should review the TD1 form (and MR-19 in Québec) you file with your employer and seek to have source withholdings reduced. You can ask your local CRA district office to permit your employer to reduce your source withholdings for deductions not normally provided for on the TD1 form, such as RRSP contributions and alimony and maintenance.

However, if your employer withholds from your remuneration RRSP contributions (up to your available RRSP contribution room—see 3.1.3), union and professional dues and alimony and maintenance payments for direct remittance to the intended recipient, the employer can take these withholdings into account in calculating your tax withheld at source without requesting permission from the CRA.

If you have a loan from your employer on which imputed interest is assessed as a taxable benefit (see 10.3 below), your source deductions of income tax will reflect that taxable benefit. If, however, you are using the funds for a purpose that allows you an offsetting deduction, you may write to the CRA, setting out that fact, and request that your employer be permitted to reduce the source withholding. An example of this is where you use the loan proceeds for investment purposes.

Many people look forward to receiving a tax refund, but it's not good tax planning to get one. If you get a refund, that means the CRA has been holding your money and not paying you interest on it for many months. Although fiscal responsibility is needed to make sure you can pay your tax when it is due, it is better to be required to send a cheque to the CRA at filing time, since it means that you have had use of the funds (for investment or other purposes) in the meantime. However, you must pay instalments if the difference between your tax payable and amounts withheld at source is more than $2,000 ($1,200 in Québec—see 17.2.24) in both the current year and either of the two preceding years. (See 9.1.2.)

Note that interest is not paid on refunds for the first 45 days of processing after the filing deadline—that is, until after June 14 for most employees. If you have a June 15 filing deadline because you have self-employment income (see 9.1.1), interest will not be paid until 45 days after April 30 or 45 days after the date that the return is actually filed, whichever is later. (See 9.1.1 and 9.3.)

10.3 Loans to employees

If you receive a low-interest or interest-free loan from your employer (or past or future employer), you are considered to have received a benefit from employment. The benefit is set at the CRA's (and Revenu Québec's) current prescribed rate of interest, which varies quarterly, minus any interest you actually pay during the year or within 30 days after the end of the year. The prescribed rate is 4% lower (3% in Québec) than the rate charged on late payments of tax—see 9.3. (There may be an offsetting deemed interest deduction, as we shall see.)

Example

Rebecca receives a loan of $10,000 from her employer on January 1, 2003. She is required to pay it back one year later, without interest. Assume the prescribed rate throughout the entire year is 4%.

Rebecca is considered to have an employment benefit of $400, and will be required to include this amount in her employment income.

But if, instead, the loan bore interest at 2%, and Rebecca made an interest payment before January 30, 2004, her taxable benefit would be calculated as 2% (the prescribed rate of 4% minus her employer's 2% rate) of $10,000, or $200.

If you have received an interest-bearing loan from your employer, consider deferring the payment of interest on the loan until January 30 of the next calendar year. This will provide you with a cash flow advantage. Make sure you do pay the interest by that date, however.

> Pay interest owing on loan from employer by January 30 of the following year.

Exceptions

A home purchase loan is taxed on the same basis as other employee loans, but the rate applied in calculating the imputed interest for the first five years of the loan will not be greater than the prescribed rate in effect at the time the loan was made. At the end of the five-year period, it is considered a new loan, and the prescribed rate at that time will be the maximum for the next five years.

> **Example**
>
> Alex receives an interest-free loan from his employer to help him buy a house. (He is not relocating, just moving from an apartment to a house.) At the time, the prescribed interest rate is 3%. Two years later, interest rates have gone up, and the prescribed rate increases to 6%.
>
> Alex will still pay tax on the interest benefit calculated at only 3% of the amount of the loan. If the prescribed rate had gone below 3%, he would, however, pay tax on imputed interest at the lower rate as long as it stayed below 3%.

If you relocate, and receive a home purchase loan to acquire a residence at least 40 km closer to your new work location, then a special deduction in computing your taxable income is available to you for the first five years of the loan equal to the interest imputed on $25,000. Note that you must still report the entire interest amount as a taxable benefit, and claim this special deduction as a separate item on your tax return.

Where you use funds borrowed from your employer to purchase investments or to purchase an automobile (or aircraft) to be used for your employment, you can obtain an offsetting deduction. The amount of imputed interest that you include in your income as a taxable benefit is deemed to have been *interest paid by you*. As a result, if such interest would otherwise have been deductible, you can deduct it. (As we saw in 7.2.3, interest paid on loans to acquire investments is deductible, and as we'll see in 12.3.1, interest paid on loans to acquire a car is deductible if the car is required by your terms of employment.) The effect is to eliminate the tax cost of the taxable benefit.

If you are a shareholder of the company as well as an employee, or if a member of your family is a shareholder, you must be especially cautious. It is possible for the *entire* amount of the loan, rather than the imputed interest, to be included in your income for tax purposes, unless stringent conditions are met. In general, you can avoid this rule if the loan is made for certain specific purposes and with arrangements for repayment within a reasonable time, provided the loan was made because of your employment relationship. Alternatively, the entire loan must be repaid within one year, and not be part of a series of loans and repayments (see 14.2.6).

10.4 Stock option plans

10.4.1 Regular stock option plans

A stock option plan is an arrangement whereby a corporation gives an employee the right (an option) to invest in its shares at a given price. The price may or may not be less than the market price at the time the option is granted. For example, suppose you work for a corporation whose stock trades at $20. In 2004, you are given an option to buy up to 1,000 shares at $20, good until 2006. If, in 2005, the stock is trading at $30, you can exercise the option, buy 1,000 shares for $20,000, and then, if you wish, turn around and sell the shares on the market for $30,000.

Stock options in certain public companies and Canadian-controlled private corporations receive preferential tax treatment—see 10.4.2 and 10.4.3. The general rule is that you are considered to receive a benefit from employment, not when the option is granted (the year 2004 in the above example), but when you exercise it (2006). The taxable benefit is the difference between the price you pay ($20,000) and the value of the shares when you exercise the option ($30,000). You would, therefore, report a taxable benefit of $10,000 in your employment income for 2005. (The adjusted cost base of the shares to you will be $30,000, so you will not be doubly taxed when you subsequently sell them.)

An offsetting partial deduction is available if certain requirements are met. The first requirement is that the shares be normal common shares (not preferred shares). Second, the exercise price must be no less than the fair market value of the shares at the time the option was granted. (Otherwise you could simply exercise the option the day you received it, so the benefit would be just like cash.) Third, you must deal at arm's length with the corporation (meaning essentially that you or members of your family do not control it). If these conditions are met, you can claim a deduction from income of one-half of the amount of the taxable benefit. The effect of this deduction is to tax the benefit at the same inclusion rate as a capital gain.

For Québec purposes, the deduction is limited to one-quarter of the amount of the benefit relating to any event relating to a stock option occurring after March 30, 2004 (three-eighths of the amount for such events occurring on or before that date).

You may wish to approach your employer about establishing a stock option plan as an employment benefit. It may cost your employer very little, and can even bring investment funds into the corporation to some extent. (The cost is the dilution of the existing shareholders' interests.)

10.4.2 Qualifying stock options in public corporations

Recognizing the increasing importance of share ownership plans and stock options for recruiting and retaining key employees, especially in the high technology sector, the government allows employees to postpone the taxation on $100,000 per year of qualifying employee stock options for publicly-listed shares to when the shares are sold instead of when the option is exercised. This measure puts employee options in public company shares on equal footing with employee options on shares in Canadian-controlled private companies (see 10.4.3).

Employees of public companies must meet several conditions to qualify for this treatment. Among other things, you must be a resident of Canada, you must deal at arm's length with your employer and you must not be a "specified shareholder" (i.e., generally, you must not own more than 10% of the company's shares). Additionally, the total of all amounts payable to acquire the shares, including the option price and any amount payable to acquire the option, cannot be less than the share's fair market value on the date the option was granted. If these conditions are met, you can include the stock option benefit on the qualifying stock options in your income in the year that the shares are sold, subject to the annual vesting limit.

The $100,000 annual limit is based on the fair market value of the shares on the date the option was granted. As well, this limit applies to the year of vesting—the year you gain the right to exercise the options under the terms of the option agreement—and not to the year in which you actually exercise the option. As a result, the vesting period can dramatically change the amount of the benefit that may be deferred.

For example, say you are granted options for 20,000 shares with an exercise price of $10 per share ($200,000 in total), which is their fair market value at the time the options are granted. All of the options vest in Year 1 and you exercise the options in that year when the share price is $25 per share ($500,000 in total).

In this case, your potential benefit is $300,000 ($500,000 − $200,000). But the deferral is only available for 10,000 shares due to the $100,000 limit, so only half of the total benefit ($150,000) can be deferred. The additional $150,000 will be taxed under the general rules as employment income in Year 1 (subject to the employee stock option deduction, if applicable).

What happens if we change the facts so the vesting period for the 20,000 shares is spread equally over Years 1 and 2 (i.e., 10,000 each year) and you exercise the options in Year 2? In this case, tax on the entire $300,000 benefit can be deferred because the fair market value of the 10,000 shares attributable to options vesting each year does not exceed the $100,000 annual limit.

If you wish to take advantage of the deferral for qualifying shares acquired in 2004, you must make an election with your employer by January 15, 2005.

Emigration or death

If you cease to be a Canadian resident, you will be required to recognize the benefit on any amounts deferred under these rules at that time. The deferral also ceases if you die and your estate becomes liable for payment of the tax.

Beware of capital losses

In cases where you acquire shares under a stock option arrangement and do not immediately sell them, the results may be severe if the value of the shares declines after acquisition. You will still be liable for tax on the difference between the exercise price and the share value at acquisition, even though you don't realize any real monetary gain until you sell the stock.

Further, the capital loss triggered on the sale cannot offset the employment benefit included in income. Despite the loss in value, tax on the benefit is still payable.

10.4.3 Stock options in Canadian-controlled private corporations

If your employer is a Canadian-controlled private corporation (CCPC) with which you deal at arm's length, you do not record the taxable benefit related to stock options in your employer's company until you sell the shares, rather than when you exercise the option and acquire them. And, if you have held them for at least two years at the date of sale, you can claim a deduction when computing your taxable income for one-half of the benefit realized in the year the shares were sold without having to meet the first two requirements outlined in 10.4.1 above. This exception is designed to stimulate employee participation in ownership of small businesses. It also recognizes that valuation of shares in a private company at the time you exercise the option may be difficult.

Be cautious about relying on CCPC shares too much for your future; shares in private corporations are generally not liquid, and can become worthless very easily if the corporation runs into trouble.

If you receive shares in a CCPC through a stock option plan, consider contributing some of them to your RRSP if the shares qualify for that purpose (see 3.1.6).

10.4.4 Share appreciation rights

The terms of some stock option plans may allow you to receive a cash payment equal to the value of the options instead of the shares. Where the plan allows the employee to make the choice, the same tax consequences apply to the cash payment as would apply to the issuance of shares—the employment benefit is included in income and the related one-half deduction is available if the required conditions are met. But if the decision is the employer's, the stock option rules will not apply and the cash payment will be treated as regular employment income.

10.4.5 Stock purchase plans

A stock purchase plan is a possible alternative to a stock option plan. In a typical stock purchase plan arrangement, a defined group of employees (which could be all employees) may purchase a limited number of shares of the company at their fair market value or at a slight discount. The plan is usually administered by a trust. You contribute a portion of your salary to the trust and in many cases your employer will make matching contributions. The trustee then uses the funds to purchase the shares at their current fair market value.

Since you make your contribution from after-tax dollars, no additional tax arises. If your company does not contribute to the plan and your contributions are simply used to purchase the shares, there will be no tax consequences. However, if the shares are issued at a discount, you will be assessed a taxable benefit on the difference between the shares' purchase price and their fair market value.

If your company contributes to the plan, the tax consequences to you will depend on how the shares are purchased. If the shares are issued from treasury, the stock option rules will apply. If the shares are purchased on the open market, you will be assessed a taxable benefit equal to the value of the shares at the time they vest.

10.4.6 Stock bonus plans

Stock bonus plans reward employees with shares of the corporation instead of cash. In most cases, the same rules apply as those outlined in 10.4.1 for stock options.

10.4.7 Phantom stock plans

A phantom stock plan avoids the requirement that you acquire shares in the corporation, and thus may be more attractive to your employer's controlling shareholders. Under such a plan, you receive bonuses based on the increase in value of your employer's shares. Such bonuses are simply taxed as employment income when they are paid to you. If they are not paid to you on an ongoing basis, you will need to determine whether they constitute a salary deferral arrangement (see 10.5.1), in which case they will be taxed in your hands even if not received. This type of plan allows you to benefit from the potential appreciation in value of your company's shares without a cash outlay and with no risk of any loss in the value of the shares.

10.5 Deferred compensation

Various techniques have been tried over the years to avoid paying tax on employment income by having some of it held back in one way or another. (In general, employment income is taxed when received.)

Registered pension plans and deferred profit-sharing plans were discussed in 3.4 and 3.5. They are accepted mechanisms for deferring employment income.

10.5.1 Salary deferral arrangements

The rules for salary deferral arrangements catch most arrangements for deferred compensation. For example, if you agree with your employer that your salary for 2004 will be $80,000, plus a further $20,000 to be paid in 2008, you will be taxed on the whole $100,000 in 2004. You can generally only escape this taxation if there is a substantial risk of forfeiting the future income.

The salary deferral arrangement rules allow certain exceptions. One is a self-funded leave of absence program, sometimes used by teachers, academics and others to fund sabbatical leaves. Provided you meet all of the conditions, you can arrange for your employer or a trustee to hold back a portion of your salary every year for up to six years, not recognize that portion as employment income each year, and receive it in the sabbatical year, paying tax on it then. Another exception is an arrangement whereby you have a right to receive a bonus to be paid within three years.

10.5.2 Profit-sharing plans

Employee profit-sharing plans do not defer the taxation of employment income. Rather, contributions are made by the employer, based on profits for the year. Although the contributions are paid to the plan, the amounts contributed are treated as income of the employees for tax purposes. Such plans can therefore operate as forced savings plans for bonuses. Income (such as interest income) earned within the plan must be allocated to specific employees, who pay tax on it as it is allocated (even if it is not paid to them).

Though these plans are not widely used, one of their tax advantages is that there is no source withholding on the amounts paid into the plan, or on the amounts paid by the plan to you. Careful

> Consider employees' profit-sharing plans for cash flow purposes.

timing of the employer's contributions and the plan's disbursements can give you better cash flow than would a straight bonus payment.

10.5.3 Supplemental ("top-hat") retirement plans

Supplemental retirement plans are usually designed to provide retirement benefits similar to those offered under registered pension plans (see 3.4) but they are not subject to the same contribution limits. As a result, they are often used to enhance the retirement compensation packages of higher-income executives and employees (which is why they are also known as "top-hat plans"). Supplementary plans may be unfunded or funded. If they are funded, they will be treated as a retirement compensation arrangement (see 10.5.4).

Under the most common type of unfunded supplemental retirement plan, the employer simply makes a promise in a letter or a more formal agreement to pay an additional amount to the employee on retirement. Because no funds are set aside, there is no immediate tax liability for either the employee or the employer. However, because the retirement benefits are not secured, their payment will ultimately depend on the employer's ability to pay on the employee's retirement.

If the payments from the supplementary retirement plan are arranged to qualify as retiring allowance payments (see 10.6), you may be able to transfer part or all the payments to your RRSP.

10.5.4 Retirement Compensation Arrangements (RCAs)

RCAs are arrangements made outside the registered pension plan system, whereby a custodian will receive funds from an employer and make payments after the employee's retirement or termination. The employer receives a deduction for contributions to such plans, but a 50% refundable tax applies to the payments made to the custodian. The tax must be remitted to the CRA when the contribution is made and refunded when the payments are made to the employee. The employee does not report the income for tax purposes until he or she receives the payments from the custodian.

RCAs may also be funded through a letter of credit or through a life insurance policy. The letter of credit's terms usually allow it to be called upon if the employer does not fulfill its obligations under the RCA. The contribution to the RCA is equal to the amount charged by the financial institution for issuing the letter of credit. A letter of credit is often viewed as a compromise between an unsecured arrangement and a fully funded RCA.

In recent years a variety of new methods have been developed for funding supplemental plans through exempt life insurance products—see 7.3.3.

10.6 Retiring allowances, wrongful dismissal payments and severance pay

A "retiring allowance", as defined for tax purposes, includes what one would normally call severance pay or termination pay, as well as a court award or settlement for wrongful dismissal. It also includes, of course, a payment by an employer for long service on retirement.

A retiring allowance, like ordinary employment income, is included in your income in the year you receive it. If you receive your retiring allowance in a year after the year you terminated employment, you may ask the CRA to determine

> Transfer retiring allowances to an RRSP.

whether it is more advantageous to you to recalculate the tax on that income as if you received it in the prior year to which the payment relates. This option relieves the higher tax liability that would otherwise result if the entire lump-sum is taxed in the year of receipt, rather than year by year as right to receive the income arose. Eligible payments must total at least $3,000 in the year and include superannuation or pension benefits (other than non-periodic benefits), wrongful dismissal and other employment-related payments arising from a court order or similar judgment, and certain other amounts.

Though damages awarded for wrongful dismissal are usually taxable as a retiring allowance, the amounts may not be taxable if the settlement includes damages related to mental anguish, humiliation, hurt feelings or loss of self-respect suffered on the job rather than as a result of losing the job. If you are suing for wrongful dismissal including damages for mental distress, ensure that any settlement contains a detailed breakdown of its components to show that it includes non-taxable general damages.

As we saw in 3.3.2, part or all of a retiring allowance can be transferred to an RRSP and thus sheltered from immediate tax. The amount that can be transferred is $2,000 for each calendar year (or part year) of service before 1996, plus $1,500 for each year (or part year) before 1989 for which employer contributions to your pension plan have not vested. (Vested pension rights are those that you can take with you on retirement or termination—see 3.4.1.)

Legal fees incurred in establishing your retiring allowance are deductible against the retiring allowance—see 10.8.5. Note that you should probably not transfer the maximum amount to an RRSP if you have incurred legal fees in obtaining your award (even if the case was settled without going to court). If you transfer the entire retiring allowance into an RRSP, the legal fees will never become deductible. (When you take payments *out* of the RRSP, they are no longer considered a "retiring allowance".) However, if you intend to leave the funds to grow tax-free in the RRSP for many years, you may want to consider transferring the maximum anyway. Legal fees can be carried forward for up to seven years and deducted against the "retiring allowance" income.

10.7 Overseas employment tax credit

If you are resident in Canada but you work outside Canada for a period of six months or more, a special tax credit may be available (if you live in Québec, see 17.2.18). To be eligible, you must be working for a Canadian employer (or its foreign affiliate) on certain kinds of projects, such as mining, oil and gas exploration or production, agriculture, construction or engineering.

The credit effectively allows you to offset the tax payable on up to $100,000 of overseas employment income per year, but is limited to 80% of that income. The details are very complicated—see the reference information in 10.10 below.

10.8 Deductions from employment income

The only deductions allowed against employment income are those specifically provided for in the federal and Québec tax rules. We look at some of them below.

10.8.1 Travelling expenses

If you are required by your employment to spend funds on employment-related travel, the amounts you pay will normally be deductible. Examples might include parking, taxis and train fares. You cannot deduct the costs of travelling between your home to your workplace. If you use your own automobile for employment-related travel, see 12.2.

If you travel for a transportation company (e.g., as a bus or truck driver or a flight attendant), you can also deduct costs of meals and lodging to the extent you are not entitled to be reimbursed. The deduction for meals will be further restricted to 50% of your cost (see 11.2.9).

10.8.2 Commission sales person's expenses

If you are employed as a sales person under a contract that requires you to pay your own expenses, and you earn commissions, you may be able to deduct the costs of your employment-related expenditures—the same kinds of costs as could be claimed if you were self-employed (see 11.2.2). To do so, you must be required by your contract of employment to pay your own expenses, and you must be ordinarily required to carry on your duties of employment away from your employer's place of business. The total expenses you claim this way cannot exceed your total commission income.

10.8.3 Supplies, assistant's salary and home office

If you are required by your contract of employment to pay for any supplies or to pay for an assistant or substitute, you can deduct the cost of the supplies or the assistant's salary.

You can also deduct expenses relating to a home office, in limited circumstances. First, you must be required by your employment contract to maintain the office, and your employer must sign a certificate (federal Form T2200, which you must keep with your records and Québec Form TP-64.3-V, which you must file with your Québec tax return). Second, either the home office must be the place where you "principally perform the duties of employment", or you must use it on a regular and continuous basis for *meeting* people (such as your employer's customers) in the ordinary course of your employment. The second restriction is parallel to that which applies to self-employed people, as outlined in more detail in 11.2.10. The effect is that the deduction is rarely available to employed individuals. You will normally only be able to claim it if you spend more of your time working at home than at your employer's premises.

10.8.4 Union and professional dues

Union dues are deductible for federal tax purposes (see 17.2.17 if you live in Québec). These are normally withheld at source and reported on the T4 and Québec Relevé 1 you receive from your employer.

Dues required to maintain a legally recognized professional status are deductible, even if you do not need to maintain that status for your current job. Your status as a lawyer, engineer, accountant, physician, architect, nurse, dentist, etc., will qualify for this purpose. Dues to voluntary associations are not deductible, unless you are self-employed (see 11.2.2).

10.8.5 Legal fees

If you spend money on a lawyer to recover unpaid wages, you can deduct the legal fees.

Legal fees you incur to establish your right to a "retiring allowance" (which includes severance pay), or to private pension plan benefits, are deductible. Under the current rules, you can only deduct the legal fees *against the income from the retiring allowance or pension benefits in that year*. To the extent you have not yet received that income, you can "carry forward" the expenses for up to seven years and claim them against such income in those later years. (See 10.6 if you transfer your retiring allowance to an RRSP.)

> **Example**
>
> Lewis was fired from his job in 2002. He retained a lawyer and sued for wrongful dismissal, spending $3,000 in 2002 and $5,000 in 2003 in legal fees. In 2004, the case is settled and his former employer pays him $50,000.
>
> Lewis can deduct his $8,000 in legal fees only in 2004 against his $50,000 "retiring allowance" income, thus recognizing only $42,000 as income in that year.
>
> Lewis could ask the CRA to recalculate his tax on the retiring allowance income as if it had been received in the year to which the payment relates—see 10.6.

See also 2.8.1 regarding the deductibility of legal fees that are not related to employment.

10.8.6 Musicians' instruments

If you are employed as a musician and required to supply your own instrument, you may deduct any maintenance, rental and insurance costs. If you have purchased the instrument, you may claim capital cost allowance (depreciation), at a rate of 10% for the first year, and 20% of the remaining balance in each subsequent year. All of these deductions can only be used to offset your income from employment as a musician, not against other income.

10.8.7 Artists' expenses

If you are employed as an artist (including, for example, a painter, sculptor, playwright, literary author, composer, actor, dancer, singer or musician), you may deduct up to $1,000 of your actual expenses incurred in order to earn income from such activities. This deduction is limited to 20% of your income from artistic employment, and the $1,000 limit is reduced by any amounts you claim as automobile expenses (see 12.3.1) and musical instrument costs (10.8.6). (No parallel deduction is allowed for Québec tax purposes.)

Of course, if you earn income from your artistic activities that is not employment income, you are self-employed, in which case all your expenses are normally deductible (see 11.2.2).

10.8.8 Northern employees

If your employer pays for you to take a vacation trip, with or without your family, the value of the taxable benefit is included in your income (see 10.1.2). If you live in northern Canada, a federal deduction is available to offset all or part of this benefit (a similar deduction is available for Québec purposes). Provided you meet certain residency requirements, the deduction can eliminate the taxable benefit associated with up to two trips per year, based on the cost of airfare to the nearest large Canadian city. (There is no limit to the number of such trips if they are taken to obtain medical services not available locally.)

See also 2.8.2, regarding the special deduction for residents of northern Canada, and 10.1.1, regarding the non-taxability of benefits relating to a remote work site.

10.9 GST rebate for employees

Claim rebate for GST paid on expenses deductible from your employment income.

In general, where you can deduct expenses from your employment income, such as those discussed in 10.8, you can also claim a rebate of GST or HST paid on those expenses. A QST rebate is available for Québec taxpayers. Documentation must be kept to support the claim for the rebate. The rebate claim is filed with your personal income tax return. That rebate will itself be considered income from employment in the year in which you receive it, except where it relates to capital cost allowance. If you drive your own car for employment-related travel, see 12.3.1.

10.10 References

The following publications can be obtained (in person or by telephone request) from your nearest CRA Tax Services Office. Forms and guides may also be available from the CRA's Internet site at *www.cra-arc.gc.c*a.

Interpretation Bulletin IT-63R5, "Benefits, including standby charge for an automobile, from the personal use of a motor vehicle supplied by an employer after 1992"

Interpretation Bulletin IT-113R4, "Benefits to employees—Stock options"

Interpretation Bulletin IT-148R3, "Recreational properties and club dues"

Interpretation Bulletin IT-158R2, "Employees' professional membership dues"

Interpretation Bulletin IT-196R2, "Payments by employer to employee"

Interpretation Bulletin IT-337R4, "Retiring allowances"

Interpretation Bulletin IT-352R2, "Employees' expenses, including work space in home expenses"

Interpretation Bulletin IT-421R2, "Benefits to individuals, corporations and shareholders from loans or debt"

Interpretation Bulletin IT-470R, "Employees' fringe benefits"

Interpretation Bulletin IT-497R4, "Overseas employment tax credit"

Interpretation Bulletin IT-508R, "Death benefits"

Interpretation Bulletin IT-522R, "Vehicle, travel and sales expenses of employees"

Interpretation Bulletin IT-529, "Flexible employee benefit programs"

Information Circular 73-21R8, "Claims for meals and lodging expenses of transport employees"

Information Circular 77-1R4, "Deferred profit sharing plans"

"Completion Guide and Form for GST/HST Rebate for Partners"

"Employment Expenses Tax Guide"

Form TD1, "20__ Personal tax credit return"

Form T626, "Overseas employment tax credit"

Form T777, "Statement of employment expenses"

Form T1212, "Statement of deferred stock option benefits"

Form T2200, "Declaration of conditions of employment"

Form GST 370, "Employee and partner GST/HST rebate"

CHAPTER 11

If you are self-employed

- Arrange to be a consultant rather than employed (11.1)

- Recover GST (or HST) and QST that you've paid by claiming input tax credits for your business (11.2.4)

- If you're a residential landlord, account for sales tax when setting rents (11.2.4)

- Be aware of your HST obligations for sales to customers in Nova Scotia, New Brunswick and Newfoundland and Labrador (11.2.5)

- Simplify your paperwork by using the "Quick Method" for GST and QST reporting (11.2.6)

- Acquire depreciable assets before year-end (11.2.7)

- Consider claiming less CCA than the maximum (11.2.7)

- Deduct public transit fares, taxis and other business travel costs (11.2.8)

- Document and claim your business meals and entertainment expenses (11.2.9)

- Write off your eligible home office expenses (11.2.10)

- If you're a partner, claim sales tax rebates on your unreimbursed partnership expenses (11.3.7)

- Use your loss carryovers to maximum advantage (11.4.1)

- Keep detailed documentation to support your write-offs for losses from rental properties (11.4.2)

- Consider the potential benefits of incorporating your business (11.5)

In this chapter we highlight some of the major topics in the taxation of business income. If you are a professional, see Chapter 16 for additional planning ideas. If you are in a partnership, see also 16.2; if you are in Québec, see also Chapter 17. It goes without saying that anyone with a substantial amount of business income should obtain proper professional advice due to the large potential for planning legitimate deductions.

11.1 Employee or independent contractor?

As you will see in this chapter, people who are self-employed, carrying on business for themselves, generally have wider scope for tax planning than do employees.

Carrying on a business has nothing to do with setting up a corporation (see 11.5 and Chapter 14). Anyone can carry on business. If you set up a second-hand clothing-for-cash exchange in your basement, you are carrying on business. If you decide to put a name to your business (say, "XYZ Second-Hand Clothing"), that is just you carrying on business under that name. You have not created a new entity. You simply have a proprietorship, which means you are the proprietor of a business.

The distinction between employee and independent contractor (i.e., self-employed) is not always clear in cases where you receive most or all of your "work" income from one source. If you provide services to an organization, you can be classed in either group, depending on the facts.

> **Example**
>
> Kathy is a computer programmer. She develops software under contract for ABC Corporation, and is paid for each hour she works. She does a lot of her work at home, though she goes to ABC's offices for regular meetings.
>
> Is Kathy an employee of ABC, or an independent consultant who carries on business and whose major (or only) client is ABC?

In cases like this, one must look at all the facts to determine the person's status. There are no hard and fast rules. In general, you are more likely to be considered an employee if you:

- work a set number of hours per day
- have to account for your time to the company
- are told what to do each step of the way
- are a member of the company's group life, drug, dental and pension plans and receive other "benefits"
- use the company's computer equipment and supplies and have an office at the company.

On the other hand, you would likely be considered an independent contractor carrying on your own business as a proprietor if you:

- agree to get the job done, but you don't make a commitment for any particular number of hours on any particular day
- work on your own with no supervision, and simply report back to the company periodically on progress
- issue invoices and receive cheques (with no source deductions for income tax, EI or CPP/QPP) and receive no employee benefits
- use your own equipment and work at home, going to the company for planning meetings only
- provide services to more than one company.

These examples are fairly extreme. Between them is a large fuzzy area, where each case will depend on its facts. It doesn't matter very much what you and the company *call* your relationship; more specifically, calling it independent contracting doesn't make it independent contracting unless the facts support such a claim.

One case where the CRA has a clear administrative policy is that of real estate agents. You will be considered self-employed if you are entitled to the full amount of commissions, and either (a) you pay only a fixed amount to your broker for administrative operating costs, or (b) you pay a percentage of your gross commissions to your broker to cover such costs, and you set your own commission rate for sales on your listings.

If you are currently employed in a position where you maintain a fair amount of independence from your employer, investigate whether you can change your relationship so that you become an independent consultant rather than an employee. You will need to document the details of your relationship carefully, in case the CRA or Revenu Québec challenges you in the future.

> Arrange to be a consultant rather than employed.

If you succeed in becoming independent, you will be able to take advantage of all of the planning tips throughout this chapter. You will lose certain advantages, however, including the right to Employment Insurance benefits, the employer's contribution to the Canada Pension Plan for you, and possibly all of the employment benefits you now have (pension plan, drug plan, etc.). You may wish to negotiate to have your cash compensation increased in exchange for any employment benefits you are giving up.

The CRA has a questionnaire, Form CPT-1, through which your employer can supply the details of its relationship with you and ask for a ruling as to whether you are an employee or not for CPP purposes (and, by extension, for income tax purposes). However, there is no requirement to apply for such a ruling, and you and your employer/client are not bound by the CRA's administrative decisions. If, after receiving professional advice, you believe that you are legally an independent contractor, then you are quite entitled to proceed on that basis. (Of course, if the CRA has expressed the view that you are an employee, your employer/client may not be willing to risk not withholding tax at source.)

11.2 Taxation of the business

In this section we review how your business income is taxed. If you are a professional, see also Chapter 16.

11.2.1 Business year-end

Until 1995, you could pick a year-end for any business when you started the business. The income was then taxed only in the taxation year in which the business year *ended*, which allowed individuals and partnerships carrying on business to defer paying tax by up to a year. Since 1995, this option is not available. Now all individuals, and all partnerships which have any individuals as members, must use a calendar year for reporting their income.

If you have been in business since before January 1, 1995 and were not already using a calendar year-end, you had to report two business "years" on your 1995 return: one ending on your normal year-end and the other ending on December 31. Since you probably would have ended up with much higher income for 1995, you have been allowed to spread the "extra" income (for the "stub period" ending December 31, 1995) over 10 years until 2004.

Andy is a lawyer in Montreal. Before 1995, his business year-end was January 31.

For the 12-month year ending January 31, 1995, Andy's income was $120,000. As well, he had to recognize the income for the 11 months running from February 1 to December 31, 1995 ($110,000). For this "stub period", Andy reported 5% of the income, or $5,500, in 1995.

In 1996, and for each year from 1997 through 2003, Andy had to include a further 10% ($11,000) of his 1995 "stub period" income. The final 15% ($16,500) must be included by 2004.

In 1995, you would have reported the full amount of the stub period income, and claimed a "reserve" (deduction) against that income of up to 95% in 1995. The amount of the reserve was then included in 1996 income, and a new reserve could be taken for 1996 of up to 85% of the original stub period income. Each following year, you would have reported an additional 10% and claim a reserve for the remainder, so that the amount of the reserve remaining in 2004 is 15%. You must include this remaining 15% of your stub period amount in your income for 2004.

If you are a proprietor or an individual who is a member of a partnership composed of individuals, you or your partnership may have elected to keep the off-calendar year-end by using an "alternative method" of eliminating the tax deferral. Under the alternative method, you or the partnership were required to add to the business income for the actual off-calendar fiscal period an estimate of income earned between the end of the 1995 fiscal period and December 31, 1995. The adjustment is determined by prorating the actual off-calendar fiscal period. For example, if your traditional fiscal year-end is January 31, 1995, the additional amount taxable in 1995 under the alternative method was 11/12 of your actual income for the fiscal period ended January 31, 1995. Similar adjustments must be made for later years. You can then claim a reserve for the 1995 adjustment amount in each year through 2004 similar to the reserve described above.

11.2.2 Business income and expenses

As a general rule, business income for tax purposes is based on generally accepted accounting principles. (Among other things, this means operating on the accrual basis: you record your income when you have billed your clients, whether or not you have been paid.) However, there are many adjustments required for tax purposes. Some of them are discussed in the sections below.

When you earn business income, there is normally no withholding of tax at source. If you are providing services to a single organization, and are able to classify your relationship as one of independent consultant rather than employee (see 11.1), you can submit invoices that will be paid in full, without tax (or EI premiums or CPP/QPP contributions) being taken off and remitted to the CRA. You may, however, be required to pay instalments of income tax. Instalments are discussed in 9.2.2.

In general, expenses are deductible if they are laid out to earn income from the business and are in reasonable amounts. There are certainly exceptions, as we shall see in the following sections. However, the underlying principle is the reverse of that for employees. *Employees can only deduct expenses that are specifically permitted under the federal* Income Tax Act *and the* Québec Taxation Act. *Someone carrying on business can deduct any expenses that are not specifically prohibited by these statutes, provided such expenses relate to the earning of business income.*

11.2.3 EI, CPP and other payroll taxes

Employment insurance is available only to those who are employed. If you carry on business for yourself, you are neither required nor permitted to pay EI premiums. This will save you up to $1,853 in 2004 when taking into account both the employee and employer's portions; on the other hand, it means that if your consulting contracts terminate and you are left without work, you cannot benefit from EI.

Canada and Québec Pension Plan contributions are split equally between employees and their employers. If you are self-employed, you are required to pay the "employer's share" to make up what is not being paid for you, as well as your own share. Since you are not employed, no CPP/QPP contributions are withheld from your income. As a result, you will find yourself required to pay up to $3,663 for 2004 in mandatory CPP/QPP contributions when you file your return. You may then claim a deduction from taxable income for the portion of CPP/QPP contributions that represents the employer's share, up to $1,831 for 2004. You can also claim the 16% federal tax credit for the employee's share of your CCP/QPP contributions (also up to $1,831 for 2004—see 2.9.1). If it's any consolation, you'll get your CPP/QPP contributions back in the form of a pension after you turn 65, or optionally as early as age 60 at a reduced amount (see 20.3.1).

Many provinces also have payroll taxes that apply to employment income. In some cases, they apply to self-employed income as well.

11.2.4 Recovering GST by claiming input tax credits

If you are self-employed (or the owner-manager of an incorporated business), the business can normally claim a full refund (an "input tax credit") of the 7% Goods and Services Tax (GST) or 15% Harmonized Sales Tax (HST; see 11.2.5) paid on most purchases. To be eligible for input tax credits, you must register with the CRA to collect GST even though you are not specifically obliged to register unless your annual sales are more than $30,000. Once you are registered, you must charge GST on all your taxable sales (or HST on taxable sales made to customers in Nova Scotia, New Brunswick and Newfoundland and Labrador), even if your annual sales are less than $30,000. You can build the tax into your prices if you wish. As is the case for income tax purposes, "personal or living expenses" are not eligible for input tax credits.

Recover GST (or HST) and QST that you've paid by claiming input tax credits for your business.

Make sure to keep accurate records so you can claim input tax credits where possible. Claims for input tax credits must be supported by receipts or other documentation of GST paid, not submitted with the GST return but held on file in case of audit. All documentation must show the vendor's name, the date (or, for a contract, the date the amounts are payable), and the total amount payable. Where the total (including all taxes) is $30 or over, the receipt must also show:

- the amount of GST, or a statement that the total includes GST, and a clear indication of which items are taxable; and
- the supplier's GST nine-digit registration number.

Where the total is $150 or over, the receipt must also show:

- the purchaser's name;
- the terms of payment; and
- a description sufficient to identify each item supplied.

Failure to have this documentation will normally lead to a disallowance of any input tax credit claim if the return is audited.

Input tax credits can only be claimed where the expenses were incurred in the course of providing "taxable supplies". A business engaged in providing supplies that are GST-exempt—such as a doctor, dentist, life insurance agent or financial institution—cannot claim input tax credits for the costs of making those supplies.

If you rent out residential real estate (whether a house or an apartment building), no GST will apply to the rent since it is GST-exempt. As a result, you cannot claim input tax credits to recover any of the GST that you pay on utilities, property management fees and other costs. You must set the rent high enough to cover your costs. (Rent for commercial real estate is subject to GST.)

> If you're a residential landlord, account for sales tax when setting rents.

In Québec, similar rules apply for QST purposes.

11.2.5 Harmonized Sales Tax

No matter where in Canada your business is located, you should be aware of your obligations under the Harmonized Sales Tax. The provincial sales taxes in Nova Scotia, New Brunswick and Newfoundland and Labrador were harmonized with the GST in 1997 to create the HST. The HST rate in these provinces is 15% (comprised of a 7% federal component and an 8% provincial component). The HST and the GST apply to the same goods and services. The only major difference is that the tax applies at the 15% rate on goods and services supplied in the three Atlantic provinces, instead of the 7% rate that applies in the rest of the country. Generally, our comments about the GST throughout this book apply equally well to the HST, though there are some exceptions.

> Be aware of your HST obligations for sales to customers in Nova Scotia, New Brunswick and Newfoundland and Labrador.

All GST registrants in Canada must collect HST on taxable supplies made to or in the above three Atlantic provinces. If you're registered for the GST, you are also registered for the HST. Collection, reporting and remittance of the HST is done through the CRA in the same way as the GST.

The HST could complicate your recordkeeping and sales tax reporting if you make taxable sales to customers both inside and outside Nova Scotia, New Brunswick and Newfoundland and Labrador. Depending on the province to which the goods or services are delivered, you will have to determine whether you should charge GST only, GST and the appropriate provincial sales tax, or HST.

11.2.6 GST—the "Quick Method" and simplified accounting

Self-employed individuals and small businesses may elect to use the "Quick Method" to simplify recordkeeping for GST. It can be used by most businesses with annual sales (including tax) under $200,000 (excluding financial services, real property, capital assets and certain other assets). Annual sales include sales of associated businesses. This method can be particularly useful for certain consultants. However, the Quick Method may not be used by anyone providing legal, accounting, actuarial, bookkeeping, financial consulting, tax consulting or tax return preparation services.

Simplify your paperwork by using the "Quick Method" for GST and QST reporting.

Under the Quick Method, a business must still charge and collect the tax at the normal rates, but instead of remitting total GST collected minus total GST paid as it would under the usual method, the business remits to the CRA a flat percentage of sales (including GST). The percentages vary depending on whether your business operates exclusively outside of Nova Scotia, New Brunswick and Newfoundland and Labrador, exclusively in those provinces, or both in and out of those provinces. The rates also vary depending on whether your business is primarily selling goods or services.

For businesses operating exclusively outside those provinces, where sales are mostly services rather than goods, the flat percentage is 5% (but only 4% on the first $30,000 of sales). For qualifying suppliers of goods whose purchases of taxable personal property (other than basic groceries) for resale are at least 40% of sales (excluding basic groceries), the flat percentage is 2.5% (but only 1.5% on the first $30,000 of sales). Input tax credits can only be claimed for capital purchases.

For businesses operating exclusively in Nova Scotia, New Brunswick and/or Newfoundland and Labrador and selling primarily services, the flat percentage is 10% (9% on the first $30,000 of sales). For businesses selling goods, the flat percentage is 5% (4% on the first $30,000 of sales). Special rules apply for businesses operating both inside and outside of these provinces.

Example

John is a computer consultant who works exclusively in Alberta. He bills his clients $100,000 in 2004, plus $7,000 GST, for his consulting services. Because he is able to use his clients' equipment and facilities, his cost of doing business is very low. He pays a total of $70 GST on $1,000 of business expenses during the year.

Normally, John would remit his GST collected minus his GST paid to the CRA for the year. This would be $7,000 minus $70, or $6,930.

By electing to use the Quick Method, however, John will be required to remit a flat 4% of the first $30,000 of his GST-included sales and 5% on the remaining $77,000 (or, to put it another way, 5% of his total sales of $107,000, minus $300). He thus remits $5,050 instead of $6,930.

Clearly, the Quick Method can be useful for businesses that have few taxable expenses. If the business' taxable expenses are high, however, the loss of the ability to claim input tax credits will offset the benefit of the Quick Method's reduced remittance rate. Input tax credits are still available on real property and capital assets purchased for use in taxable activities.

As an alternative to the Quick Method, the streamlined input tax credit method allows you to total up your GST-bearing purchases—including GST, provincial sales tax, late payment penalties and tips—and claim 7/107 of the total for input tax credit purposes (or 15/115 for expenditures on which HST was paid). Your business' annual sales (including sales of associated businesses) must not exceed $500,000 and taxable purchases must be less than $2 million (including purchases of associated businesses) for you to use this method. Not only does it make accounting for input tax credits simpler, but it gives you a slightly larger claim than you can make by totalling up individual amounts of GST paid.

For QST reporting in Québec, you can use a similar "Quick Method" and simplified accounting (however, the rates under the QST system are somewhat different).

11.2.7 Capital cost allowance

The treatment of capital expenses is one of the major differences between business income based on accounting principles and income calculated for income tax purposes. In both cases, you cannot simply write off the cost of purchasing major capital assets (furniture, buildings, computers, automobiles, etc.). You must spread the cost over several years.

For accounting (not tax) purposes, a professional will make a judgment call as to the appropriate depreciation to claim. Various methods of depreciation can be used.

For tax purposes, depreciation is subject to strict rules and limitations, since it reduces your income (and thus the tax you pay). The income tax system of depreciation is called capital cost allowance (CCA); the rules are numerous and complex.

In general terms, your capital assets are grouped into classes, and capital cost allowance can be claimed annually against each class. The "declining balance" method is used for most classes; the maximum you can claim against each class is a fixed percentage of the "undepreciated capital cost". What you claim then reduces that balance for next year's claim.

Some common CCA rates	
Automobiles (class 10 or 10.1)	30%
Buildings:	
acquired after 1987 (class 1)	4%
acquired in 1979 – 1987 (class 3)	5%
Computer hardware:	
acquired after March 22, 2004 (new class)	45%
acquired on or before March 22, 2004 (class 10)	30%
Most computer software (class 12)	100%
Furniture and fixtures (class 8)	20%
Tools costing less than $200 (class 12)	100%

Acquire depreciable assets before year-end.

For most acquisitions, only one-half of the CCA you could otherwise claim for the asset will be allowed in the year of acquisition. As a result, acquiring an asset just before your year-end will accelerate the timing of your tax write-off, while acquiring the asset at the beginning of the year will delay your CCA claim. Assets are normally required to be available for use and not simply "on the books" to be eligible for CCA, unless you have owned them for at least two years. (The term "available for use" has a specific and complex definition, and professional advice should be sought if you are unsure as to how it applies in your case.)

Note that you are never required to claim the maximum CCA. You may in any year choose to claim less than the maximum, or nothing at all, for any given class of assets. The undepreciated capital cost for that class will remain intact, so you can make claims in later years based on that carried-forward balance.

Consider claiming less CCA than the maximum.

In some circumstances you may wish to claim less CCA than you are entitled to. For example, if you have old non-capital losses or investment tax credits that will otherwise expire, you are better off to not claim CCA, use up the losses or credits, and save your "undepreciated capital cost" balances for CCA claims in future years.

You might also choose not to claim CCA if you are in a low-income year and expect your income to be much higher (and thus taxed at higher marginal rates) in later years. Such a decision should only be made after careful analysis of the present value of the future tax savings, including the impact on your ability to make an RRSP contribution in the subsequent year.

11.2.8 Transportation expenses

If you rely on modes of travel other than an automobile for your business travel, you can generally deduct the related expenses. Keep records of all such business trips, and deduct the

> Deduct public transit fares, taxis and other business travel costs.

appropriate costs of public transit, taxicabs, and so on. (If you use your own car, see 12.3.)

You cannot consider transportation from your home to your own office as a business expense. However, if you have an office in your home, and you travel from there to your major client (who might happen to provide you with an office on its premises), you are engaging in business travel.

11.2.9 Meals and entertainment

If you take a client or potential client (or a group of such people) to lunch or dinner, you can normally consider the cost of the meal as a business expense. The tax rules restrict the amount you can claim to 50% of the amount

> Document and claim your business meals and entertainment expenses.

paid; the restriction is designed to deny a deduction for some of the personal benefit you receive (since you would need to eat anyway). The same 50% limitation applies to entertainment expenses, such as taking a client to a sports event. (If you pay Québec tax, see 17.2.19.)

Similarly, if you are registered for GST purposes, you can only claim input tax credits for half of the GST paid on such expenses (see 11.2.4).

Make sure you claim all lunches and dinners that you can justifiably relate to your business. For audit purposes, you should make a notation on your receipt of the individual(s) entertained and the reason for the meeting.

11.2.10 Home office expenses

If you have an office in your home, you can claim a portion of your ongoing home expenses as business expenses, subject to the restrictions discussed below. The portion will normally be based on the fraction of the home that is used for your office (you can usually exclude common areas, such as hallways, kitchen and washrooms, when making the calculation).

Mary is a computer programmer and works as a consultant to various companies. She works in her home, where her office is a room that is 200 square feet. The total area of the rooms in her house (bedrooms, living room, dining room and the office) is 2,000 square feet.

Provided her home office qualifies (see below), Mary can claim 10% of her costs such as mortgage interest, property taxes, house insurance and utilities as expenses for tax purposes.

The expenses you can claim include:

- rent, if you are a tenant
- mortgage interest (but not the principal portion of blended mortgage payments)
- property taxes
- utilities, such as electricity, heat, water, gas
- telephone (if you have a separate business telephone which is fully deductible, consider whether you also use your personal phone for business calls)
- home insurance.

Also make sure to claim your business portion of some of the less obvious expenses, such as garden service, driveway snowplowing, and minor repairs. You will need to keep receipts on file; do not simply estimate your expenses.

Write off your eligible home office expenses.

You may also claim capital cost allowance on the appropriate fraction of your home, but this is often not advisable. If you claim CCA, the CRA will take the position that that fraction of your home is not part of your principal residence, and will disallow your claim for the principal residence exemption (see 6.5.2) for that portion of the home. Any CCA you claimed can also be "recaptured" into income when you sell your home. (If you bought your home at the top of the housing market and do not expect to recover your costs when you sell, claiming CCA may be a good idea, however.)

The home office expenses are subject to restrictions. First, you can only claim the expenses against your income from the business. You therefore cannot use home office expenses to produce an overall business loss that is applied against other income. However, losses disallowed because of this rule can be carried forward and used in any later year against income generated from the same business.

Second, the home office will only be allowed if:

- your home is your principal place of business—that is, you do not have an office elsewhere (if you have one major client and that client provides you with an office on its premises, it is still the client's premises and it will not disentitle you to your claim for a home office)

- the home office is used exclusively for your business, and is used "on a regular and continuous basis for meeting clients, customers or patients".

> **Example**
>
> Les is an optometrist and has an office outside his home. He also has an office in his basement, where he does a lot of his business' paperwork and occasionally sees patients (usually neighbours who come over for treatment in the evening).
>
> Les will not be able to claim any expenses in respect of his home office unless he can show that he uses it "on a regular and continuous basis" to see patients.

Of course, supplies that relate exclusively to your home office are fully deductible and not subject to the above restrictions. Fully deductible expenses would normally include a separate business phone line; fax and printer paper; laser printer or photocopier toner cartridges; computer repairs (assuming your computer is used only for your business); and so on.

If you pay Québec tax, see also 17.2.20.

11.2.11 Health and dental premiums

Self-employed individuals may write-off premiums paid for supplementary health care coverage against their business income. For the premiums to be deductible, your coverage must be no greater than the benefits provided to your arm's length employees. If you have no such employees, your deductible premiums are limited to $1,500 for yourself, $1,500 for your spouse and $750 for each child.

11.2.12 Convention expenses

The CRA will allow you to deduct the costs of attending two conventions a year in connection with your business or profession. A portion of your expenses may be subject to the limitation on the deductibility of meals and entertainment expenses discussed at 11.2.9.

For the expenses to be deductible, the convention must be held at a location that can reasonably be considered to be within the scope of the host organization. For example, if the convention's sponsor is a business or professional body that is provincial in scope, the convention must be held in that province. Under the Canada-U.S. tax treaty, expenses to attend a Canadian-sponsored convention in the U.S. are deductible, but only if the Canadian organization is a national one. (The CRA will not allow you to deduct any costs for attending a convention held during an ocean cruise, no matter who sponsors it.)

11.2.13 Capital gains

Any capital gains that you realize are accounted for directly, through the capital gains system discussed in Chapter 6. They are not counted within the business' income.

11.2.14 Investment tax credits

Federal investment tax credits (ITCs) are available for investment in certain regions of the country (for example, parts of the Maritimes) and for investment in scientific research and experimental development.

ITCs are claimed in the return for the calendar year in which they are generated. Unused ITCs can be carried back three years or carried forward for up to 10 years.

11.3 Partnerships

If you join together to carry on business with one or more other people—which could include your spouse—you will be in partnership. You are still, for tax purposes, carrying on business. (As well as the discussion below, see 16.2, where we discuss some special rules applying to professional partnerships.)

11.3.1 How partnership income is taxed

Partnerships do not pay tax. Partnerships with more than five partners are required to file "information returns" with the CRA, reporting partnership income, but these are not tax returns.

The individual partners must each report their share of the partnership's income (or loss) as their own, *whether or not they have taken any of the profits out of the partnership.* The partnership is required to report income on a December 31 year-end basis. (Resource allowances and certain other resource-related expenses are claimed by the individual partner rather than at the partnership level.)

Note that a partnership cannot pay a "salary" to a partner. Even if you, as a partner, receive something called a "salary", it is really partnership drawings (withdrawal of profits or capital from the partnership). You are *not* taxed on your partnership drawings, but on your share of the partnership's income, which may be very different.

If the partnership suffers losses, you can normally claim your share of those losses against your other sources of income. (This may not be the case where the partnership is a limited partnership.)

11.3.2 Adjustment of partnership allocation

The allocation of partnership income (or losses) among the partners is normally left up to the partners to resolve. If you set up an unreasonable allocation for income-splitting purposes (see Chapter 5), however, the CRA may disallow your allocation and substitute a reasonable one.

For example, if you and your spouse are in partnership together and you supply all of the capital and do almost all of the work in your business, while your spouse does almost nothing, the CRA could be expected to disallow a 50/50 allocation of the business' income between the two of you.

11.3.3 Capital gains

Capital gains or losses realized by a partnership are allocated to the individual partners at the end of the partnership's taxation year. This continues to be the case where the partnership elects to follow the alternative method and keeps its off-calendar year-end (see 11.2.1). However, for partnerships that must use a December 31 year-end, such gains or losses will always be reported by the individual partners in the calendar year in which they are realized.

11.3.4 Allocation of investment tax credits

Investment tax credits (see 11.2.14) earned by a partnership are allocated to the individual partners and claimed in the year in which the partnership's year ends.

11.3.5 Gain or loss on partnership interest

When you are a member of a partnership you own a "partnership interest", which has an adjusted cost base for capital gains calculation purposes (see 6.2.1). If you sell your interest in the partnership (or are deemed to dispose of it at fair market value on death or emigration—see 6.5.4 and 13.3.2), the adjusted cost base will determine whether you have a capital gain or capital loss.

Your initial cost base is the capital you put into the partnership. Each year, when you report your share of the partnership's income, that amount is added to your cost base (since you have already been taxed on it, it should not be taxed again if you sell your interest without withdrawing the profits). When you withdraw profits from the partnership (see 11.3.1), the amount you withdraw reduces your adjusted cost base. Thus, in simplified terms, your adjusted cost base is your contributions, plus all partnership profits, minus all partnership losses and your withdrawals. (The details are much more complicated and there are many special rules, but that is the essence of it.)

A partnership is a "flow-through entity" for purposes of the 1994 capital gain election, so you may have an "exempt capital gain balance" that you can use against the capital gain on a partnership interest, but only until the end of 2004 (see 6.4.4).

11.3.6 Assessment of partnership

The CRA is able to issue a "determination" of a partnership's income or loss. This "determination" is much like an assessment of a taxpayer's tax (see 9.4.1), in that it will be binding on the partners unless a Notice of Objection is filed. One partner will have to be designated by the partnership to file any such Notice of Objection, and the other partners will not be able to object directly to the determination.

11.3.7 Partners' sales tax rebates

Like employees, partners who are not registered for GST purposes and who have unreimbursed expenses such as automobile expenses that are deductible for income tax purposes can generally claim a rebate for the GST, HST or QST paid on those expenses (see 12.3.2 for an example).

> If you're a partner, claim sales tax rebates on your unreimbursed partnership expenses.

Make sure to keep records through the year and obtain invoices that indicate the amount of tax paid. The rebate is claimed with your individual income tax return.

11.4 Losses

11.4.1 Business losses

If your business expenses claimed for tax purposes exceed the revenues from the business, you have a loss. You also have a loss for tax purposes if you share in a portion of a partnership's loss.

You can only claim a business loss or loss arising from a limited partnership against other income if your business activity is clearly commercial and undertaken in pursuit of profit. If the activity has a personal element or has the aspect of a hobby, such as breeding race horses, the venture is considered to be in pursuit of profit if it is undertaken in a sufficiently commercial manner.

In October 2003, a draft change to the tax law was proposed to introduce a test for assessing whether an activity has a reasonable expectation of cumulative profit over the business's expected life cycle. In the past, the CRA relied heavily on such a test as an administrative policy, but its application in hindsight often prevented people from deducting losses from misguided business activities that failed to produce anticipated returns. In 2002, the Supreme Court downgraded the test, saying it is only one of many factors the CRA should evaluate in determining the activity's commercial nature. The October 2003 proposals, once enacted, will make it mandatory for the CRA to apply the test to determine whether business losses are deductible for 2005 and later years.

A business loss must first be used in the year in which it arises, to offset income from other businesses and other types of income, such as employment income, interest, (grossed-up) dividends and taxable capital gains. You do not have any choice in this matter; even if, for example, the tax on your dividend income could be offset by the dividend tax credit anyway, you must apply your business losses against any income you have in that year.

Business losses not deductible in the year they arise are called non-capital losses. They can be applied to other years' income. They can be carried back for up to three years and, for tax years ending after March 22, 2004, they can be carried forward for up to ten years (seven years for earlier tax years). They can be applied against any source of income in those years. All such claims are optional.

> Use your loss carryovers to maximum advantage.

Example

Judy had no income in 2001, and she earned $40,000 in 2002 and $50,000 in 2003 as an employee. In 2004, she goes into business for herself, and for her 2004 business year she suffers a loss for tax purposes of $100,000.

Judy can file a form requesting that her non-capital loss from 2004 be applied against any amount of her 2002 and 2003 income. She will then receive a refund for the tax she paid in those years. If she wipes out all of her 2002 and 2003 income, she will still have a $10,000 non-capital loss, which can be carried forward to future years.

Judy should not, however, use up $90,000 of her loss. She only needs to use enough to bring her 2002 and 2003 income so low that she pays no tax at all (about $7,700). If she wishes, she may choose to use even less, and leave some of the 2002 and 2003 income taxed at relatively low rates.

This example shows the need to use any non-capital losses carefully. When using non-capital losses against income for any given year, consider whether you want to keep some of the income taxed at a low rate. For example, if you have a loss in 2004 and are carrying it back to 2003, bear in mind that taxable income below $32,000 in 2003 was taxed at only about 24%. If you (confidently) expect to have a large income within the next few years, so that you can apply the loss against income which will otherwise be taxed at approximately 45%, you may be better off not bringing your 2003 taxable income below the $32,000 level.

Of course, you should never use loss carryovers to reduce your taxable income below the level ($8,012 for 2004, or more depending on the credits you can claim—see Chapter 2) where no tax is payable anyway.

11.4.2 Losses from rental properties

If you are a residential landlord, your losses from your rental property are deductible in the same way as other business losses as long as your rental business meets the general tax law requirements for business deductions. The CRA is quite aggressive in targetting rental loss deductions, so you should be sure to have adequate supporting documentation on hand to support your rental loss deductions.

> Keep detailed documentation to support your write-offs for losses from rental properties.

The CRA is likely to question your rental losses if your ownership of the property has a personal-use element, for example, if you or one of your relatives live there rent-free, or if you plan to live there in the future. The CRA may ask for detailed documentation such as a floor plan of the building showing which areas you use, rent out and share with your tenants. You should also be prepared to show which of your expenses relate to the whole property as opposed to the rental portion only. If you rent to a relative, your losses may be disallowed if you charge a lower rent than you would charge another tenant.

You should be prepared to prove the commercial nature of your rental activities. Where possible, keep complete records to show that you did thorough research on rental properties before you chose one to buy and complete records of the information that led you to believe your rental property would be a profitable investment. The tax courts have ruled that rental businesses may take several years—up to eight years in one case—to turn a profit. An explanation for your losses and description of steps taken to increase revenue or reduce expenses would also help support your case.

As discussed in 11.4.1, the Supreme Court has ruled that the tax system should not penalize taxpayers for lack of business acumen. Even if you do not have detailed profit projections and market research on hand, you should seek professional tax advice if the CRA seeks to deny your rental losses.

11.5 Should you incorporate your small business?

If you have an unincorporated business, you may be considering incorporation to save on taxes. But whether you and your business will gain a tax benefit from incorporation will depend on your personal cash flow needs, the personal and corporate tax rates in your province and the status of your business. (If you are considering setting up a corporation for the sole purpose of holding your investments, see 14.6.)

If you rely on all of your business' profits to support your personal cash flow needs, incorporation may not be a good idea—the cost of setting up and maintaining the corporation could outweigh the tax benefits. But if you can leave some of your profits in the corporation to be reinvested, incorporation could result in significant tax savings.

The taxation of corporations is discussed in 14.1. Generally, if you earn income through a corporation, the income will be taxed at the corporation level and then again at the personal level when the corporation distributes its after-tax income to you as a shareholder in the form of a dividend. Theoretically, the total corporate and personal income tax incurred by using a corporation to earn income should be the same as the personal tax that would result if the income were earned directly by an individual who was taxable at the top marginal rate. But in practice, this is not always the case. Before you incorporate your business, ask a professional tax adviser to help you compare the total amount of tax you will pay if you earn your business income directly or through a corporation.

Some advantages of incorporating your business include the following:

> Consider the potential benefits of incorporating your business.

Creditor-proofing your personal assets — Incorporation can limit your liability by keeping your personal and corporate assets separate. But since banks often ask small business owners for personal guarantees before they'll provide financing, incorporation may not protect you from all creditors.

Deferring expenses — You may be able to defer certain expenses if you incorporate. For example, if you report a bonus paid to an employee for tax purposes, you do not have to pay out the money until six months later.

Fiscal year flexibility — As we saw in 11.2.1, an unincorporated business must use the calendar year for tax purposes. An incorporated business can choose a non-calendar fiscal year, which may work better for your business cycle. If the fiscal year-end is in the later part of the calendar year, the payment of a bonus six months after the end of the year would put the payment into the next calendar year.

Access to the small business deduction and manufacturing and processing credit — With a corporation, you may be able to take advantage of the special lower tax rates for the first $300,000 of active business income of small "Canadian-controlled private corporations" and for income from manufacturing and processing (see 14.1).

Income splitting — If your spouse and adult children are shareholders in the corporation, any dividends they receive will be taxed in their hands.

179

Your corporation can also employ your family members as long as the amount paid is reasonable for the work performed (see 5.3.2).

Capital gains exemption — If your corporation is a qualifying small business corporation, the $500,000 capital gains exemption discussed in 6.4.1 is available to shelter your gain and the gains of each of your family members that will arise when the shares of the corporation are sold or transferred through a will.

Group insurance and retirement benefits — Once you incorporate, you can create a registered pension plan and obtain tax-deductible group health and life insurance for yourself and your employees, which could include family members. (Unincorporated businesses can also deduct group health insurance premiums if certain conditions are met and within certain limits—see 11.2.11.)

Against these potential advantages, you will need to weigh the legal and administrative costs of setting up and maintaining the corporation, keeping separate books and filing corporate federal and provincial tax returns. Also bear in mind that once you incorporate you will no longer be able to deduct business and capital losses against your other sources of income. Your decision about whether and when you should incorporate your business should be made with appropriate professional advice.

11.6 References

The following publications can be obtained (in person or by telephone request) from your nearest CRA Tax Services Office. Forms and guides may also be available from the CRA's Internet site at *www.cra-arc.gc.ca*.

Interpretation Bulletin IT-79R3, "Capital cost allowance—Buildings or other structures"
Interpretation Bulletin IT-131R2, "Convention expenses"
Interpretation Bulletin IT-232R3, "Losses—Their deductibility in the loss year or in other years"
Interpretation Bulletin IT-514, "Work space in home expenses"
Interpretation Bulletin IT-518R, "Food, beverages and entertainment expenses"
Interpretation Bulletin IT-521R, "Motor vehicle expenses claimed by self-employed individuals"
Interpretation Bulletin IT-525R, "Performing artists"
Interpretation Bulletin IT-533, "Interest Deductibility and Related Issues"
Information Circular 89-5R, "Partnership information return"
Guide, "Business and Professional Income Tax Guide"
Guide, "GST/HST Rebate for Partners"
Guide, "Employee or Self-Employed?"
Guide, "General Information for GST Registrants"

Guide, "Guide for Canadian Small Businesses"
Guide, "Guide for the Partnership Information Return"
Guide, "GST/HST Calculation Guide"
Guide, "General Application for GST/HST Rebates"
Guide, "The Quick Method of Accounting for GST/HST"
Guide, "Rental Income Tax Guide"
Guide, "Paying Your Tax by Instalments"
Form CPT1, "Request for a ruling as to the status of a worker"
Form T1A, "Request for loss carry-back"
Form T776, "Statement of real estate rentals"
Form T2038, "Investment tax credit (Individuals)"
Form T2124, "Statement of business activities"

If you use an automobile for business

- Keep track of—and maximize—business use of your car (12.1, 12.2.1, 12.3.1)
- Check to see if you qualify for a reduced standby charge benefit (12.2.1)
- Reduce the amount of time your company car is available for personal use (12.2.1)
- Avoid employer-owned vehicles costing over $30,000 (12.2.1)
- Take steps to minimize the taxable benefit from car operating costs (12.2.2)
- Claim rebate for GST paid on expenses deductible from your employment income (12.3.2)

If your employer provides you with an automobile, you may be assessed a taxable benefit for your personal use of the car. If you drive your own car in the course of your job or your business, you may be able to write off your work-related automobile costs against your employment or business income. In this chapter, we map out the complex rules that the CRA uses to arrive at your automobile-related taxable benefit or deduction. Along the way, we also point out some tax-saving opportunities.

12.1 Keeping a log

Whether you drive your employer's car or your own in the course of your work, keep careful track of the distance you drive for work-related purposes to verify your automobile-related tax

> Keep track of—and maximize—business use of your car.

claims with the CRA. You may wish to keep a log book on the dashboard, or record your business driving in your daily appointment calendar. The log must show the total number of kilometres driven and total business kilometres for the year. It should also include the date, destination and distance driven for each business trip.

Starting in 2005, Québec employees using employer-provided automobiles will be required to provide their employers with a copy of such a log book within 10 days of either the end of the year or the end of the period the automobile was available to them, or they will face a $200 penalty.

12.2 Using a company automobile

Special rules apply for determining the taxable benefit when your employer provides you with an automobile. (If you use your own car for employment purposes, see 12.3.1.)

There are two elements to the benefit that must be reported for tax purposes: a standby charge, and the benefit in respect of operating costs. These will normally be reported together on your T4 (and Québec Relevé 1) statement from your employer as a single amount, and included in your total "income from employment" for tax purposes.

12.2.1 Standby charge

The standby charge is, essentially, 2% of the original cost of the car for each month that it is available to you—that is, 24% per year. (For automobile sales persons, it can instead be 1.5% per month of the average cost of the dealer's cars acquired in the year.)

You can have your standby charge reduced if you can show both that:

- your business use of the car is 50% or more of the kilometres driven, and

- your personal use of the car is less than 1,667 km per month, or 20,000 km in total during the year.

> Check to see if you qualify for a reduced standby charge benefit.

If you meet these conditions, your employer can reduce your reported standby charge by a percentage equal to the number of person-use km driven divided by 20,000 (assuming the car was available to you for a full 12 months). For example, if you drive an employer-owned car 25,000 km for business purposes and 15,000 km for personal purposes, your standby charge can be reduced to 75% (15,000 ÷ 20,000) of the regular standby charge.

Note that driving between your home and your place of employment is normally *not* considered business use. It can thus be very difficult to satisfy the above tests for a reduction in the standby charge.

Where the car is leased, the standby charge is two-thirds of the monthly leasing cost instead of 2% of the purchase price. Up-front, lump-sum leasing charges (or "balloon" payments) are pro-rated over the term of the lease for purposes of the calculation.

Lease termination charges are normally considered a lease payment in the year paid. If you and your employer agree, a lease termination payment may be retroactively spread over the term of the lease for purposes of the standby charge, as long as the years are not statute-barred and your employer issues amended T4 slips (Relevé 1 for Québec) for those years. This will generally be advantageous if your income in the year that the lease is terminated is taxed at a higher rate than in previous years, although you will need to factor in the non-deductible interest that will be payable on the increase in your taxes for the prior years.

An extra 7% (15% in Nova Scotia, New Brunswick and Newfoundland) must be added to the employee's taxable benefit to reflect the GST or HST embedded in the value of the automobile to you (7% GST plus an extra 7.5% QST on the GST-included price if you live in Québec).

The standby charge is based on the number of 30-day periods in the year that a company car is "made available" to you or a member of your family. However, the actual calculation is based on the number of *days* during which the car is available. This number is divided by 30 and rounded to the nearest whole number, and rounded down if it is exactly in the middle.

> Reduce the amount of time your company car is available for personal use.

If you can get the number of "available days" down to 345, which is 11.5 30-day periods, the standby charge will therefore be reduced to only 11 times 2% of the automobile cost instead of 12 times 2%.

If you take three weeks or more of vacations or business trips during the year, leave the car at the company's premises during those times. If the car cost $30,000 new in 2004, you can thus reduce your taxable income for the year by $600 (and save about $270 in tax if you are in the highest tax bracket) by getting the number of "available days" down to 345. Note, however, that the CRA holds the view that the car is still made available to you during this time unless you are *required* to return the car and control over its use to your employer. You might wish to arrange for your employer to impose this requirement on you.

As we will see in 12.3.1, there is a ceiling on the capital cost of cars for capital cost allowance purposes that creates an element of double taxation. For example, if you drive a company car

> Avoid employer-owned vehicles costing over $30,000.

that was purchased in 2004 and cost more than $30,000 (plus GST and PST), your taxable "standby charge" benefit is 2% per month of the actual cost of the car. However, only $30,000 (plus GST and PST) can be written off (over time) as capital cost allowance by your employer. As such, it may be more economical for you to purchase the car yourself and arrange for an appropriate increase in remuneration from your employer.

12.2.2 Operating cost benefit

The taxable benefit for operating costs is 17¢/km of personal use for 2004. If your employer pays any operating costs during the year in respect of your personal use of an employer-provided car (and you don't fully reimburse your employer by the following February 14), the 17¢ rate applies. If you are employed principally in selling or leasing automobiles this rate is 14¢.

An alternative calculation is available for the operating expenses where your business use of the car exceeds 50%. If you notify your employer in writing *by December 31* that you wish this option, the operating costs benefit will be a flat 50% of the standby charge.

If you qualify for a standby charge reduction (see 12.2.1), you should look into whether you could also benefit from the alternative operating cost benefit calculation. A benefit of one-half of the standby charge will also be to your advantage where the cost of the car is relatively low (for a small car, or a car that was purchased used), and the number of personal kilometres is relatively high even though it is used for personal purposes less than 50% of the time.

> Take steps to minimize the taxable benefit from car operating costs.

If your employer pays only part of the operating costs of an employer-owned car that you use, the taxable benefit from operating costs can cost you more than the amount the employer pays. Sometimes the employer pays only the insurance and the employee pays for all gas and repairs, or the employer does not pay most operating expenses but might cover an occasional major repair bill.

For example, suppose you put 20,000 km on your company car over the year, all of which is personal use (including driving to work and back). Your employer pays the insurance ($800 per year) and you pay the rest of the operating expenses. Your taxable benefit for operating costs will be 17¢ per personal-use kilometre, or $3,400, which will cost you about $1,530 in tax if you are in the top tax bracket. So having the employer pay for the insurance is very disadvantageous.

In such a case you should repay the $800 to the employer *by February 14* of the following year, so that the "17¢ per kilometre" rule will not apply. Of course, your employer can pay you sufficient additional salary so that the after-tax amount will be enough to offset your repayment of the insurance costs.

12.2.3 Allowances and advances for automobile expenses

If you receive a reasonable allowance for automobile expenses, the allowance will not be included in your income if it is based solely on the number of kilometres driven in the performance of your employment duties. If it is a flat amount not calculated in terms of your employment-related driving, it will be taxable (though you may be able to claim offsetting automobile expenses—see 12.3.1).

The CRA will agree to consider a flat periodic amount to be an accountable advance (rather than a taxable allowance) if you and your employer agree at the beginning of the year that you will receive a reasonable stated amount for each employment-related kilometre driven and you and your employer settle up at the end of the year regarding the difference between your actual business-related kilometres and the stated amount.

For 2004, the CRA and Revenu Québec accept as a "reasonable allowance" of 42¢/km for the first 5,000 km and 36¢/km for each additional kilometre driven (4¢ more in the Yukon and Northwest Territories); in some cases you may be able to justify a higher amount as "reasonable".

If you receive an allowance from your employer that is a combination of flat-rate and reasonable per-kilometre allowances that cover the same use for the vehicle, the total combined allowance is taxable as an employee benefit.

12.3 Using your own automobile for business purposes

12.3.1 Automobile expense deductions for employees

If you are required by the terms of your employment to use your own automobile and are not receiving a (non-taxable) reasonable allowance based on the number of kilometres you drive for employment purposes (see 12.2.3), you can deduct a portion of your automobile expenses from your employment income. (Your employer must certify that you were required to use your own vehicle on federal Form T2200, which you must keep on file, and Québec Form TP-64.3-V, which you must file with your Québec tax return.)

You can deduct operating costs, such as gas, repairs and car washes, to the extent they relate to your employment. As noted in 12.1, you will need to keep a detailed log of your driving to track your employment-related use as opposed to your personal use.

You can also deduct capital cost allowance (depreciation), or your monthly lease payments for the proportion of employment-related use. The allowable rate of capital cost allowance is 15% in the year of acquisition of the car, followed by 30% *on the remaining balance* in each subsequent year. However, there is a cap on the cost of the car for this purpose:

Year car purchased	Limit
1998 – 1999	$26,000*
2000	$27,000*
2001 – 2004	$30,000*

Example

Michelle buys a new car in Ontario in January 2004 for $35,000 plus 7% GST and 8% Ontario sales tax. She is required to drive 10,000 km for employment-related purposes during the year. She also drives 10,000 km on personal trips.

Since half of her driving is employment-related, Michelle can claim half of the capital cost allowance normally allowed for a car. Although she spent $35,000, the cost is capped at $30,000, plus $2,400 Ontario sales tax and $2,100 GST (total of $34,500), for tax purposes. The maximum capital cost allowance for the year of acquisition is 15%. Fifteen per cent of $34,500 is $5,175. Michelle can therefore claim half of this amount, $2,588 as a deduction against her employment income for 2004.

Further, because she uses her car partly for business, Michelle can claim a GST rebate for 2004 from the CRA equal to 7/107 of her capital cost allowance claim—see 12.3.2. (If she had purchased the car in Nova Scotia, New Brunswick or Newfoundland and Labrador, the rebate would be equal to 15/115 of her capital cost allowance claim.)

If you lease the car, your deduction for the lease payments is restricted to parallel the dollar limit on purchases:

Year lease entered into	Limit
1998 – 1999	$650*
2000	$700*
2001 – 2004	$800*

*plus GST/HST and PST on this amount

Your maximum deductible monthly lease charge is the lesser of the maximum lease limit set out above and an amount determined through a complex formula that takes into account your leasing charges and cumulative payments, the manufacturer's suggested list price, the prescribed purchase limit for CCA purposes and refundable deposits.

Example

James bought a new car in January 2004 for $60,000, and is paying $1,100 per month on his car loan. He paid $5,000 down and the loan interest rate is 7%. One-half of his driving is related to his employment.

Calculations show that James pays $320 per month in interest for the first month, and slightly less over the following months. His interest for tax purposes over the year will be limited to $300 per month, or $3,600. Of this, he can deduct half, or $1,800, to reflect the proportion of his driving which was employment-related.

If you lease the car and you make an up-front lump-sum payment (or "balloon" payment), the CRA will normally consider the amount to be part of your normal lease charge in the year paid and your deduction may be restricted by the lease deduction limit—see 12.3.3.

You can also deduct interest on any loan you have taken out to purchase the car (including financing on the purchase itself, where you make monthly payments that combine interest and capital). Your monthly interest is limited to $300 ($250 for cars purchased in 1997 – 2000).

If you are reimbursed by your employer for employment-related use of your automobile, the reimbursement payments are not taxed. Of course, you cannot deduct your own expenses to the extent you have been reimbursed for them.

Driving between home and work is normally considered personal use. If, however, you travel from your home to a business call (to visit a client or supplier, for example), that will constitute business use. You can maximize your employment-related travel by making all of your business calls at the beginning and end of your day, before you go to work and after you leave work. You can thus make your entire trip from home to work count as travel for employment purposes.

12.3.2 GST rebate for employees' auto expenses

Where you can deduct expenses from your employment income, you can also generally claim a rebate of GST or HST paid on those expenses (see 10.9). If you have auto expenses you're deducting from your employment income, you

> Claim rebate for GST paid on expenses deductible from your employment income.

may be entitled to a GST or HST rebate, as the following example shows.

Example

Continuing our first example in 12.3.1, Michelle is required to drive 10,000 km for employment-related purposes during the year. She also drives 10,000 km on personal trips. She spends $2,140 (including GST) over the course of the year on gas and repairs for her car, and does not receive any reimbursement from her employer. All the expenses are paid in Ontario.

Since one-half of Michelle's expenses are required by her employment, she can claim $1,070 as a deduction from employment income. That figure, however, already includes $70 in GST that applied to the gas and repairs. Michelle can claim a rebate of the $70 on a form filed with her income tax return. The $70 rebate is taxable in the year she receives it.

Further, because she uses her car partly for business, Michelle can claim a GST rebate in 2004 from the CCRA equal to 7/107 of her capital cost allowance claim. That is, 7/107 of the $2,588 Michelle can deduct as capital cost allowance, or $169, is refunded to her. This $169 is deducted from the undepreciated capital cost of the car at the beginning of 2005.

In the above example, we assume that Michelle's employer is a GST registrant and is not a financial institution. If, instead, she is employed by a financial institution or by a non-GST registrant, she would not be entitled to the employee GST rebate which, as shown, amounts to $239 in the first year.

We have also assumed that Michelle did not receive a per kilometre allowance from her employer. If she had, she would not be able to claim a GST rebate on any of her automobile expenses unless her employer certified on her Form GST 370 that the allowance was "unreasonable" and that her employer would not be claiming a GST tax credit with respect to her allowance. However, in the unlikely case that Michelle's employer certifies that her per kilometre allowance is unreasonable, the amount will be included in her income and her employer must withhold income tax and other source deductions on the amount.

A rebate is only available where GST was paid on the purchase. Michelle cannot receive a rebate in respect of the deductible portion of her car insurance, since insurance is not subject to GST. Similarly, there is no rebate for GST paid on gas purchased in the United States, because no GST is included in its price.

Finally, note also that if Michelle's expenses were incurred in Nova Scotia, New Brunswick or Newfoundland, she would have paid the 15% HST (instead of the 7% GST) and would be entitled to claim a rebate of 15/115 of her HST-included expenses. (GST or HST rebates are also available to members of partnerships—see 11.3.7.)

12.3.3 Automobile expense deductions for the self-employed

If you're self-employed, you can generally deduct the proportion of your automobile expenses that represents your business use of the vehicle, normally based on kilometres driven.

If half of your driving is done for your business (excluding driving from your home to your own place of business) and half is personal use, you can deduct one-half of the expenses of the car for that year. The expenses would include gas, washes, repairs, insurance, interest on financing the vehicle, leasing costs if the car is leased and capital cost allowance if you own it.

However, there are limits to how expensive a vehicle you can write off. Your claims for CCA and leasing costs will be based on a maximum cost:

Year car purchased	Purchase limit	Lease limit
1998 – 1999	$26,000*	$650*
2000	$27,000*	$700*
2001 – 2004	$30,000*	$800*

*plus GST/HST and PST on this amount

For most businesses, since you get back all GST paid as an input tax credit (see 11.2.4), "before GST and PST" effectively means "plus PST". (However, if you are a sole proprietor, you can only claim an input tax credit for the GST portion of your CCA. For other businesses, no input tax credits are available if the vehicle is driven 90% or more of the time for personal use.)

Where you have financed the purchase of a car, your monthly interest expense before determining the business portion will be limited to $300 ($250 for cars purchased in 1997 – 2000).

If you lease the car and you make an up-front lump sum payment (or "balloon" payment), the CRA will normally consider the amount to be part of your normal lease charge in the year paid and your deduction may be restricted by the lease deduction limit. However, the full balloon payment amount may be deductible if the sum of:

- the amount of the balloon payment divided by the number of months in the term of the lease, plus
- your monthly lease payment

does not exceed your maximum monthly lease deduction limit.

The CRA counts lease termination payments as normal lease payments in the year paid, and their deductibility is also subject to your lease limit for the year. However, the CRA will make the adjustment at your request over the term of the lease (instead of just in the year of sale), provided none of the years to be adjusted are statute-barred.

The $30,000 purchase limit also applies for purposes of calculating your GST input tax credit (see 11.2.4). The limit is $20,000 for purposes of the refunds of QST.

See the planning tips suggested for employees in 12.3.1—the same techniques can help maximize your deductions for business-related use of your own car.

12.4 References

The following publications can be obtained (in person or by telephone request) from your nearest CRA Tax Services Office. Forms, guides and interpretation bulletins may also be available from the CRA's Internet site at *www.cra-arc.gc.ca*.

Interpretation Bulletin IT-63R5, "Benefits, including standby charge for an automobile, from the personal use of a motor vehicle supplied by an employer after 1992"

Interpretation Bulletin IT-521R, "Motor vehicle expenses claimed by self-employed individuals"

Interpretation Bulletin IT-522R, "Vehicle, travel and sales expenses of employees"

Form T2200, "Declaration of conditions of employment applicable to expense claims"

Form GST 370, "Employee and partner GST/HST rebate"

CHAPTER 13

If you are moving

- If you're planning to move, arrange to meet the tests for deducting your moving expenses where practical (13.1.1)

- Arrange to avoid a taxable benefit on your employer-paid moving expenses where possible (13.1.3)

- Before moving to Canada, consider setting up a foreign trust to hold your non-Canadian investments (13.2)

- Take steps to cease Canadian residency if you are moving abroad (13.3.1)

- Beware of Canadian departure tax on emigration (13.3.2)

- Obtain a clearance certificate from the CRA if you sell your Canadian home after you emigrate (13.3.5)

- If you wish to wind up your RRSP, consider waiting until after you become non-resident (13.3.6)

- Repay Home Buyers' Plan and Lifelong Learning Plan withdrawals within 60 days of becoming non-resident (13.3.6)

Moving expenses are often overlooked as a deduction. Depending on your circumstances, many of your expenses may be tax-deductible if you're moving within Canada to start a new job or business or attend school. If you're immigrating to or emigrating from Canada, there are complex tax rules that you'll need to consider before and after your move. In this chapter we discuss the tax treatment of moving expenses and other tax rules related to moving, including some planning opportunities to help make your move as tax-efficient as possible.

13.1 Moving within Canada

13.1.1 Work-related moving expenses

If you start working at a new location of employment, or start a new business, and you move to a home that is 40 km closer to your new work location than your old home was, you can deduct substantial amounts for tax purposes. The 40-km distance is measured by the shortest normal route of travel, including roads, bridges and ferries, rather than "as the crow flies". Expenses incurred in moving from another country to Canada, or from Canada to another country, are not deductible for Canadian tax purposes (unless you are a student receiving scholarship or grant income—see 13.1.2).

Except to the extent you are reimbursed by your employer, you can deduct the following:

- Reasonable travelling costs, including meals and lodging, to move you and the members of your household
- The moving costs for your household effects, including storage charges
- The cost of meals and lodging near either the old or the new home for up to 15 days
- Lease cancellation costs
- The costs of revising legal documents to reflect your new address, replacing driver's licences and automobile permits, and connecting and disconnecting utilities
- Selling costs in respect of your old home, including real estate commissions
- Where you are selling your old home, the legal fees and land transfer tax payable when you buy a new home (but not GST and QST)
- Mortgage interest, property taxes, insurance premiums and utility costs related to your old residence (provided it remains unoccupied), to a maximum of the actual costs, or $5,000, whichever is less.

The real estate commissions alone can easily run into many thousands of dollars.

> If you're planning to move, arrange to meet the tests for deducting your moving expenses where practical.

So when considering a move, ensure if possible that your move coincides with a new employment location or a new place of business, and that your move meets the 40-km test.

13.1.2 Students' moving expenses

If you are a student, you can claim moving expenses if you move when you begin a job (including a summer job) or start a business. If you are moving to attend full-time post-secondary education (in Canada or abroad), you can deduct the expenses but only to the extent you have scholarship or research grant income.

13.1.3 Moving allowances and reimbursements paid by your employer

If your employer is paying your moving expenses, you may be assessed a taxable benefit for the payments, depending on how they are structured. Generally, if your employer pays you an allowance related to relocation expenses without asking you to account for the use of the money, the CRA considers it to be a taxable benefit but you will be able to deduct your actual qualifying expenses incurred (as listed in 13.1.1). If your employer reimburses you for your documented expenses or pays you an accountable advance, the payment is usually not considered a taxable benefit. Your employer can reimburse you for certain moving expenses for you and your family without conferring a taxable benefit, including:

- The cost of house-hunting trips to the new location
- Travelling costs, including meals and lodging, while you and members of your household are moving from old to new homes
- The cost of transporting or storing your household effects and other personal property such as cars and boats while moving from old to new homes
- The costs of revising legal documents to reflect your new address, replacing driver's licences and automobile permits and connecting and disconnecting utilities
- Selling costs of the old residence (advertising, legal fees, real estate commissions and mortgage prepayment or discharge fees)
- Where the old residence has been sold, legal fees to purchase the new residence and any taxes on the transfer or registration of title on the new residence
- Mortgage interest, property taxes, insurance premiums and utility costs related to the former residence (provided it remains unoccupied), to a maximum of the actual costs for three months or $5,000, whichever is less.

If your employer pays a non-accountable moving expenses allowance of up to $650, it is not a taxable benefit as long as you certify in writing that you used the allowance for moving expenses. Any amount over $650 paid as a non-accountable moving allowance is considered a taxable benefit and you can deduct your actual moving expenses.

Where possible, you should try to avoid being assessed a taxable benefit by arranging for your employer to reimburse you for your moving costs or pay you an accountable advance or a non-accountable moving allowance that does not exceed $650, rather than paying you a non-accountable allowance over $650.

> Arrange to avoid a taxable benefit on your employer-paid moving expenses where possible.

Moving allowances are treated differently for Québec tax purposes. If you are relocated by your employer and receive a moving allowance, you do not have to include in your Québec income an amount equal to two weeks' worth of your salary (based on your new salary after your relocation).

If you relocate and receive a home purchase loan from your employer, a special deduction is available for the imputed interest on the loan—see 7.2.3.

13.1.4 Other relocation payments

Your employer may make certain types of relocation payments to help you defray higher home financing costs in your new location. Most direct or indirect financing support payments are considered taxable benefits. These payments include:

- Mortgage interest differential payments made by your employer to compensate you if the interest rate on your new mortgage is higher than the interest rate on the old one.
- Mortgage subsidy payments to offset the larger mortgage interest payments created by a higher mortgage principal amount due to higher housing prices in the new location for homes of the same size as your previous one.
- One-half of the excess of reimbursements over $15,000 for a loss on the sale of a former residence, calculated as the difference between the employee's cost of the home and the selling price, or the difference between the selling price of the home and its fair market value, as determined by an independent appraisal.
- Tax equalization payments and cost-of-living payments made to compensate you for higher taxes and higher living costs in your new location.

13.2 Moving to Canada

When you immigrate to Canada, most property you own is deemed to be acquired by you at its fair market value as of your date of immigration. This means that Canada will tax only the capital gain that accrues while you are resident in Canada.

If you are moving to Canada to settle permanently for the first time or, if you are coming to Canada for temporary employment for a period of more than three years, you can bring your personal and household effects free of duties and taxes if you owned and used these goods before arriving in Canada (leased goods are subject to regular duties). But if you sell or give the goods away within the first year, duty and tax will apply.

> Before moving to Canada, consider setting up a foreign trust to hold your non-Canadian investments.

If you have significant non-Canadian investments, it may be worthwhile to set up a foreign trust before you become resident in Canada. A foreign trust can be exempt from Canadian tax for up to five years after you become resident. (See 7.4 for a discussion of some special Canadian tax rules that apply to investments in property outside Canada.)

If you are being relocated to Canada by your employer, you may wish to negotiate for a payment to cover the higher taxes imposed in Canada. Note, however, that "tax equalization payments" are considered a taxable benefit for Canadian tax purposes.

If you are moving to Canada, you should obtain professional advice regarding strategies for minimizing your tax burden. There may be steps you should take before you arrive in Canada.

13.3 Moving from Canada

13.3.1 Ceasing Canadian residence

Generally, Canada imposes tax on the worldwide income of its residents but only on the Canadian-source income of non-residents. So whether you are considered resident in Canada can make a significant difference to your potential Canadian tax liability after you move.

If you move to another country, you may still be considered a Canadian resident for tax purposes if you keep certain ties with Canada such as maintaining a home, club memberships, credit cards or medical plans or if your spouse or dependants remain in Canada. If you're moving to another country permanently or for an extended period, you may want to take steps to cease Canadian residency.

The CRA has no hard and fast rules for determining residency. Each situation is assessed on its own merits. Generally, you will be considered a non-resident of Canada if your stay abroad has a degree of permanence, you sever your residential ties to Canada and establish new ties elsewhere, you are considered a resident of another country, and your visits to Canada after your departure are occasional and sporadic.

> Take steps to cease Canadian residency if you are moving abroad.

Starting in the year of your departure, you should spend significantly less than 183 days in Canada per year. Days during any portion of which you are physically present in Canada count as full days.

Other steps that will show you have ceased Canadian residency include:

- Selling your personal property such as furniture or cars or taking it with you to your new country
- Cancelling or suspending club memberships
- Cancelling your Canadian driver's licence and plate (you may want to obtain a driver's licence in your new country before you give up your Canadian licence)
- Closing your Canadian bank accounts or putting them on non-resident status
- Cancelling credits cards issued in Canada and having them re-issued in your new country
- Changing your mailing address for all correspondence
- Cancelling your Canadian medical plans and taking out new ones in your new country
- Situating your primary place of business outside Canada.

As a non-resident of Canada, you will still be subject to Canadian tax if at any time during a calendar year you:

- Are employed or perform services in Canada;
- Carry on business in Canada;
- Dispose of property not subject to Canadian departure tax (see 13.3.2) such as rental real estate;
- Receive Canadian sourced dividend or interest income; or
- Receive rental income from rental properties in Canada.

A tax treaty between Canada and your new country will reduce or eliminate your Canadian tax liability in many circumstances.

13.3.2 Canadian departure tax

If you leave Canada and become non-resident, you are deemed to have sold most of your assets at fair market value, and will have to recognize any resulting income or capital gains. The range of assets treated as having been sold for fair market value on emigration includes *all* property, except for:

- Canadian real estate
- Property that you already owned when you became resident in Canada, if your residence in Canada totalled no more than five years out of the last 10
- Pension entitlements, including RRSPs or RRIFs
- Property used in a business in Canada
- Certain stock options
- Certain interests in Canadian trusts

Beware of Canadian departure tax on emigration.

For other property, the deemed disposition will result in an immediate tax liability on the resulting income or gains, although the CRA will allow you to defer paying the tax on gains as long as you post acceptable security. Acceptable security could be a letter of credit, a mortgage or a bank guarantee. You will not have to post security for departure tax on the first $100,000 in capital gains. The tax will still be due but not until the assets are sold.

If you decide to post the security, interest will not be charged for the period up to the actual disposition of the property or death of the owner (whichever occurs first). If the security subsequently becomes deficient (e.g., due to a decline in value of the assets posted), you will have 90 days after you're notified by the CRA to make up the deficiency.

If you are an active or retired partner of a professional partnership and you are leaving Canada, see 16.2.5.

Security for private Canadian company shares

If you're a private Canadian company shareholder and you give up your Canadian residency status but retain your shares, the new rules may create valuation and financing problems if your shares have significantly appreciated in value. For example, determining the fair market value of your shares will generally require professional assistance, possibly resulting in significant valuation costs. If you don't have your shares valued, the CRA will fix the value. Financing your tax liability may also pose a problem if it is not advisable or possible to use the business's banking facilities and you do not have other liquid resources available to satisfy the debt.

In the past, the CRA has not normally accepted non-liquid assets such as shares of private corporations as security for future tax liabilities. However, recognizing the dilemma many taxpayers will face, the CRA officials say that they may accept such shares as security for the debt. The CRA will act as any other commercial lender and expect the normal representations, warranties and covenants to ensure that the shares retain their value. To satisfy the CRA, you may have to change existing collateral arrangements and shareholder agreements.

13.3.3 Capital gains exemption on emigration

Once you are non-resident, you cannot use the $500,000 capital gains exemption discussed in 6.3. So if you still have room in your exemption, and you own qualifying farm property (which includes Canadian real estate), you may wish to take steps to "crystallize" your gain before you emigrate. That way, you will trigger a gain that is absorbed by the $500,000 exemption which would not otherwise be available after you have emigrated, and only the increase from the current fair market value will be taxed in Canada when you, as a non-resident, eventually dispose of the property.

Alternatively, if you realize gains on the deemed disposition of certain qualified farm property or shares in a qualified small business corporation, you will want to make sure you apply any of your remaining $500,000 exemption against these gains.

For small business shares and certain qualifying farm property, the deemed disposition on emigration will occur automatically. You will not need to make a special election and you can claim the exemption on your return in the year of your emigration.

13.3.4 Reporting rules for emigrants with property worth over $25,000

If you emigrate from Canada and you own property with a total value of $25,000 or more, you are required to file an information form (T1161) listing all your significant assets with your final Canadian tax return in the year of emigration. In determining whether your property exceeds the $25,000 reporting threshold, the following assets are not included:

- Cash, including bank deposits;
- RRSPs, private company pension plans (RPPs), RRIFs, retirement compensation arrangements (RCA), employee benefit plans and deferred profit sharing plans (DPSPs); and
- Items for personal use (such as household effects, clothing, cars, collectibles) whose fair market value is less than $10,000.

13.3.5 If you rent or sell your Canadian home after emigration

Real property that you own in Canada will not be subject to the deemed disposition rules discussed above when you emigrate. If you decide to rent your property, you will generally have to remit a 25% non-resident withholding tax on your gross rental income. If you will be incurring expenses to earn your rental income, you can file Form NR6 before your first non-resident tax payment is due and the withholding tax will be assessed on your net rental income. If you file the form, you will have to file an annual rental income tax return by June 30 of each following year.

> Obtain a clearance certificate from the CRA if you sell your Canadian home after you emigrate.

Generally, there is no Canadian income tax levied on the gain from selling a principal residence (see 6.4.2). If you sell your former principal residence while you are a non-resident of Canada, you must notify the CRA (and Revenu Québec if the property is in Québec) of the disposition and request a clearance certificate. If you don't obtain a clearance certificate before the disposition, the purchaser must withhold and remit one-quarter of the gross proceeds to the CRA and a further 12% to Revenu Québec, where applicable. You should file the CRA's Form T2062 at least 30 days before the property is sold or within 10 days of the sale to obtain the clearance certificate. (You must also file Revenu Québec Form TP-1097-V if the property is located in Québec.)

If you sell your former principal residence more than one year after the year of your move, only a portion of the gain would be exempt under the principal residence exemption. As we saw in 6.4.2, the principal residence exemption calculation is based on the fraction of one plus the number of taxation years ending after 1971 for which the property was a principal residence and during which you are a resident of Canada over the total number of years (after 1971) it was owned by you. So for each additional year that you do not sell your principal residence after you cease Canadian residency, the denominator increases while the numerator stays constant and a smaller portion of the gain is exempt from Canadian tax.

If you plan to rent out your former principal residence, the property's use will change from personal to income-producing and will be subject to a deemed disposition at fair market value. Any gain accruing up to the date of the change in use will be taxable but the tax may be reduced or completely eliminated by the principal residence exemption.

You may be able to make an election not to deem a change in use of the property. You will not be able to claim depreciation on the property while the election is in effect. However, the election could be beneficial if you expect the property to increase significantly in value since you will be able to shelter some of the resulting capital gain with the principal residence exemption because of the proration calculation.

13.3.6 If you have RRSPs

As noted in 13.3.2, your RRSPs are not subject to the deemed disposition rules when you leave Canada. For Canadian tax purposes, you can continue to make deductible contributions to your RRSP as long as you have contribution room available. Of course, if you have no income subject to Canadian tax, you will not realize any current tax savings from making contributions.

If you need to collapse your RRSP, you may want to wait until you are a non-resident of Canada to do so. As a non-resident, you will be subject to a 25% withholding tax on the proceeds received

> If you wish to wind up your RRSP, consider waiting until after you become non-resident.

from the plan. Many tax treaties reduce the Canadian withholding tax rate if the payments are periodic rather than lump-sum. If you collapse the plan while you're a resident of Canada, the proceeds will be taxed at your marginal tax rate, which will be about 45% if you are in the top tax bracket, depending on the province you live in.

If you withdrew funds from your RRSP under the Home Buyers' Plan (see 3.3.6) or Lifelong Learning Plan (see 3.3.7) and you become a non-resident, you should repay the entire withdrawal within 60 days of becoming non-resident. To the extent you do not make the repayment within 60 days, the unpaid balance will be included in your income on your Canadian income tax return for the year of your departure.

If you move to the U.S., your RRSP contributions will not be deductible for U.S. tax purposes and the income earned inside your RRSP is technically subject to U.S. taxation in the year it is earned. However, the Canada-U.S. tax treaty provides an election to defer the U.S. taxation until an actual distribution is made.

> Repay Home Buyers' Plan and Lifelong Learning Plan withdrawals within 60 days of becoming non-resident.

13.4 References

The following publications can be obtained (in person or by telephone request) from your nearest CRA Tax Services Office. Forms and guides may also be available from the CRA's Internet site at *www.cra-arc.gc.ca.*

Interpretation Bulletin IT-178R3, "Moving expenses"

Interpretation Bulletin IT-221R3, "Determination of an individual's residence status"

Form NR6, "Undertaking to file an income tax return by a non-resident receiving rent from real property or receiving a timber royalty"

Form NR73 "Determination of residency status (leaving Canada)"

Form NR74 "Determination of residency status (entering Canada)"

Form T1-M "Moving expenses deduction"

Form T1161, "List of properties by an emigrant of Canada"

Form T2062, "Request by a non-resident of Canada for a certificate of compliance related to a disposition of taxable Canadian property"

CHAPTER 14

If you have your own corporation

- Keep the corporation a small business corporation at all times (14.1)
- Consider crystallizing your $500,000 capital gains exemption (14.1)
- Multiply your access to the capital gains exemption (14.1)
- Defer income to the next calendar year by accruing bonuses (14.2.2)
- Maximize capital dividend payments (14.2.4)
- Consider a tax-free repayment of capital (14.2.5)
- Crunch the numbers to calculate your optimum salary/dividend mix (14.2.9)
- Consider the tax benefits of setting up a holding corporation (14.3)
- Look into the potential advantages of a corporate partnership (14.3.1)
- Weigh the potential advantages of incorporating your investments (14.6)
- Be cautious about having investment income in your corporation that carries on an active business (14.6)

In this chapter we suggest some tax planning techniques that are available if you are an owner/manager—that is, you carry on your business through a corporation. We will not discuss tax planning for the corporation itself, except in relation to how to most effectively get its profits into your hands. If you are thinking about setting up a corporation for running your business, see 11.5 for a discussion of some of the pros and cons. The tax rules in this area are substantially the same for both federal and Québec tax purposes.

14.1 Taxation of the corporation

A corporation is a distinct legal entity, and if you have an incorporated business, the corporation's profits are not yours simply to take. You, as a director of the corporation (even if you are the sole director), act in a different capacity from yourself as a shareholder of the corporation. Legally, as a shareholder your only right is to elect the board of directors, who then cause the corporation to take specific actions.

To extract funds from the corporation you must follow one of the "correct" methods we discuss in 14.2 below. If you do not, the tax system will penalize you.

For tax purposes, the corporation's business and investment income will be calculated in much the same way as your own. (See 11.2 regarding the calculation of business income.) As with individuals, certain deductions (such as loss carryforwards) are available in computing taxable income. The corporation then pays federal tax and provincial tax on its taxable income.

For 2004, the federal general corporate tax rate (excluding federal surtax) is 22% for income from manufacturing and processing, active business income and investment income. (In 2003 and earlier years, higher rates applied to active business income and investment income.)

For small "Canadian-controlled private corporations", the federal rate on the first $250,000 of "active business income" is 13% and 22% on active business income between $250,000 and $300,000. (A Canadian-controlled private corporation is a corporation that is resident in Canada and is not controlled in any manner by any combination of non-residents or public corporations.) The amount of active business income subject to the reduced rate of 13% is scheduled to rise to $300,000 for 2005 and later years. The federal small business rate is not available for large corporations. It begins to be phased out once the corporation's capital exceeds $10 million.

Provincial tax varies, but the general corporate rate is typically around 13%. Most provinces (except Québec) have reduced rates for the first $250,000 of business income and many of them have lower rates on business income between $250,000 and $300,000 or $400,000; the reduced rates range from 3% to 7.5%. The combined federal and provincial tax burden ranges from about 16% to 22% on the first $250,000 of a small business corporation's income and from about 25% to 38% on income between $250,000 and $300,000. The remainder is taxed at about 31% to 39%, unless the corporation earns income from manufacturing and processing, in which case the combined tax burden ranges from about 27% to 38%.

| Keep the corporation a small business corporation at all times. | If possible, ensure that your corporation remains a "small business corporation" (see 6.2.3) and that your shares are "qualified small business corporation shares" (see 6.3.1) at all times. This will preserve, respectively, your ability to claim allowable business investment losses in respect of |

any loss on the corporation's shares, and the $500,000 capital gains exemption on any gain.

Note that you cannot always predict when the sale of the shares will be triggered for tax purposes. On the death of any shareholder, there will be a deemed disposition of that shareholder's shares at their fair market value unless the shares are transferred to a spouse or a qualifying "spousal trust" (see 21.5.2).

As an alternative, you may wish to "crystallize" your capital gains exemption. "Crystallizing" means triggering a capital gain on your shares of a qualified small business corporation, while continuing to own (or at least control) the corporation. This will permanently increase your adjusted cost base of the shares and possibly eliminate the need for the corporation to retain its qualified small business corporation status. Several techniques (such as selling shares to a family member) can be used to crystallize an exemption; professional advice should be sought. Crystallization may be a good idea given that the federal and Québec governments could eliminate the $500,000 exemption at some point in the future.

> Consider crystallizing your $500,000 capital gains exemption.

If you arrange for your spouse to invest in common shares of your corporation, you can effectively double the available exemption by each claiming $500,000. Your spouse's own funds must be used for the investment, to avoid the attribution rules discussed in 5.2.2. You may also be able to multiply the exemption by transferring shares to your children.

> Multiply your access to the capital gains exemption.

On death, it is possible to double the available capital gains exemption by leaving shares to your spouse or to a trust for your spouse. See 22.2.3 and 21.5.2.

14.2 Ways of extracting funds from the corporation

Since the corporation is legally a separate "person", you must follow one of the methods described below to get your hands on the corporation's income.

14.2.1 Dividends

Dividends are the distribution of a corporation's profits to its shareholders. They are not deductible to the corporation. In your hands, dividends will be grossed up by one-quarter and eligible for a dividend tax credit worth approximately the same amount (one-quarter of the actual dividend). See 7.1.2 for details.

If the corporation earns income, pays tax on it and pays what is left to you as a dividend, the combined effect of the corporation's tax and your personal tax will be about the same as if you had earned the income directly, if the corporation's tax rate is 20%. This is called "integration".

Where the corporate rate (federal plus provincial) is more than 20%, the combined effect of the two levels of tax will normally be that more tax is paid than if you had earned the same income directly. Conversely, where the corporate tax rate is less than 20%, paying dividends results in less tax than if you were to pay tax directly on the business income.

Example

Jac owns all the shares of Jac Ltd. Jac Ltd. earns $100,000 in small business income, which is taxed at a combined federal/provincial rate of 20%. Jac Ltd. then pays the remaining $80,000 as a dividend to Jac.

Jac will "gross up" the $80,000 dividend by one-quarter, or $20,000, and will pay tax on $100,000, which conceptually represents the corporation's original income. Jac will then receive a combined federal/provincial dividend tax credit worth about $20,000, equal to the amount of tax the corporation paid. So Jac and the corporation will together be taxed as if Jac had earned the $100,000 as salary income.

Note that Jac's gross-up and dividend tax credit will be 25% of the dividend regardless of the rate of tax that Jac Ltd. actually paid.

14.2.2 Salary

Where the corporation pays you a salary, the amount paid is deductible to the corporation and taxable to you as employment income. If the corporation pays all of its profits to you as salary, you are therefore in much the same position as you would be if you earned the income directly, without having a corporation.

Although your salary may become quite high in such situations, the CRA's general policy is not to consider it an unreasonable deduction (for the corporation) where you are the owner/manager of the corporation. It is usually acceptable to consider the corporation's income is due to your efforts, and therefore a salary equal to that income is a reasonable one. Of course, you are paying tax on the salary anyway.

> Defer income to the next calendar year by accruing bonuses.

You may decide on a base salary followed by a bonus, to be paid to you after the corporation has calculated its income at the end of the year. In general, you are taxed on employment income only when you receive it, while the corporation can accrue salary or bonus, counting it as deductible in the year even though it is paid after year-end.

However, any salary or bonus that is deducted by the corporation must actually be *paid* to you no later than 179 days after the end of the year. (Administratively, the CRA allows you 180 days.) Otherwise, it is not deductible by the corporation until the year in which it is actually paid.

If the corporation's year-end occurs after early July, it can declare a bonus to you as of its year-end, but pay the bonus within 180 days which will be after December 31. The corporation can thus get a deduction from its income, but you do not have to recognize the income personally for tax purposes until the next calendar year.

14.2.3 Payments on loans from shareholders

If you lend funds to the corporation (or if you did so when originally setting up the business), the corporation can repay any amount of the loan without tax consequences. Such a repayment is neither deductible to the corporation nor taxable to you.

You could arrange to have the corporation pay you interest on your loan. The interest paid will normally be taxable to you as investment income. The tax effect would be about the same as if the corporation paid you that amount in salary. However, if your loan to the corporation does not *require* that interest be paid or there is no formal loan document, there is a danger that the interest will not be deductible to the corporation since it has not been paid pursuant to a legal obligation to pay interest. (Conversely, if you arrange for documentation requiring that interest be paid, the annual interest accrual rule discussed in 7.2.1 may require you to include interest in your income even in years when it is not paid!)

14.2.4 Capital dividends

We mentioned capital dividends in 5.3.8 and 7.1.4. As you will recall from Chapter 6, only one-half of capital gains are taxed. When a "private" (i.e., non-public) corporation realizes a capital gain, the untaxed portion is added to its "capital dividend account". Similarly, one-half of capital losses reduces the capital dividend account.

Any amount in the corporation's capital dividend account may be paid out entirely tax-free to its shareholders. This preserves the non-taxability of the appropriate fraction of the capital gain. So if the corporation has realized any capital gains, you should cause it to pay out capital dividends as your first choice for extracting funds.

> Maximize capital dividend payments.

> **Example**
>
> Tod owns all the shares of Todcorp Inc. In March 2004, Todcorp Inc. sells some land for a capital gain of $120,000, one-half of which is brought into Todcorp's income and taxed as a taxable capital gain.
>
> Todcorp can pay a dividend of up to $60,000 (one-half of the capital gain) to Tod in 2004 or any later year, provided he elects beforehand to make the dividend a "capital dividend". The capital dividend will then be completely tax-free to Tod. (Of course, because it is a dividend, it is not deductible to Todcorp.)

Note also that if you allow a capital dividend account to build up in the corporation without paying capital dividends, the account can be reduced or wiped out by future capital losses. Once you have paid out capital dividends, however, they are safely out of the corporation, and subsequent capital losses will have no effect on them.

14.2.5 Repayment of capital

Consider a tax-free repayment of capital.

Any amount that is less than the corporation's "paid-up capital" may be paid out to the shareholders as a repayment of capital, generally with no tax consequences, if the paid-up capital is reduced by that amount.

Paid-up capital (PUC) is essentially the amount of capital contributed to the corporation in exchange for its shares. However, the figure can be adjusted in various ways for tax purposes, as a result of transactions involving the corporation. As such, the legal PUC often differs from the tax PUC.

> **Example**
>
> ABC Corp. was capitalized with $500,000, the amount that the original shareholders contributed when subscribing for 1,000 common shares.
>
> If the directors of ABC approve a reduction in paid-up capital to $200,000 and a simultaneous repayment of $300,000 in capital to the shareholders, there will be no adverse tax consequences for either ABC or its shareholders. The $300,000 simply comes out tax-free. ABC then has 1,000 common shares issued with a paid-up capital of $200,000 and an adjusted cost base to its shareholders of $200,000.

If the corporation was originally funded with a substantial amount of capital, consider extracting funds by a reduction of the paid-up capital of the corporation. Make sure the corporation remains sufficiently capitalized to satisfy any requirements of its creditors or bankers.

14.2.6 Loan to shareholder

All of the mechanisms we have looked at so far—dividend, salary, repayment of a shareholder loan, capital dividend and repayment of capital—are legitimate ways to get your hands on the corporation's income or funds. We now turn to some of the rules designed to prevent you from doing so without following the normal routes.

Suppose the corporation simply lends you its funds. If you do not fit within certain exceptions, the entire amount of the loan will simply be included in your income. This is a very serious penalty, because the corporation receives no deduction for the amount of the loan, and you do not benefit from the dividend tax credit. The same rule applies if you become indebted to the corporation in some other way (e.g., you buy property from it, but pay for the property with a promissory note rather than cash). However, where a loan has been included in your income and you subsequently repay it, you will be allowed a deduction from your income.

To avoid this provision, bona fide repayment arrangements must be made at the time the loan is made and the loan must fall into one of the following exceptions:

- a loan to an employee who (along with family members) does not own 10% of the shares of any class of the corporation, where the reason for the loan is the individual's employment rather than the shareholding
- a loan to an employee, where the reason for the loan is the individual's employment rather than the shareholding, to help the employee purchase a home, shares in the employer or a related corporation, or a car to be used in employment duties (note that the rules do not specify a threshold for the percentage interest owned in the corporation for purposes of determining the reason for the loan)
- a loan that is repaid within one year of the end of the corporation's taxation year in which the loan was made, and which is not part of a series of loans and repayments.

If the loan falls into one of the above exceptions, but is made at no interest or at a low rate of interest, you will be considered to be receiving a taxable benefit from the corporation based on the difference between the CRA's current "low rate" prescribed rate of interest (see 9.3) and the rate that you are paying. This rule is exactly the same as for loans to employees, which we saw in 10.3. As in the case of employees, you may be allowed an offsetting deduction as a notional interest expense (which affects your entitlement to the capital gains exemption—see 6.3.3) if such expense would otherwise meet the rules concerning the deductibility of interest.

14.2.7 Deemed dividends

Certain types of actions that involve changes to a corporation's capital structure will deem you to have received a dividend from the corporation. Generally, this happens when the corporation takes actions that would otherwise allow you to extract profits as a repayment of capital.

For example, if the corporation redeems shares that you own, any amount paid by the corporation in excess of the paid-up capital of the shares is deemed to be a dividend (and not part of your proceeds of disposition for capital gains purposes). The return of the paid-up capital on the redemption is generally tax-free.

14.2.8 Shareholder appropriations

We have covered all of the "proper" mechanisms for extracting funds from a corporation. Suppose you don't follow any of the legalities and you simply take the corporation's funds or property, and use them as your own. If you are the sole shareholder, there will be no one to object to you doing this.

In such cases, the *Income Tax Act* deems that any benefit the corporation confers on you will be brought into your income for tax purposes. So, for example, if you simply take $10,000 out of the corporation's bank account without declaring a dividend, that $10,000 will be added to your income (without you benefiting from the dividend tax credit).

Clearly, it is to your advantage to follow the more conventional mechanisms for extracting funds. In the next section, we explore some of the considerations that will affect your decision as to the appropriate mix between salary, dividend and other forms of remuneration for yourself.

14.2.9 Determining your salary/dividend mix

Crunch the numbers to calculate your optimum salary/ dividend mix.

Careful analysis will be needed to calculate the best mix of salary and dividends for your case. It will depend on your cash flow needs, your income level, the corporation's income level, the corporation's status for tax purposes, and many other factors. Computer spreadsheets and planning tools are available to assist in this task.

In many cases, the best strategy for a small business corporation is to pay enough salary to reduce the corporation's income to $250,000. This maximizes the amount of income that is taxed at the low small business rate, without having corporate income taxed at the higher rates that apply to income beyond $250,000.

However, you will usually want to pay yourself enough salary to allow the maximum possible contribution to an RRSP (see 3.1.3). The same goes for any family members you've employed for income splitting purposes (see 5.3.2).

Note also that if you are in a business that can suffer a downturn, paying out a large salary can prevent you from carrying back a later year's loss. Suppose, for example, your business earns $1 million in 2004, and you pay out $750,000 to yourself as a salary, leaving $250,000 as the business's income. If in 2005 the business loses $1 million, you will have no way of carrying back the loss against your personal income. If you had left the funds as business income and paid out dividends, you would be able to carry back the 2005 loss to 2004, retroactively wiping out the business's 2004 corporate tax, and obtain a refund of that tax from the CRA.

14.3 Effect of having a holding company

You may choose to interpose a holding company between yourself and your corporation for various reasons. One reason for doing this is to pay out dividends from the operating business to make the funds harder for creditors to reach, while keeping the income subject to a lower level of taxation than would apply if it were paid out to you personally.

For example, you own 100% of the shares of ABC Holdings Ltd., which owns 100% of the shares of ABC Manufacturing Ltd. In general, dividends can be paid from the manufacturing company to the holding company without any tax effects.

> Consider the tax benefits of setting up a holding corporation.

If your children do not have any ownership in the business, you can consider bringing them in as shareholders at the time you set up the holding corporation. (See the estate planning example in 21.6.2 for one way of doing this.) This may be desirable for several reasons including income splitting as well as planning for your succession. However, if your children are under 18 you must be particularly careful about the attribution rules (see 5.2.3 and 5.2.4).

A holding company is often appropriate where you have family members involved in ownership of your share of the business (perhaps for income-splitting purposes), and there are other shareholders not related to you. If you and your family members own shares in the holding corporation, and the holding corporation owns all of your family's interest in the operating company, the other shareholders of the operating company need not be concerned with your internal family arrangements.

You should be cautious about accumulating funds in a holding company, however. If you intend to treat the holding corporation as qualifying for the $500,000 capital gains exemption (see 6.3.1), you can run into trouble if the corporation begins to have a substantial amount of funds that are used for generating investment income, rather than owning only the shares in the operating corporation. You may also be caught by the attribution rules or the income splitting tax on certain income received by minor children (see Chapter 5), depending on when and how you introduced family members as shareholders of the corporation. Note also that investment income in a corporation is subject to an extra refundable tax that makes the up-front cost of earning the income very high (see 14.6).

14.3.1 Corporate partnerships

An alternative to the use of holding companies is a corporate partnership. This is a partnership between your corporation and one or more other corporations (owned by other people).

There are a number of advantages to this form of corporate structure, including the deferral of tax in the initial years and increased flexibility concerning remuneration. Professional advice should be obtained to determine whether this structure is appropriate.

> Look into the potential advantages of a corporate partnership.

14.4 Shareholders' agreements

Where you share the ownership of a private corporation, it is usually wise to have a shareholders' agreement. Such an agreement can set out rights and obligations of the shareholders that go beyond the basic ownership of shares.

Typically, a shareholders' agreement will provide for the orderly termination of the relationship between the shareholders if there is a future disagreement, or death or disability of one of the key shareholders.

> **Example**
>
> Euan and Jonathan start a small manufacturing business together. Each owns 50% of the shares of the corporation. Over the years, the business becomes very successful, but Euan and Jonathan cannot get along and decide that one of them must leave.
>
> Euan and Jonathan signed a shareholders' agreement that contains a "shotgun" clause. Euan now offers Jonathan $1 million for Jonathan's shares in the corporation. If Jonathan refuses to sell, the agreement provides that Jonathan must buy Euan's shares for the price Euan is offering ($1 million).

The "shotgun" clause is just one example of a provision that can resolve (or prevent) major disputes between key shareholders. Typical provisions in a shareholders' agreement deal with:

- desire of a shareholder to sell his or her shares
- dissension among shareholders
- death or disability of a shareholder
- agreement as to who the directors and/or officers of the corporation will be
- agreement to vote the shares in a particular way on certain issues
- what will happen if the corporation's shares are awarded to a key shareholder's spouse on separation or divorce.

Tax considerations play a major part of planning for shareholder agreements. The tax treatment of life insurance payments, the availability of the $500,000 capital gains exemption, the valuation of shares, and many other issues must be considered. Clearly, shareholder agreements should always be drafted with proper professional advice as to both the legal and tax issues.

14.5 Pension plans for small business owners

Registered pension plans were discussed in 3.4.1. Both "money-purchase" and "defined-benefit" pension plans can be used to accrue benefits for major shareholders who are employees (see also 3.4.2, regarding individual pension plans). As an alternative to saving for retirement exclusively through an RRSP, consider having your company establish an individual pension plan, which we discussed in 3.4.2. However, this is a complex area and professional advice is essential.

If you are a small business owner and you don't want the trouble of administering a pension plan, you may simply want to set up an RRSP for yourself and ensure that you have sufficient "earned income" (i.e., salary from the corporation) to be able to make adequate contributions (see 3.1.3).

14.6 Investment income earned in a corporation

In the past, it was generally advantageous to have investment income earned in a corporation. Since the regular corporate tax rate (combined federal/provincial) was substantially lower than the rate that applies to high levels of personal income, you could often achieve a significant tax deferral in the current year, assuming you were already paying tax at the top personal rate.

But since 1995, a federal 6 2/3% refundable tax has applied to interest and other investment income in a Canadian-controlled private corporation. Most dividends received by a private corporation from public companies are also subject to a 33 1/3% refundable tax (Part IV tax). These refundable taxes are paid back to the corporation only when it has paid out sufficient taxable dividends (resulting in tax being paid by the shareholders). The combined corporate tax rate has thus risen to about 50% (combined federal and provincial).

As a result of this increase and provincial personal tax rate cuts over the past several years, there is generally no tax deferral advantage to earning investment income in a corporation. In some cases a tax prepayment results. The precise calculation depends on your province of residence, your level of personal income, the extent to which you need to extract the funds from the corporation, and the way in which you extract those funds. It may well be cheaper to hold your investments personally.

Looking beyond the potential tax deferral advantages and absolute costs, there are other possible benefits of holding investments in a corporation. For example, incorporating your

> Weigh the potential advantages of incorporating your investments.

investments can help you to shield your investments from creditors, reduce probate fees on your death (see 21.4), and protect your assets from U.S.

estate tax (see 19.4). Incorporation will also give you control over the timing of dividend payments and thus the timing of income receipts in your own hands, allowing you to:

- maximize Old Age Security (OAS) benefits (if your income from sources other than investments for 2004 is less than $59,760) (see 20.3.2);
- reduce your exposure to alternative minimum tax (see 7.6);
- manage the timing of dividend payments in order to manage your cumulative net investment loss (CNIL) account balance (see 6.3.3); and
- increase your earned income and RRSP contribution room (see 3.1.3) through the payment of directors' fees and/or salaries.

Against the potential benefits, you'll also need to weigh the incremental costs of forming and maintaining the corporation, including substantial start-up and ongoing legal and administrative costs and the corporation's potential liability for federal Large Corporations Tax and provincial capital taxes.

> Be cautious about having investment income in your corporation that carries on an active business.

Be particularly wary of moving investments into a corporation carrying on an active business. You will likely jeopardize the status of the corporation's shares from being eligible for the $500,000 capital gains exemption (see 6.3.1 and 14.1). In addition, the creditors of the active business will have access to the investments.

14.7 Selling the business

If you decide to sell your incorporated business, there are two general approaches that can be taken. One is for the corporation to sell the assets of the business. The other is for you to sell the shares of the corporation.

If your shares are "qualified small business corporation shares" (see 6.3.1), you may be able to claim an exemption for up to $500,000 of your gain on the sale. No capital gains exemption is available to the corporation if it sells the assets. From your point of view, it may therefore be preferable to sell the shares.

The buyer of your business, however, will often prefer to purchase the assets. One reason is that this will normally allow the buyer to claim higher capital cost allowance on the cost of depreciable assets (see 11.2.7).

No GST or other sales tax applies on a sale of shares. On a sale of assets, GST (or HST) and QST will usually apply, but can almost always be recovered by the purchaser in the form of an input tax credit (see 11.2.4). Alternatively, in many cases on the sale of part or all of a business an election can be made to have no GST (or HST) or QST apply to the sale. However, provincial sales tax will generally apply to the sale of tangible assets other than manufacturing equipment, but the rules vary depending on the province.

Needless to say, any purchase and sale of a business must be done with detailed professional advice.

If your business goes public without you selling the shares, you can make a special election to "crystallize" part or all of your accrued capital gain, and get the $500,000 exemption as if you had sold the shares (see 6.3).

14.8 References

The following publications can be obtained (in person or by telephone request) from your nearest CRA Tax Services Office. Forms and guides may also be available from the CRA's Internet site at *www.cra-arc.gc.ca*.

Interpretation Bulletin IT-66R6, "Capital dividends"
Interpretation Bulletin IT-67R3, "Taxable dividends from corporations resident in Canada"
Interpretation Bulletin IT-73R6, "The small business deduction"
Interpretation Bulletin IT-109R2, "Unpaid amounts"
Interpretation Bulletin IT-119R4, "Debts of shareholders, certain persons connected with shareholders, etc."
Interpretation Bulletin IT-432R2, "Benefits conferred on shareholders"

Farming

- Establish that your farming business is undertaken solely in pursuit of profit (15.1)
- Classify farming as your chief source of income (15.1)
- Claim deductions available for the self-employed (15.2)
- Consider using the "cash method" of accounting to defer taxes (15.2.1)
- Make the most of the $500,000 capital gains exemption for qualified farm property (15.4.1)
- Take advantage of the intergenerational transfer rules (15.4.2)

The income tax system has a number of special rules to deal with farming. We outline some of them in this chapter.

15.1 Farming—a business or not?

No matter what kind of activity you undertake, you are only allowed to write off losses for tax purposes if you are engaged in a business that is clearly undertaken in pursuit of profit (see 11.4.1). This issue comes up repeatedly in the case of part-time farmers.

"Farming", for tax purposes, includes a number of activities ranging from growing crops to raising livestock, fur farming, fruit growing, keeping bees and training horses for racing. The *Income Tax Act* classifies people engaged in farming into three groups. The principal difference among the groups is the extent to which they can deduct expenses relating to their farming activities.

At one extreme are the full-time farmers, for whom farming is **a chief source of income**. Such people are allowed to treat their farming business like any other business, and can therefore claim losses against other income for tax purposes if they suffer losses in any given year (see 15.3.1).

> Establish that your farming business is undertaken solely in pursuit of profit.

At the other extreme are people whose farming activity is a personal pursuit. Such people are sometimes called "hobby farmers", as farming is considered to be their hobby rather than something they are doing in order to make money. Hobby farmers may not deduct any losses from their farming activity.

In the middle are the people who undertake farming activities in pursuit of profit, but whose "chief source of income is neither farming nor a combination of farming and some other source of income", to quote the

Income Tax Act. Such people are allowed only **"restricted farm losses"**, limited to certain dollar amounts (see 15.3.2).

Example 1

Darryl lives on his farm and raises dairy cattle. Almost all his income comes from selling the cows' milk. In 2004, Darryl's dairy business has a bad year and he loses $30,000.

Darryl will be able to deduct his $30,000 against any other income he has (such as investment income) and carry it forward or back to be used in other years (see 15.3.1). His farming loss is very much like a loss from any other kind of business, such as manufacturing or retailing.

Example 2

Bob is a jeweller who lives and works in Toronto. He spends his weekends on his ranch, where he keeps a stable of racehorses. In past years, Bob's horses have won a fair amount of prize money. In 2004, Bob has a bad year and spends $30,000 on maintaining his horses without winning any prize money at all.

Bob's loss will likely be considered a "restricted farm loss", and only a portion of it (see 15.3.2) will be deductible against his jewellery business income. Although his horse-racing business (which for income tax purposes is considered farming) is clearly a commercial venture, it is not a chief source of income to him and therefore falls into the "restricted" category.

> **Classify farming as your chief source of income.**

You will need to keep records that establish that your farming business is carried on in a sufficiently commercial nature on an objective basis. If your activities never actually turn a profit over many years, a claim that your activity is clearly commercial may be hard to sustain in court.

Many court cases have considered the question of whether farming, or farming in combination with some other source, constitutes a taxpayer's "chief source of income". You may wish to consult a tax professional to determine what facts will best establish a claim that will entitle you to a full deduction for farm losses, rather than the more limited deduction for "restricted farm losses".

15.2 Computing farming income

If you are engaged in a farming business—whether or not your losses will be "restricted" as we saw in 15.1—you may take advantage of a number of special rules when calculating income for tax purposes.

In addition to the specific rules for farmers discussed in this chapter, see 11.2 for ideas as to deductions that can be claimed by the self-employed. If you successfully establish that your farming business is a commercial venture, such deductions will be available to you.

> Claim deductions available for the self-employed.

15.2.1 The cash method

Businesses are generally required to follow the accrual method of accounting for income. That is, you take your sales for the year into income, even though you may not have been paid for some of those sales until after your business year-end. You claim expenses the same way (see 11.2.2).

For a farming business, you may choose to use the **"cash method"** instead. In general, this means you will count payments received, rather than your sales—and only deduct amounts that you have paid, but not still-unpaid expenses that you have incurred. This usually provides a certain amount of deferral of income, and may result in lower tax payable. Once you have chosen the cash method, you are normally required to continue to use that method for the farming business for all subsequent years.

> Consider using the "cash method" of accounting to defer taxes.

When you are using the cash method, you may, if you wish, include in income any amount up to the fair market value of your inventories on hand at year-end (subject to the mandatory inventory adjustment discussed in 15.2.2). The amount you include will then be deductible in the following year. You might wish to do this for 2004, for example, if you had very low income in 2004 and can see by the spring of 2005 (when you file your return) that your 2005 income will increase substantially, enough to put you into a higher tax bracket.

15.2.2 Purchases of inventory and prepaid expenses

If you are using the cash method of accounting, it is clearly possible to generate a loss for tax purposes by purchasing large amounts of inventory. Special rules have been introduced to deal with this possibility and to limit the loss you can claim.

Darryl, from our example in 15.1, purchased dairy cows for $5,000 just before his year-end on December 31, 2004. This purchase was included as an expense in arriving at his farming loss of $30,000. He had no other purchased inventory on hand at the end of the year. For income tax purposes, he will be required to include $5,000 as a mandatory inventory adjustment to his 2004 income, reducing his farm loss to $25,000. In 2005, this $5,000 mandatory inventory will be treated as a farm expense.

In general, you will be denied the portion of a loss that is attributable to purchases of inventory. However, for horses and certain registered bovine animals, you can deduct a portion of the loss. Professional advice should be obtained when dealing with these complex rules.

Claims for prepaid expenses will also be restricted if the expenses relate to a year that is two or more years after the year of payment.

15.2.3 Cost of improving land for farming

Normally, when calculating income from a business, the cost of work done to improve land is considered a capital expense and is not deductible. However, for a farming business, amounts paid for clearing land, levelling land or installing a land drainage system are deductible.

15.2.4 Sales of livestock in a drought region

If you are farming in a region designated for the year as a "drought region", special relief is available if you sold a significant portion of your breeding herd. This rule is designed to allow you to defer paying tax if you are forced to sell off part or all of your herd because of drought. The list of regions designated for the year is determined by Agriculture Canada's Prairie Farm Rehabilitation Administration in Saskatoon each September.

The rule only applies if, by the end of the year, you have sold off (and not replaced) at least 15% of your "breeding herd". When it applies, some or all of your sales of the breeding animals are not counted into your income, but are deferred until a later year when your area is no longer designated as a drought region.

15.2.5 Forced destruction of livestock

If you have diseased livestock, the government may force you to destroy it under the *Animal Contagious Diseases Act* or similar legislation. If you receive compensation for the destruction, the compensation is included in your income. A special rule allows you to deduct all or part of this compensation and include it in your income in the next year. This allows you to defer paying tax on the compensation by one year.

15.2.6 Canadian Agricultural Income Stabilization (CAIS) Plan

The CAIS program was introduced in 2003 as a stabilization and disaster relief program to help agricultural producers respond to income decline. The CAIS plan replaces the Net Income Stabilization Account (NISA), which ended after 2002. Over a five-year transition period, producers must close their NISA accounts, which may have tax implications. Producers must also submit coverage levels under the CAIS plan. Consult your tax adviser for details about the transition to CAIS and how it may affect your farming business.

15.3 Farming losses

15.3.1 Ordinary farm losses

As we saw in 15.1, if your chief source of income is farming, or your chief source of income is "a combination of farming and some other source of income", you may deduct your farm losses as though they were ordinary business losses.

The carryover available for such losses is somewhat more generous than that for normal business losses (non-capital losses), which we saw in 11.4.1. Like normal losses, farm losses can be carried back and used against income of the past three years. They can also be carried forward, and used against income in any of the next 10 years.

15.3.2 Restricted farm losses

As noted in 15.1, a loss from farming cannot *all* be used if you do not meet the "chief source of income" test. In this case, the loss you claim is limited to the first $2,500, plus one-half of the next $12,500 (that is, up to an additional $6,250).

> Example
>
> Bob the jeweller, who we met in 15.1, loses $30,000 on his racehorses in 2004.
>
> Bob's "restricted farm loss" will be $2,500, plus one-half of the next $12,500. Since his total loss is more than $15,000, he reaches the maximum, and he can only deduct $8,750 against the income from his jewellery business for 2004.

Any amount of loss that cannot be used because of the "restricted farm loss" rules can be carried back for three years and forward for 10 years, but can be used only against farming income. So, in our example, Bob has $21,250 that can be used to offset income from his horse operations during the years 2001 to 2003 and 2005 to 2014.

15.4 Transfers of farming assets

A number of special rules, as outlined below, are available to alleviate the tax burden of selling or transferring a farm and the assets of a farming business.

15.4.1 The $500,000 capital gains exemption

Make the most of the $500,000 capital gains exemption for qualified farm property.

As discussed in 6.3.2, a $500,000 exemption from capital gains is available on the disposition of "qualified farm property"—if you are disposing of farm property, investigate whether it qualifies. In general terms, farm land and buildings, shares of farm companies and interests in farming partnerships may qualify for the exemption if they meet certain tests; equipment, inventory and most other assets do not qualify. In some circumstances you may be able to take action, such as delaying the sale, so you can gain time to reorganize your affairs in order to take advantage of the exemption. You also may be able to take steps to increase the cost base of your qualifying farm property to reduce the tax liability that will arise in the future on the property's sale. The tax rules in this area are quite complex so you should seek professional tax advice if you own farm property that qualifies for the exemption.

15.4.2 Transferring farm property to your children or grandchildren

Normally, if you sell or give property to members of your family other than your spouse, you are deemed to have sold the property for its "fair market value", and will thus have to recognize as a capital gain or income the difference between your original cost (or the value on February 22, 1994 if you elected to use your capital gains exemption on the farm property) and the property's current value. (See 6.3.4 and 6.4.5.)

Take advantage of the intergenerational transfer rules.

If you transfer property used in a farming business to a child, grandchild or great-grandchild (including a spouse of your child, a child of your spouse, etc., where "spouse" includes a common-law or same-sex spouse as outlined in 2.2.1), you can avoid this rule. If you simply give the property, it will be deemed to be transferred at your cost (adjusted cost base [see 6.2.1] for capital property, or undepreciated capital cost [see 11.2.7] for depreciable property). Any gain on the property will thus be deferred.

For this "rollover" rule to apply, you or your spouse or one of your children must have used the property "principally" in a farming business in which you, your spouse or children were actively engaged on a regular and continuous basis.

When the rollover applies, the recipient (your child, grandchild, etc.) will be deemed to have acquired the farm property for the amount at which you are deemed to have sold it, so the gain will eventually be taxed, when the child sells the property at some later time.

> **Example**
>
> Flo operates a wheat farm in Saskatchewan. In 2004, Flo decides to retire and gives the farm to her grandson Daniel. The farmland cost her $10,000 in 1979 and is now worth $150,000.
>
> Flo is deemed to receive $10,000 for the land, and so has no capital gain. Daniel is deemed to have acquired the land for $10,000; if he ever sells the land, the $10,000 figure will be used as his cost for capital gains calculation purposes. (Of course, if Daniel transfers the farm one day to his child, a further rollover will be available, assuming the rules have not changed.)

If you are transferring farm property to a child, grandchild, etc., you may wish to realize a partial capital gain, in order to use up your $500,000 capital gains exemption and give your child a higher cost base in the property. If you sell the property for something in between your cost and the current market value, that amount will be accepted for tax purposes. (Where land is being transferred, don't forget to consider the possible cost of provincial land transfer tax. GST, HST or QST may apply as well, depending on the circumstances.)

Note that the tax rules do not let you transfer farm inventory to a child on a tax-free basis. Gifting farm inventory results in the same income inclusion as a sale of farm inventory at fair value.

15.4.3 Capital gains reserve on sale of farm to your child

We discussed capital gains reserves briefly in 6.4.1. It was noted there that the capital gain must be recognized at a cumulative rate of one-fifth each year, so that no reserve can last for more than four years after the year of sale.

Where you sell property used in a farming business (including land) to your child, grandchild or great-grandchild, the allowable reserve is 10 years rather than five. As with the rules discussed in 15.4.2, a spouse of your child, grandchild or great-grandchild, and a child, grandchild or great-grandchild of your spouse also qualify. (For this purpose, "spouse" includes a common-law or same-sex spouse as outlined in 2.2.1.)

15.5 References

The following publications can be obtained (in person or by telephone request) from your nearest CRA Tax Services Office. Forms and guides may also be available from the CRA's Internet site at *www.cra-arc.gc.ca.*

Interpretation Bulletin IT-232R3, "Losses—Their deductibility in the loss year or in other years"

Interpretation Bulletin IT-268R4, "*Inter vivos* transfer of farm property to a child"

Interpretation Bulletin IT-322R, "Farm losses"

Interpretation Bulletin IT-349R3, "Intergenerational transfer of farm property on death"

Interpretation Bulletin IT-373R2, "Woodlots"

Interpretation Bulletin IT-425, "Miscellaneous farm income"

Interpretation Bulletin IT-427R, "Livestock of farmers"

Interpretation Bulletin IT-433R, "Farming or fishing—Use of cash method"

Interpretation Bulletin IT-485, "Cost of clearing or levelling land"

Interpretation Bulletin IT-526, "Farming—Cash method inventory adjustments"

"Farming Income Tax Guide"

Guide, "Farming Income and NISA"

Form T1163, "NISA account information and statement of farming activities for individuals

Form T2042, "Statement of farming activities"

If you practise a profession

- Defer tax by electing to follow the modified accrual method for computing income (16.1.1)

- Maximize your deductible interest (16.2.1)

- Pay retiring partners income or capital as appropriate (16.2.2)

- Consider paying club dues at the partnership level (16.2.3)

Most of income tax planning for professionals is the same as that for other self-employed people (see Chapter 11). Self-employed professionals are, after all, carrying on business. However, a number of special rules exist which we consider in 16.1. Since many professionals carry on their practice in partnership, we also look at some rules that apply to partnerships in 16.2.

16.1 Specific rules for professionals

16.1.1 The modified accrual method of accounting for income

As we noted in 11.2.2 and 15.2.1, businesses other than farming businesses are generally required to report income on the accrual basis. That is, you take your sales into income even though you may not be paid until after your year-end.

Most businesses must also account for work in progress—work that has been done but not yet billed. However, there is an exception for the professional practice of an accountant, dentist, lawyer, medical doctor, veterinarian or chiropractor. If you are practising one of these professions, you may elect to exclude work in progress from your income.

This method of accounting is sometimes called the "modified accrual" method. It is not the cash method, since once an amount has been billed, it must be reported as income even if not yet paid.

> Defer tax by electing to follow the modified accrual method for computing income.

But excluding work in progress is a step away from the full accrual method.

> **Example**
>
> Dianne is a lawyer who is in sole practice. She spends almost the entire month of December 2004 preparing for a major trial to defend her client Michael. The trial takes place in January. She does not bill Michael until the conclusion of the trial, in January 2005.
>
> If Dianne elects to exclude work in progress from her income for 2004 she will not have to recognize as income any amount in respect of her work in preparing for the trial until her business year ending December 31, 2005.

As you can see, electing to exclude work in progress from your income can create a substantial deferral of tax. If you are practising one of the eligible professions, you will almost certainly want to follow this method. The only reason not to do so might be if you are in your first year or two of practice, with relatively low income, and you wish to recognize income earlier while it can be taxed at relatively low rates.

Once you choose to exclude work in progress, you must normally continue to do so for all future years.

On retirement or withdrawal from the business, the remaining work in progress is brought into your income. Such income is considered to be "earned income" for RRSP contribution limit purposes (see 3.1.3).

16.1.2 Professional corporations

Some provinces allow certain professionals to incorporate their professional practices. For example, lawyers in Alberta and physicians in Nova Scotia can be incorporated. Ontario allows incorporation by all regulated professionals, including accountants, lawyers, members of regulated health professions, social workers and veterinarians.

For tax purposes, a professional corporation is generally treated like any other small business corporation—see Chapter 14. If you are considering incorporating your practice, see 11.5 for a discussion of some of the pros and cons.

Professional corporations which are members of partnerships must use a December 31 business year-end (see 11.2.1). Other professional corporations may use an off-calendar year-end.

16.2 Specific rules that apply to partnerships

In 11.3 we discussed the taxation of partnerships in general. In this section we shall look at some rules applicable to partnerships that are of particular relevance to professionals.

16.2.1 Deductibility of interest paid by the partnership

As we saw in 7.2.3, interest paid is normally deductible as long as the funds borrowed are used to earn income from business or property. Where a partnership borrows funds for working capital, the interest is therefore clearly deductible.

Maximize your deductible interest.

As a member of a partnership, consider whether you can accelerate your drawings or have the partnership repay a portion of your capital contribution. You could then use the funds to pay off non-deductible debt (such as a home mortgage), while the partnership can borrow funds to replace the lost working capital. The interest would then become deductible. Alternatively, you yourself could borrow funds to inject back into the partnership. However, the CRA could challenge such an arrangement under the general anti-avoidance rule (discussed in 5.2.6) if it considers this type of refinancing technique to be a misuse or abuse of the Income Tax Act.

If the partnership borrows funds in order to make a distribution of profits and/or capital to the partners, the interest paid on such borrowings is normally deductible, but only up to the amount of the partnership's "net equity" as determined under generally accepted accounting principles.

16.2.2 Income payments to retired partners

Normally, if you withdraw from a partnership, and you receive a payment to compensate for your interest in the partnership, the payment will be considered capital. That is, any excess over your adjusted cost base in the partnership will be a capital gain, and taxed as discussed in Chapter 6. (Your adjusted cost base is essentially the amount you contributed to the partnership, plus your share of the profits on which you have been taxed, minus your drawings. See 11.3.5.)

Another option is available under the *Income Tax Act*, however. If your partners agree to pay you a share of the income from the partnership, and to treat it explicitly as an income payment, you will be considered as still being a partner for tax purposes. You will therefore be taxed on that income, but your former partners will effectively pay less tax, since part of their partnership income will be allocated to you.

When you (or a partner of yours) decide to withdraw from a partnership, you will need to calculate the best way of paying out the retiring partner's interest.

> Pay retiring partners income or capital as appropriate.

To avoid confusion or dispute, ensure your partnership agreement specifically addresses the tax treatment of payments to retired partners.

Example

Joel, an accountant, retires from his firm at the beginning of 2004. There are three other partners, who share equally in profits. The firm's income for 2004 is $600,000. The partners agree to pay Joel $120,000 on his retirement, and declare the $120,000 to be a share of the income from the partnership (rather than as a repayment of his capital interest).

Joel will be required to report the $120,000 as income. However, each of the partners will effectively get a deduction of $40,000, since after Joel's allocation, there is only $480,000 to be divided three ways. Each partner will thus report $160,000 in income instead of $200,000.

If you have a 10-year reserve in respect of your 1995 "stub period" income due to the 1995 budget's calendar-year reporting rules for unincorporated business income (discussed in 11.2.1), you will have to report the remaining balance of your 10-year reserve in 2004. In most cases, the amount remaining will be 15% of your 1995 "stub period" income.

16.2.3 Club dues

Most club dues are not allowed as business expenses. Many professional partnership agreements provide that such dues should be paid by the partners personally (since they are not deductible in computing the partnership's income anyway).

Consider paying club dues at the partnership level.

There may be an advantage to having the partnership pay these dues even though they are not deductible. The individual partners' adjusted cost bases in the partnership are not reduced by such disallowed expenses, even though the assets of the partnership are reduced by making the payments. (As noted above, your adjusted cost base is essentially the amount you contributed to the partnership, plus your share of your after-tax profits, minus your drawings. See 11.3.5.) As a result, having the partnership pay the club dues can reduce the capital gain (or increase the capital loss) on an eventual sale of the partnership interest.

16.2.4 RRSP contribution limit

As discussed in 3.1.3, the amount you can contribute to an RRSP is generally limited to 18% of your "earned income" for the previous year or $15,500 for 2004, whichever is less (minus your pension adjustment, if any). Whether partnership income (and related stub period income—see 16.2.1) is considered earned income depends on whether the partner is active in the partnership during the year.

Partnership income of active partners is included in earned income for purposes of calculating your RRSP contribution limit.

Continuing income payments to retired partners are not included in earned income. Retiring partners are deemed to be active for the entire calendar year in which they withdraw from the partnership, but any allocation of partnership income in following years will not be eligible for RRSP purposes.

For example, if you withdraw from a partnership in September 2004, your partnership income reported on your 2004 tax return will be included in earned income for purposes of computing your 2005 RRSP contribution limit. However, partnership income reported in 2005 and later years will not create new RRSP contribution room.

16.2.5 Emigration of a partner

If you emigrate from Canada, as either an active or a retired partner, any income allocated to you from the partnership will continue to be taxable in Canada. If the income is also taxable in your new home country, you should be able to claim a foreign tax credit (see 18.2.2) for any taxes paid in Canada to fully or partially offset taxes paid in the foreign jurisdiction.

As we saw in 13.3.2, when you become a non-resident of Canada, you are deemed to have sold most of your assets at fair market value at the time of emigration. You then have to pay tax on any resulting income or capital gains or post acceptable security for the tax with the CRA. If you are a retired partner and you retain a right to continue receiving partnership income, this right may also be considered to be an asset. On emigration, the right would be deemed to be sold and Canadian departure tax would apply on the present value of your future income entitlements.

If you hold your partnership interest through a professional corporation (see 16.1.2), the shares of the corporation will be deemed sold when you emigrate, and the value of the shares will have to be determined to compute your Canadian departure tax liability. If the shares are qualifying small business corporation shares, you can apply any of your remaining $500,000 capital gains exemption against the gain on the deemed sale of the shares—see 13.3.3. Note that if your professional corporation retains a right to continuing partnership income, the CRA takes the position that this right is not active income, and thus may deny your claim for the exemption in respect of the shares.

If you are an active or retired partner emigrating from Canada, it is strongly recommended that you review your situation with a tax professional before you leave Canada, both to plan for the tax consequences of your departure and to determine the tax consequences to you in the foreign country.

16.2.6 Death of a partner

When an active or retired partner dies, the partner is subject to the tax rules that generally apply on death. As we will see in 22.2.3, capital assets, such as stocks and real estate, are deemed for tax purposes to have been sold at fair market value on the date of death. Any accrued gains or losses on the assets are realized at that time, unless the assets are left to the deceased's spouse or to a spousal trust, in which case the assets transfer at your tax cost (unless you elect otherwise—see 22.2.3) and your spouse or the trust inherits the accrued tax liability.

A deceased partner's capital interest in the partnership is such a capital asset if the full amount of the partner's capital contribution has not been paid out to the partner before death. However, continuing income payments of retired partners and other income rights of partners are not capital assets. Various options are available for reporting these items for tax purposes.

A deceased partner's share of partnership income can be included in the partner's terminal return or in a second, separate tax return (also known as a "right or things" return). The advantage of claiming this income in a separate tax return is that the income may be subject to lower marginal tax rates and some of the same personal tax credits can be claimed as on the terminal return.

Similarly, continuing income payments of retired partners can be reported on the terminal return or on a separate return, or they can be included in the income of the partner's estate or beneficiary as they receive these amounts.

In light of the various choices for reporting income entitlements of deceased partners, you should ensure your will gives your executors sufficient discretion to file whatever tax elections and separate returns are necessary to take full advantage of any tax saving opportunities in settling your estate. (For a general discussion of tax-oriented will planning, see 21.2.3.)

16.3 References

The following publications can be obtained (in person or by telephone request) from your nearest CRA Tax Services Office. Forms and guides may also be available from the CRA's Internet site at *www.cra-arc.gc.ca*.

Interpretation Bulletin IT-90, "What is a partnership?"
Interpretation Bulletin IT-242R, "Retired partners"
Interpretation Bulletin IT-278R2, "Death of a partner or retired partner"
Interpretation Bulletin IT-457R, "Election by professionals to exclude work in progress from income"
Information Circular 89-5R, "Partnership information return"
"Business and Professional Income Tax Guide"
"Guide to the Partnership Information Return"
Form T2032, "Statement of professional activities"
Form GST 370, "Employee and partner GST/HST rebate application"
Form T5013, "Statement of partnership income"

If you live in Québec

- Calculate your Québec taxes under the general and simplified systems to find out your best filing option (17.1.2)

- Be aware of differences between the federal and Québec tax systems (17.2)

- Claim a refundable credit if you adopt a child or have infertility treatment (17.2.3)

- Claim the caregiver credit if you provide in-home care for your parents or other relatives (17.2.6)

- Boost your Québec business entertainment expense deduction by subscribing to eligible Québec cultural performances (17.2.19)

Unlike the other provinces, Québec administers its own tax system and Québec residents must file a separate provincial tax return. The Québec Taxation Act (Loi sur les impôts) is largely modelled on the federal Income Tax Act, but, as we will see in this chapter, there are a number of differences.

17.1 Québec income tax rates

17.1.1 2004 Québec tax rates

Québec's 2004 provincial income tax rates are listed in Appendix I.

Québec residents are allowed a Refundable Québec Abatement on their federal tax return, which reduces their federal tax by 16.5% of basic federal tax. As a result, Québec residents earn federal non-refundable tax credits at a rate of about 13.4%, instead of at the 16% rate earned in the other provinces. Québec non-refundable tax credits are earned at a 20% rate, so an amount that is eligible for federal and Québec credits is effectively worth about 33% of the related amount.

17.1.2 Québec's optional simplified tax filing system

When you file your Québec tax return, if you are a Québec resident on December 31 of that year, you can choose between the province's general tax filing system and a simplified system. Obviously, your choice will depend on which system will give you the greater tax savings, so you will need to estimate your taxes payable under both systems.

Under the simplified system, several Québec deductions and non-refundable tax credits are replaced by a single, lump-sum amount for 2004 of $2,925 per person (worth $585). Whether you stand to benefit under the simplified system will depend on whether the lump-sum amount under the simplified system is greater than the sum of the replaced deductions and non-refundable credits. The simplified system will be eliminated as of 2005.

Since 2003, certain deductions that were previously only allowed in calculating net income under the general system are also allowed in calculating net income under the simplified system. These include deductions for support payments, moving expenses and certain expenses incurred to earn investment income.

Québec's tax return package includes a workchart for figuring out your taxes under both systems. If you choose to file your return using the general system, Revenu Québec will calculate your taxes payable under both systems and return any additional tax savings that you would have obtained by following the simplified system.

> Calculate your Québec taxes under the general and simplified systems to find out your best filing option.

If you and your spouse both opt to use the simplified system, the two of you can elect to file a joint Québec tax return. (Under Québec tax law, same-sex couples are treated the same under tax law as opposite-sex common-law couples.)

17.1.3   Income tax reduction for Québec families

Québec offers a non-refundable tax reduction for couples or single-parent families with at least one dependent child. The tax reduction for families is worth up to $1,195 for a single parent and up to $1,500 for cohabiting spouses, less the "designated" child's income over $6,275. If you have more than one child, you should designate the child with the lower net income in order to maximize the tax reduction.

If a single parent's or couple's Québec family net income is over $27,635 the tax reduction is reduced by 3% of family net income over $27,635.

In 2005, the tax reduction for Québec families and certain other Québec tax measures will be replaced with a new quarterly child assistance payment.

17.2   Differences from federal tax

In this section we highlight the principal differences between Québec and federal tax law that affect personal tax.

> Be aware of differences between the federal and Québec tax systems.

You should review the differences between the federal and the Québec income tax systems, as highlighted below. Be cautious of the possible Québec tax implications of any step you take for federal tax purposes.

17.2.1   Basic personal and family credits

Like the federal basic credit discussed in 2.2, Québec offers a basic personal tax credit of $1,255 in 2004.

Instead of a spousal tax credit, however, Québec allows for the transfer of the unused portion of non-refundable tax credits between spouses (under the general or simplified tax system). Under this mechanism, you may only claim the deduction resulting from the transfer after all other non-refundable credits have been deducted from Québec tax otherwise payable. This transfer mechanism is also be followed on the principal tax return for the year of death of one of the spouses.

If you have dependent children 18 and under, or over 18 and attending school full-time, a non-refundable Québec tax credit is available of up to $553 for the first child and $510 for each additional child.

You can claim an additional single-parent family credit of $276 for the first dependent child if you did not live with, support or receive support payments from your spouse at any time during the year. If you made support payments to your spouse that are tax-deductible, you may still claim the single-parent family credit. You cannot claim the credit if you claim a deduction for the unused portion of non-refundable tax credits transferred from your spouse.

No eligible dependant credit is available in Québec. Instead a credit is available for "other dependants" who are related to you by blood, marriage or adoption. The person must ordinarily live with you unless the person is your dependant due to infirmity. For example, an "other dependant" could be a parent, grandparent, aunt or uncle, or a child over 18 who does not attend school full-time. Except for dependent children and grandchildren, infirm dependants must live in Canada to be eligible. The credit is worth up to $510, plus $745 if the person is infirm. The $2,550 or $3,725 amount used to calculate the credit is reduced by the dependant's net income and then multiplied by the 20% credit rate.

In 2005, the tax credits for dependent children and certain other Québec tax measures will be replaced with a new quarterly child assistance payment.

Québec also allows a non-refundable tax credit of $223 for a "person living alone". To qualify, you must have lived by yourself for the entire calendar year in a self-contained home with no person other than dependent children whom you claim for tax purposes. If you are separated but you support your spouse, you cannot claim this credit; however, if you pay only alimony which you deduct on your tax return, you and your spouse can both claim the credit. The credit is reduced by 15% of Québec family net income over $27,635 so that the credit is fully eliminated if your family net income is $35,070 or more in that year.

The $27,635 family net income test is used to reduce the tax credit for persons living alone, the Québec age credit and the Québec pension income credit (see 17.2.5). Your amounts eligible for claiming all three of these credits will be totalled and then reduced by 15% of your family net income over $27,635.

17.2.2 Child care expenses

There are a number of differences between the federal rules discussed in 2.3.2 and the Québec rules. Child care expenses give rise to a refundable credit in Québec instead of a deduction. (See 2.1.2 for a discussion of refundable credits and the difference between a deduction and a credit.) The credit is on a sliding scale, worth 75% of the expenses of low-income families, down to 26% for families with Québec family net income over $79,725. Thus, the Québec credit for child care expenses is more valuable to lower-income families, such as where both parents are attending school full-time.

For federal purposes, only the lower-income spouse can claim the deduction for child care expenses. Either spouse may claim the child care expenses credit for Québec purposes.

For Québec purposes, eligible child care expenses are limited to 100% of earned income, instead of the federal limit of two-thirds of earned income. Québec disregards any income earned by the child in determining whether child care expenses are eligible. Québec child care expense claims are capped at $7,000 per child under seven, at $4,000 per child aged seven to 16 and at $10,000 where a child, at any age, has a severe and prolonged mental or physical impairment for which the disability credit can be claimed (see 2.3.2).

> **Example**
>
> Nicole and Daniel have two pre-school children. In 2004 Daniel earns $70,000, and Nicole earns $10,000 working part-time. They pay $5,500 in day care, required to enable them both to work.
>
> For federal purposes, Nicole can claim the least of (a) the amount paid—$5,500; (b) $7,000 per child—$14,000; and (c) two-thirds of her earned income—$6,666. She can thus deduct $6,666 from income.
>
> For Québec purposes, Nicole's credit will be based on the least of (a) the amount paid—$5,500; (b) $7,000 per child—$14,000; and (c) 100% of Nicole's earned income—$10,000. Since Nicole's and Daniel's Québec family net income is more than $79,725, the credit is 26% of $5,500, or $1,430.

In other circumstances, child care expenses are subject to weekly limits of $175 per child under seven, $250 per child of any age suffering from an impairment, and $100 per child aged seven to 16.

The $5 per day contribution that has to be paid by parents of children attending the province's early childhood centres is not eligible for purposes of the Québec child care expense credit.

17.2.3 Adoption and infertility treatment expenses

Québec offers a refundable credit for adoption expenses to help finance the expenses associated with adopting children from overseas, but is available even for local adoptions. The credit is 30% of up to $20,000 in expenses paid by you, or by you and your spouse, to a maximum credit of $6,000 per child. Qualifying expenses include court fees, legal fees, travelling and translation expenses (for adoptions from other countries), and fees charged by approved agencies.

Since the credit is refundable, it is available even if you have no tax to pay for the year. You will have to keep records of your expenses and claim only those that qualify. The credit is available under the general and simplified systems.

> Claim a refundable credit if you adopt a child or have infertility treatment.

If you're being treated for infertility, you may be able to claim a refundable credit for the costs associated with artificial insemination and *in vitro* fertilization paid by you or your spouse. The credit is equal to 30% of all the eligible expenses, to a maximum annual credit of $6,000 per couple.

17.2.4 Tuition fees and interest on student loans

Tuition fees qualify for a 20% non-refundable credit for Québec tax purposes. Unlike the federal tuition fees credit (see 2.4), Québec does not allow the transfer of undeducted tuition fees to the parent. Since 1997, unused tuition fees can be carried forward indefinitely and claimed as a credit in later years.

Québec does not have a credit to parallel the federal education amount. Instead, Québec increases the parents' non-refundable credit for dependent children and other dependants (see 17.2.1) by $351 per semester (for up to two semesters) if the dependant is a full-time student at a post-secondary institution.

A non-refundable tax credit is available of 20% of interest paid in the year on a student loan that you received under a federal or Québec student loan program. You can carry forward any unused portion of the credit to a later year. To claim the credit, you must file under Québec's general system (see 17.1.2) and you must include a voucher from your financial institution showing the amount of interest paid.

17.2.5 Seniors

Québec offers a 20% non-refundable tax credit similar to the federal credit for persons who are 65 and older (20.3.4) and for pension income (see 20.3.5). The Québec age credit is worth up to $440 and the Québec pension credit is worth up to $200.

The amounts available for claiming each of these credits and the credit for persons living alone are added together and then reduced by 15% of your Québec family net income over $27,635 (see 17.2.1).

17.2.6 Home support for elderly persons living alone

Québec allows a refundable tax credit for the home support of persons age 70 or older living alone who are losing their autonomy. The credit equals 23% of eligible expenses paid to obtain certain home support services. The credit is capped at $2,760. If the expense also qualifies for the Québec medical expense credit, you cannot claim it for purposes of both credits—you will need to determine which credit will be worth more to you.

17.2.7 Adults housing parents and certain other relatives

> Claim the credit for housing parents and certain other relatives.

Québec provides a refundable tax credit of $550 for taxpayers who have parents and certain other relatives living with them. This includes parents, grandparents, great-grandparents, uncles, aunts, great-uncles or great-aunts (including in-laws). Since the credit is refundable, it is available even if you have no tax to pay for the year and regardless of whether you file under the general or simplified system

To claim the credit, your relative must be 70 or older (or 60 or older and disabled), but there is no requirement that the relative be financially dependent on you or in a low-income bracket. (In fact, the relative could be financially supporting you. However, the person making the claim must own or rent the home.)

17.2.8 Legal fees for establishing support payments

Under the federal system, you may deduct legal costs to establish or enforce a right to child or spousal support, or to obtain an increase in child or spousal support amounts (see 2.6). For Québec purposes, fees paid in connection with a court application to increase the level of support are deductible if you file under the general system and simplified systems.

You can also deduct judicial and extrajudicial expenses paid regarding an initial right to receive or obligation to pay a support amount, as long as the expenses are not reimbursed and you did not deduct them from income in a previous year.

17.2.9 Charitable donations

In addition to the federal credit for charitable donations discussed in 8.1, you can claim a Québec credit of 20% for the first $2,000 of charitable donations and 24% for amounts over $2,000. You can claim annual donations of up to 75% of your Québec net income on your Québec return, or higher in some cases, if you donate gifts of cultural property, property with ecological value, or, for 2004 and later years, gifts of capital property that have increased in value. In the year of death and the year before, the limit is increased to 100% of Québec net income. The inclusion rate for capital gains arising from gifts of publicly traded securities and other appreciable property is limited to 25% (see 8.3). The credit is available under both the general and simplified systems.

For Québec purposes there is a special restriction on the credit for gifts of works of art. The valuation of the gift is limited to the price the charity receives when it sells the art plus 25% of that amount and the credit can only be claimed (by the donor) if the charity sells the art within the next five years of accepting the donation. This rule does not apply to donations to certain museums and galleries, recognized artistic organizations, governments or municipalities.

17.2.10 Medical expenses

Like the federal credit for medical expenses (see 2.7.1), the parallel Québec credit is reduced by 3% of Québec family income. For Québec purposes, the maximum reduction is not capped at $1,813. The list of allowable expenses is similar to the federal list.

For 2004, you can claim the Québec medical expense credit even if you are filing under the simplified system. However, as the net income amount is based on the combined income of *both* spouses, many Québec residents are no longer eligible for the credit.

Québec also offers a refundable tax credit for medical expenses similar to the federal medical expense supplement for low-income workers discussed in 2.7.1. For Québec purposes, the credit is reduced by 5% of your Québec family income over $18,600. Also, as noted in 17.2.16 below, the taxable benefit for employer-paid private health insurance premiums qualifies as a medical expense for Québec purposes.

17.2.11 Credit for people with disabilities

Québec offers a non-refundable tax credit for persons with severe and prolonged physical or mental impairment. You can claim this credit whether you file under the general or simplified system (see 17.1.2). The Québec credit is similar to the federal credit discussed at 2.5.1 and you must meet essentially the same criteria to be eligible. You are entitled to the Québec disability credit if, because of chronic illness, you undergo physician-prescribed therapy essential to the maintenance of a vital function two or more times a week, and must devote a total of at least 14 hours a week to the therapy, including post-treatment recovery time. The supplementary credit for a child with a disability is not available in Québec.

To claim the Québec credit for the first time, you must file Form TP-752.0.14-V with your Québec tax return for that year. The maximum amount available for the credit is $2,200, which means it may be worth up to $440 to you. If you have a dependant who suffers from an impairment, your dependant's unused disability credit can be transferred to your Québec return.

17.2.12 Political contributions

As noted in 2.7.2, many provinces, including Québec, provide credits for contributions to provincial political parties, riding associations and election candidates. In Québec, municipal electoral contributions are also eligible. You can claim a non-refundable tax credit of up to $405, which equals 75% of the total of: (a) the first $140 of contributions to municipal political parties and (b) the first $400 of contributions to provincial political parties. This credit can be claimed under both the general and simplified systems.

17.2.13 Québec Sales Tax credit

Québec offers a sales tax refund similar to the GST credit available to low-income families (see 2.9.3). The refund is $163 each for you and your spouse, plus an extra $110 if you have no spouse and ordinarily live in a self-contained domestic establishment where no other person entitled to the QST credit for the year lives.

The total credit is reduced by 3% of your Québec family income (see 17.2.1) over $27,635. The credit is refundable and is claimed on your Québec tax return (whether you file under the general or simplified system).

Québec also offers a sales tax rebate that parallels the GST rebate for employees (see 10.9) and partners (see 11.3.7).

17.2.14 Real estate tax refund

You may be entitled to a refund of a portion of the property taxes that apply on your dwelling. If you own the property, taxes eligible for the refund include school, water and municipal taxes. If you rent, the eligible amount is indicated on the Relevé 4 supplied to you by your landlord each year. The credit is claimed on your Québec tax return whether you file under the general or simplified systems.

The eligible property tax is reduced by $455 for each spouse. The refund is 40% of this amount, to a maximum of $546, minus 3% of your Québec family net income over $27,635, subject to various adjustments. Since it is refundable, the real estate tax refund is paid to you even if you have no Québec tax to pay for the year.

17.2.15 Cumulative net investment loss

As we saw in 6.3.3, investment expenses and tax shelter write-offs create a cumulative net investment loss (CNIL), which reduces your ability to claim the $500,000 capital gains exemption.

For Québec tax purposes, certain special Québec investment incentives are not included in your CNIL calculation. That is, they will not affect your ability to claim the capital gains exemption on your Québec tax return. These incentives include deductions for the Québec Stock Savings Plan, the Cooperative Investment Plan, Québec Business Investment Corporations, certain research and development incentives, certified Québec film and television productions and resource exploration expenses incurred in Québec.

17.2.16 Employer-paid private health insurance

As we saw in 10.1.1, employer contributions to a private health services plan are non-taxable employee benefits for federal purposes. These contributions are, however, taxable for Québec tax purposes. Thus, if your employer pays for your group sickness, drug or dental plan, the value of the benefit will be included in your employment income on your Relevé 1 and must be reported on your Québec tax return, even though it does not appear on your T4 for federal income tax purposes. As a result, employer health plan contributions will normally make your employment income for Québec tax purposes higher than it is for federal purposes. You (or your spouse) can claim the taxable benefit as a medical expense on your Québec tax return (see 17.2.10).

17.2.17 Union and professional dues

Union and professional dues (excluding professional insurance), which are deductible for federal tax purposes (see 10.8.4), are not deductible on your Québec tax return but instead entitle you to a 20% non-refundable tax credit (under the general system only). This rule applies to employees and self-employed individuals alike. The cost of professional insurance is deductible under both the general and simplified systems.

17.2.18 Overseas employment tax deduction

We discussed the federal overseas employment tax credit in 9.8. The Québec rules accomplish essentially the same goals of not taxing certain income earned while working on projects outside Canada, but do so rather differently.

First, the Québec system allows the overseas income as a deduction (under the general system only), rather than allowing a tax credit for a percentage of it. For each consecutive 30-day period that the employee works outside Canada on a qualified project, 1/12 of the income earned abroad in the year can be deducted.

Second, foreign living allowances are completely tax exempt, provided they do not exceed one-half of the income earned abroad.

Third, the recognized activities for purposes of the deduction are broader than under the federal system. As well as the projects that qualify for federal purposes, the installation of computer or office automation systems or data communications systems, and the provision of scientific and technical services, entitle you to the deduction for Québec purposes.

17.2.19 Meals and entertainment expenses

As under the federal rules (see 11.2.9), if you are self-employed and you take a client or business contact out for a meal or to an entertainment event, your deduction for your costs as a business expense is limited to 50% of the amount paid for Québec tax purposes.

For tax years ending after March 30, 2004, entertainment expenses are further limited for Québec purposes to:

- 2% of total sales, if your total sales are $32,500 or less
- $650, if your total sales are between $32,500 and $52,000
- 1.25% of total sales, if your total sales are $52,000 or more.

Relief from these limits is available for certain sectors, such as businesses requiring frequent travel and sales agencies.

Boost your Québec business entertainment expense deduction by subscribing to eligible Québec cultural performances.

Some business entertainment expenses for cultural events held in Québec are still 100% deductible for Québec tax purposes. These include the cost of a subscription to a symphony orchestra, classical or jazz ensemble, and opera, dance, theatre, and vocal performances. To qualify for this special deduction, the subscription must be for at least three performances in eligible artistic disciplines.

17.2.20 Home office expenses

The federal tax rules governing deductions for home office expenses are discussed in 10.8.3 and 11.2.10. For Québec tax purposes, the deduction for self-employed individuals is limited to 50% if the expenditures relate to the cost of maintaining a residence (e.g., maintenance and repair costs, rent, mortgage interest, property and school taxes, insurance premiums and depreciation). The home office expense claims of employees are not subject to this restriction.

17.2.21 Rental expenses—documentation

If you use a building located in Québec to earn rental or business income and you claim any expenses for renovation, improvement, maintenance or repair of the property, you must include with your Québec income tax return Form TP-1086.R.23.12-V with the contractor's name, address, social insurance number (if an individual) and QST registration number (if available) as well as the amount paid for the work carried out. This measure is designed to combat tax evasion in the contracting and renovation sectors.

17.2.22 Limit on deductibility of investment expenses

For Québec purposes, as of March 30, 2004, your ability to deduct expenses incurred to earn income from property is limited to your income from such investments earned in the year. Investment expenses that cannot be used in the current year can be carried back to offset investment income earned in the three preceding tax years and they can be carried forward indefinitely, as long as the investment income in that year exceeds the investment expenses.

For 2004, the limitation applies only to the portion of investment expenses that exceeds investment income, calculated in proportion to the number of days in the year following March 30, 2004.

17.2.23 Minimum tax

For 2003 and later years, the Québec minimum tax rate was reduced to 16% (from 20%) and the basic exemption was increased to $40,000 (from $25,000). These parameters are now the same as the federal ones (see 7.6). In addition, the portion of a capital gain realized in a year that must be included for the purposes of calculating adjusted taxable income was raised to 75% (from 70%).

Certain tax benefits, such as deductions for resource exploration in Québec, investment tax credits for research and development, a portion of the deduction for certain investments under Québec incentive plans and employee stock option deductions are not considered tax preferences for Québec minimum tax purposes.

Note that Québec minimum tax will not apply if you file under the simplified system. The deduction for the unused portion of non-refundable tax credits transferred from a spouse for 2003 and later years (see 17.2.1) will not be taken into account in the calculation of the basic minimum tax exemption.

17.2.24 Instalments

Québec instalment requirements are parallel to those for federal tax described in 9.2.2, with some minor differences.

The penalty for late or insufficient instalments is an extra 10% in addition to the normal interest rate. This penalty is substantially higher than the federal penalty, so if you can only pay part of your instalments, you are better off to pay your Québec instalments on time.

The determination of who has to pay instalments is the same as under the federal system, as outlined in 9.2.2. Instalments are required where your balance of Québec tax owing at the end of the year exceeds $1,200 for both the current year and either of the previous two years.

For Québec residents, quarterly *federal* tax instalments are payable if you have federal taxes owing of $1,200 in the current year and either of the previous two years. Since Québec tax can be higher or lower than federal tax for any individual (depending on many factors including those outlined throughout 17.2 above), there can be cases where you must remit federal instalments but not Québec instalments, or vice versa.

17.2.25 Health Services Fund contribution

Your income from all sources (other than employment income) is subject to a "contribution" to the Health Services Fund (i.e., another tax). The income taxed is generally the total shown on your income tax return including business income, investment income, pension or retirement income and taxable capital gains, but not employment income, Old Age Security or alimony.

Certain specific deductions are permitted to arrive at the base amount for the contribution, and a further $11,905 exemption is allowed. If your income is between $11,905 and $41,400 your Health Services Fund contribution is 1% of income over $11,905, to a maximum of $150. If your income is over $41,400, your contribution is $150 plus 1% of your income over $41,400, to a maximum of $1,000. Your contribution is then offset by a non-refundable tax credit of 20%.

If you are required to pay income tax instalments (see 17.2.24), you must also pay quarterly instalments on your Health Services Fund contribution.

17.2.26 Self-employed QPP/CPP deduction

Self-employed individuals are eligible to deduct 50% of their QPP or CPP contributions on pensionable self-employed earnings in calculating their income (whether they file under the general or simplified system). The remaining 50% of these contributions remains eligible for a non-refundable tax credit. This deduction also applies when calculating the income used to determine the 1% contribution to the Health Services Fund (see 17.2.25).

17.3 References

Revenu Québec produces a number of publications to assist taxpayers, the most notable of which is the *Guide to the Income Tax Return* that accompanies the provincial income tax return. Québec tax forms and guides are also available in French and English from the government of Québec's Internet site at *www.revenu.gouv.qc.ca*.

CHAPTER 18

If you are a U.S. citizen in Canada

- Claim the foreign earned income exclusion if beneficial (18.2.1)
- Claim the maximum foreign tax credit (18.2.2)
- Keep records of expenses deductible on your U.S. return (18.3.1)
- Beware of differences between Canadian and U.S. rules governing retirement income (18.3.4)
- Elect to defer U.S. taxation of income accruing in your RRSP and other Canadian retirement plans (18.3.4)
- Watch out for ownership of Canadian corporations earning passive income (18.3.6)
- Be cautious of using the Cdn$500,000 capital gains exemption (18.4.3)
- Watch out for U.S. minimum tax (18.5)
- Review income splitting arrangements to prevent double taxation (18.6.2)
- If you're married, file a joint return where appropriate (18.7.1)
- Consider using the annual $11,000 U.S. gift tax exclusion to transfer wealth to children (18.8.2)
- Beware of U.S. gift and foreign trust reporting rules (18.8.4)

In this chapter we address the difficult and complicated tax problems of the United States citizen who lives in Canada. We can only scratch the surface, due to the interaction of two highly complex tax systems that are both subject to continual change. You should seek professional advice if you are a U.S. citizen living in Canada.

18.1 Two systems of taxation

The income tax systems of the United States and Canada are similar in some general ways, but very different in their details. A U.S. citizen resident in Canada must deal with both systems.

The United States is one of the few countries in the world that taxes its citizens on their worldwide income, whether or not they are physically in the United States. Canada taxes only Canadian residents on their world income; non-residents (including Canadian citizens) are taxed by Canada only on certain income from Canadian sources.

The result is that U.S. citizens living in Canada must file returns under both systems, and often must pay tax to both governments. Safeguards exist to prevent double taxation: clearly, you could not afford to pay a large percentage of your income to each country. But the safeguards, which are outlined in 18.2 below, are not perfect. Much of this chapter deals with the double taxation problems that arise due to differences between the two systems' ways of calculating income and tax.

In general, you will find that U.S. taxation is lower than Canadian. U.S. federal tax currently reaches a maximum rate of 35%. Canadian federal tax reaches 29%, but as a resident of Canada you also have a provincial tax liability, which raises the top rate to about 45%, depending on your province of residence. As a U.S. citizen not resident or domiciled in any state, you have no liability for any U.S. state tax except, perhaps, to the extent you have income arising in a state.

The 2004 U.S. income tax rates for single persons with no dependants and for married couples filing joint returns (see 18.7.1) are:

Single (see 18.7.1)	
Taxable income	Federal tax
$0 – 7,150	10%
$7,150 – 29,050	$715 + 15% of the amount over $7,150
$29,050 – 70,350	$4,000 + 25% of the amount over $29,050
$70,350 – 146,750	$14,325 + 28% of the amount over $70,350
$146,750 – 319,100	$35,717 + 33% of the amount over $146,750
$319,100 and up	$92,530 + 35% of the amount over $319,100

Married filing joint income tax returns (see 18.7.1)	
Taxable income	Federal tax
$0 – 14,300	10%
$14,300 – 58,100	$1,430 + 15% of the amount over $14,300
$58,100 – 117,250	$8,000 + 25% of the amount over $58,100
$117,250 – 178,650	$22,788 + 28% of the amount over $117,250
$178,650 – 319,100	$39,980+ 33% of the amount over $178,650
$319,100 and up	$86,328 + 35% of the amount over $319,100

(The rates for other types of taxpayers are different; see 18.7.1 for a discussion of the types of filers.)

The highest effective marginal rate is thus 35% for most taxpayers. Due to certain adjustments such as a phaseout of personal exemptions and a limitation on itemized deductions for high-income taxpayers, the effective marginal rate can be higher still in some cases.

The 35% marginal rate applies to taxable income over US$319,100 regardless of filing status. However, married individuals filing separately (see 18.7.1) become subject to the highest rate at taxable income in excess of US$159,550.

18.2 Basic mechanisms for avoiding double taxation

There are three mechanisms in place to help you avoid paying tax twice on the same income.

18.2.1 Foreign earned income exclusion (U.S. tax law)

The simplest way to avoid double taxation is the U.S. "foreign earned income exclusion." On your U.S. tax return, you may exclude from your income up to US$80,000 of "earned income" (employment or services income) earned from services provided outside the United States.

If you do not have any income other than your employment or professional services income, and your annual income is under US$80,000, this exclusion will be all you need to escape U.S. tax entirely. You must still file a U.S. return (see 18.7.2 below) and claim the exclusion.

> **Example**
>
> Cathy is a U.S. citizen who lives in Calgary. She works as an accountant and earns Cdn$100,000 in 2004. (Assume the Canadian dollar is worth an average of US70¢ through 2004.) She has no other income.
>
> On her U.S. tax return, Cathy will report her income of approximately US$70,000. She will then elect to use the foreign earned income exclusion, and will deduct the same $70,000, to show a total income of $0. As a result she will pay no tax to the United States. Her Canadian tax return will not be affected by her U.S. citizenship.

Note that if you file as "married filing jointly" (see 18.7.1 below), you and your spouse can each claim up to US$80,000 for purposes of the exclusion against your respective earned incomes. This can be done even if your spouse is not a U.S. citizen.

The regulations make it possible to elect the foreign earned income exclusion on late-filed returns in a number of cases. If you are eligible for the foreign earned income exclusion, you should normally claim it. However, there are some unusual circumstances (mostly involving carryovers of foreign tax credits—see 18.2.2) where claiming a foreign tax credit can be more beneficial than claiming the exclusion. If you claim the exclusion and then, in a later year, elect not to claim it, you cannot normally claim it again for five years.

> Claim the foreign earned income exclusion if beneficial.

18.2.2   Foreign tax credit (both U.S. and Canadian law)

The foreign tax credit is a unilateral mechanism provided by many countries to prevent double taxation. Both the U.S. and Canada provide foreign tax credits. While the details differ, the concept is basically the same for both.

Consider the U.S. foreign tax credit as an example. If you are subject to U.S. taxation (because you are a citizen), but you have paid tax to Canada on Canadian-source income, you can, in general, claim a foreign tax credit to offset your U.S. tax on that income. Your credit cannot be greater than the Canadian tax you paid.

> **Example**
>
> Dave is a U.S. citizen who lives and works in Vancouver. He earns Cdn$1,428 (equivalent to US$1,000) in interest on his Vancouver bank account in 2004. He also receives a salary in Canada and income from investments in the United States.
>
> Dave will be required to include the US$1,000 in his income for U.S. tax purposes. (Because it is investment income and not earned income, it is not eligible for the foreign earned income exclusion.) Assume that he is in the 28% bracket (i.e., his taxable income is less than US$146,750 and he is single), so his additional U.S. tax is US$280. If he is in a 45% tax bracket in Canada, so that he has paid the equivalent of US$450 to Canada (and British Columbia) on the income, he can receive a foreign tax credit for the full US$280 on his U.S. return. On the other hand, if his Canadian tax rate were lower and he paid only US$260 to Canada (and British Columbia), he could only claim US$260 as his foreign tax credit.

The above example is highly simplified, but it demonstrates the basic effect of the credit. When you total up the tax to both countries (including provincial and state tax) and the foreign tax credits of each, you should end up paying a total that is equal to the higher of the two countries' rates of tax.

The Canadian foreign tax credit follows essentially the same principles. Since Canada taxes Canadian residents on their worldwide income, Dave in our example will have to report his U.S.-source investment income on his Canadian tax return. He will then be eligible for a foreign tax credit for U.S. taxes paid on his U.S.-source investment income to offset the Canadian tax that applies, but only up to the amount of U.S. tax he would have paid if he was not a U.S. citizen. Canada only allows foreign tax credits for the amount of U.S. tax payable by non-U.S. citizens and therefore Canadian-resident U.S. citizens earning U.S.-source dividends and interest may pay more tax on such income than Canadian residents who are not U.S. citizens.

The U.S. will then allow an additional credit under the treaty, which many taxpayers neglect to claim. (Note that each country's foreign tax credit applies only to foreign taxes on income from sources outside that country.)

The details of the foreign tax credit rules are very complicated. If you receive income for personal services performed in both the U.S. and Canada, it is a good idea to keep a diary to record U.S. and Canadian work days.

For U.S. foreign tax credit purposes, excess (non-creditable) foreign tax can be carried back two years and forward five years. For Canadian foreign tax credit purposes, certain excess foreign tax can be deducted from income in the current year. If the excess foreign tax relates to business income, the excess generally can be carried back three years and forward seven years.

If you have various sources of income and need to claim a foreign tax credit under one or both systems, you should consult a professional adviser.

> Claim the maximum foreign tax credit.

18.2.3 Canada-U.S. tax treaty

The third safeguard against double taxation is the Canada-U.S. tax treaty (also known as a tax convention). Both Canada and the U.S. have such treaties with many countries. The purpose of a tax treaty is twofold: to prevent double taxation, and to reduce tax evasion by allowing exchange of taxpayer information between the two governments.

The Canada-U.S. treaty, for the most part, does not apply to United States citizens resident in Canada except in specific circumstances.

For example, the treaty allows a U.S. citizen resident in Canada to defer U.S. taxation of funds accruing in an RRSP or other pension plan, which are not qualifying deferral plans under U.S. rules. Absent this provision, U.S. tax could apply to the accruing funds, which are specifically exempt from Canadian tax (see 3.1.5 and 18.3.4).

If you are using the treaty to reduce your U.S. tax liability, you are generally required to disclose the specific details of the treaty benefits you are claiming on your U.S. tax return. If you do not, the treaty benefits can be denied.

Under the treaty, if you are a Canadian resident and you receive U.S. social security benefits, you are not subject to U.S. tax on these amounts. However, 85% of the amount received is subject to tax in Canada.

18.3 Differences in calculating income

In theory, the foreign tax credit mechanism prevents you from paying tax twice. However, there are many differences between U.S. and Canadian calculations of income for tax purposes. These differences can lead to unexpected tax liabilities.

18.3.1 Deductions available in the U.S. but not in Canada

While you can normally deduct home mortgage interest and property taxes on your U.S. tax return, it is not deductible in Canada, except to the extent you can claim an office in your home (see 7.2.3 and 11.2.10).

State taxes, which may be imposed to the extent you reside in or have income arising in a U.S. state, are generally deductible for U.S. income tax purposes, while provincial income taxes are not deductible in Canada.

Keep records of expenses deductible on your U.S. return.

Certain employment-related expenses not available in Canada can also be deducted on your U.S. return. If you are claiming deductions on your U.S. return that are not allowable in Canada, make sure to keep records sufficient to establish your claim.

18.3.2 Deductions available in Canada but not in the U.S.

As we saw in 7.2.3, interest paid may be deducted for Canadian tax purposes where the funds were borrowed for the purpose of earning income from investments. There is no strict requirement that you actually earn more income from your investments than you spend in interest.

For U.S. tax purposes, your investment expense deduction is limited to your investment income. You cannot write off interest expense against other income such as employment or business income. This principle extends, under a separate set of complex rules, beyond interest expenses to all deductions relating to "passive" activities, including limited partnership and most rental losses.

Certain other expenses and deductions permitted for Canadian purposes such as RRSP contributions and certain tuition fees will not be allowed on your U.S. return.

18.3.3 Limitations on U.S. deductions for high-income taxpayers

Two limitations apply to high-income taxpayers.

First, personal exemptions (US$3,100 for you, your spouse and each dependant) are phased out once adjusted gross income (AGI) exceeds a threshold. (Adjusted gross income is gross income minus certain deductions such as the foreign earned income exclusion, alimony, and IRA [Individual Retirement Account] or Keogh plan contributions.) For married persons filing jointly, the threshold is US$214,050; for single taxpayers it is US$142,700; for married filing separately, it is US$107,025. For each $2,500 ($1,250 for married individuals filing separately) or part thereof by which AGI exceeds the threshold, *each* exemption is reduced by 2% (not to exceed 100%).

Second, itemized deductions are reduced once AGI exceeds a threshold, which is US$142,700 for single taxpayers and married filing jointly, and US$71,350 for married filing separately. For each dollar over the threshold, itemized deductions that could otherwise be claimed are reduced by 3% (other than medical expenses, investment interest, casualty or theft losses and gambling losses). However, even for very high-income taxpayers, a base amount of 20% of itemized deductions can always be claimed (i.e., the reduction cannot go beyond 80% of the deductions).

18.3.4 Retirement and profit-sharing plans

RRSPs, RPPs and DPSPs (see Chapter 3) can cause problems for U.S. citizens, because they are not given any special status in the U.S. Internal Revenue Code.

Employer contributions to a registered pension plan or a deferred profit-sharing plan are exempt from immediate Canadian tax (see 10.1.1). As we saw in 3.4.1, you are taxed on the funds only when you receive them (usually on retirement).

> Beware of differences between Canadian and U.S. rules governing retirement income.

For U.S. tax purposes, there is no such exemption. The amount contributed by your employer is treated as an employment benefit and is taxed, once the contributions have vested (that is, you are entitled to them even if you leave your employment). Furthermore, these amounts are explicitly excluded from the definition of "foreign earned income" under U.S. tax law, so you cannot make use of the foreign earned income exclusion (see 18.2.1). You may have to pay U.S. tax on these contributions, depending on the circumstances and the amount of your unused foreign tax credit carryover. When you later withdraw the funds, they should not be taxable in the U.S.

Your own contributions to an RRSP or RPP, which are deductible on your Canadian return, are not deductible for U.S. tax purposes.

Income accruing in your RRSP, RRIF and other Canadian retirement plans (see Chapter 3) would normally be taxable in the U.S. As noted in 18.2.3, the Canada-U.S. tax treaty allows you to elect each year to defer the taxation of the accruing income until you actually receive the

> Elect to defer U.S. taxation of income accruing in your RRSP and other Canadian retirement plans.

funds from the plan. This allows you to report the income in the same year for Canadian and U.S. purposes, provided you file an appropriate election under the Canada-U.S. tax treaty with your tax return. The IRS is expected to issue a prescribed form for disclosing RRSP contributions, distributions and investments in the coming years.

If you contribute to a regular IRA (U.S. Individual Retirement Account), your contributions are not deductible for Canadian tax purposes. Income accruing in an IRA is not taxed by Canada. When you withdraw funds from an IRA, Canada will generally tax the same amount that you would have had to include in your income under U.S. laws if you were a resident of the U.S. at the time of withdrawal. While you may be able to transfer lump sum payments received from an IRA into an RRSP free of Canadian tax, the amount transferred would be subject to U.S. tax. Foreign tax credits may alleviate double taxation.

Contributions to a U.S. deferred income plan by a U.S. employer may be taxable in Canada as an employment benefit or "retirement compensation arrangement" (see 10.5.4).

18.3.5 Dividends

As we saw in 7.1.2, Canada taxes dividends from Canadian corporations using the "gross-up and credit" system, which results in less tax being levied than on other kinds of income. For U.S. purposes, most dividends are taxed at a lower rate (i.e., 15%). The actual amount that you receive, rather than the grossed-up amount, is included in income for U.S. purposes.

18.3.6 Canadian corporations earning passive income

Owning an interest in a Canadian corporation that earns passive income can result in an unexpected U.S. tax liability. Under U.S. law, if you invest in a non-U.S. corporation that earns a substantial part of its income from investments (a "passive foreign investment corporation"), and then sell the stock or receive an "excess" distribution, there may be a theoretical deferral of U.S. tax (which would have applied if you had earned the investment income directly). In such a case, an interest charge on this "deferred tax" may be imposed under U.S. tax law.

> Watch out for ownership of Canadian corporations earning passive income.

There is no minimum U.S. ownership required in a Canadian corporation to be subject to these rules. Most mutual funds and REITs are considered foreign corporations under U.S. law. As a result, the passive foreign investment company rules could apply to these investments depending on the income and assets of the entity. Additionally, the income distributed would be considered dividend income instead of retaining the same character (as it does for Canadian tax purposes). Thus capital gains allocated from a Canadian mutual fund would be treated as ordinary income for U.S. purposes.

There are ways to avoid the interest charge, however; one way is to elect to include your *pro rata* share of the corporation's earnings in your income on a current basis each year (which may result in a mismatching of income for Canadian and U.S. purposes).

18.3.7 U.S. taxation of income fund investments

Most income fund investments are considered foreign corporations for U.S. purposes. The earnings distributed would be taxable as ordinary income for U.S. purposes. Capital distributions should not be taxable for U.S. purposes, provided all of the earnings had been distributed. (The Canadian taxation of income fund investments is discussed at 7.3.2.)

18.3.8 Charitable donations

As discussed in 8.1, charitable donations of up to 75% of your net income entitle you to a credit for federal Canadian and Québec tax purposes.

For Canadian tax purposes, charitable donations must normally be made to a Canadian charity to qualify (subject to certain specific exceptions). The Canada-U.S. tax treaty, however, provides that donations to U.S. charities will qualify, up to a limit of 75% of U.S.-source net income. You will need to obtain receipts from the U.S. charities and file them with your Canadian return.

Similarly, charitable donations are normally deductible in the U.S., subject to a limit of 50% or 30% of income for most charities. However, donations to Canadian charities may only be deducted for U.S. tax purposes to the extent of 50% of your *Canadian-source* "adjusted gross income". If you are excluding much or all of your Canadian-source income due to the foreign earned income exclusion (see 18.2.1), this limitation can cause problems.

18.3.9 Moving expenses

Moving expenses paid by your employer are not taxable benefits for Canadian purposes (see 13.1.3). For U.S. purposes only, no taxable benefits arises if your employer pays for the cost of moving your household goods and for transporting you and your family. If your employer pays additional amounts for you, such as real estate commission on the sale of your home, this amount will be included in your taxable employment income for U.S. tax purposes.

18.4 Differences in taxation of capital gains

18.4.1 Basic calculation

It is in the field of capital gains that one finds the most glaring differences between the Canadian and U.S. tax systems. Not only are many details different, but the basic scheme of taxation of capital gains is itself fundamentally different, which creates a large number of problems for U.S. citizens resident in Canada.

For Canadian tax purposes, only one-half of capital gains are taxed (see 6.2.1).

For U.S. tax purposes, short-term capital gains from property held for one year or less are normally taxed like other income, at your marginal rate (see table in 18.1 above). However, the rate for long-term capital gains (generally from property held more than 12 months) was limited to 15% or 5%, depending on your tax bracket. Certain gains and depreciation recapture are subject to a maximum rate of 25%.

18.4.2 Use of capital losses

For Canadian purposes, allowable capital losses (one-half of your capital losses) can only be used to offset taxable capital gains, though they can be carried back three years and forward indefinitely against such gains (see 6.2.2). An exception exists for allowable business investment losses (on shares or debt of small business corporations), which can be used against any income (6.2.3).

For U.S. purposes, capital losses can be used against capital gains. In addition, US$3,000 of capital losses can be written off against other income (US$1,500 for a married person filing separately). Unused capital losses can be carried forward (but not back), to be applied against capital gains or against US$3,000 per year of other income in any future year.

18.4.3 The Canadian capital gains exemption

A Cdn$500,000 capital gains exemption is available in Canada for certain small business shares and farm property (see 6.3.1 and 6.3.2). No such exemption exists for U.S. tax purposes.

> Be cautious of using the Cdn$500,000 capital gains exemption.

The Canadian foreign tax credit is calculated so as not to apply to any portion of a gain on foreign property for which the capital gains exemption was claimed. In other words, if you sell U.S. property and pay U.S. tax on the sale, you cannot claim a Canadian foreign tax credit for the portion of the

> **Example**
>
> Jeff purchases 100 shares of XYZ Corporation on the Toronto Stock Exchange when the Canadian dollar is at US70¢. He pays $20 per share including commission, or Cdn$2,000 (US$1,400). He sells the shares several years later, when the Canadian dollar is at US78¢, for $19 each (after commission), or Cdn$1,900 (US$1,482).
>
> For Canadian tax purposes, Jeff has a $100 capital loss, one-half of which can be deducted against taxable capital gains. For U.S. tax purposes, however, Jeff has an $82 capital gain, which is taxed. Since he does not pay any Canadian tax on the gain, no foreign tax credit is available to offset his tax (maximum 15%) on US$82.

U.S. tax that relates to the gain on which you or your spouse previously claimed the capital gains exemption for Canadian purposes.

If you sell small business corporation shares or farm property, the Cdn$500,000 capital gains exemption won't protect you from U.S. tax on the gain, even if you are not subject to Canadian tax. Generally, you should steer clear of the planning ideas discussed in 14.1 to "crystallize" your gains and use up your exemption.

18.4.4 Foreign exchange gains or losses

When you sell Canadian property, your gain for U.S. tax purposes must be calculated using the U.S. dollar equivalent of your cost, as of the date you purchased the property. This can lead to a foreign exchange gain or loss that is independent of your (Canadian-dollar) gain or loss on the property.

Similarly, when you sell U.S. property, your gain for Canadian purposes must be calculated in Canadian dollars.

18.4.5 Pre-1972 holdings

As noted in 6.4.4, Canada taxes only capital gains accrued since 1972. The U.S. does not have any such rule. If you are a U.S. citizen and have owned property since before 1972, your gain for U.S. tax purposes could be substantially higher than your gain for Canadian tax purposes.

18.4.6 Principal residence

As we saw in 6.4.2, a gain on a "principal residence" is normally completely exempt from tax in Canada. The U.S. rules related to sales of a principal residence are very different from the Canadian rules and more restrictive.

Under the U.S. rules, you may claim an exclusion of US$250,000 of gain on a principal residence. The exclusion is increased to US$500,000 for spouses filing jointly.

Certain requirements must be met to claim the exclusion; for example, you and your spouse must have actually occupied the home for at least two of the past five years, and neither you nor your spouse must have claimed this exclusion in the past two years.

If you and your spouse file jointly but do not share a principal residence, the US$250,000 exclusion is available on the sale of one of the principal residences. Similarly, you can claim the US$250,000 exclusion if you marry someone who has used the exclusion in the past two years.

Be careful if you and your spouse buy more than one home during the two-year period. You will have to pay tax on any gain arising on one of the homes.

A further difference between Canadian and U.S. exemptions for a principal residence lies in the definition of the term. As we saw in 6.4.2, a vacation property such as a cottage will generally qualify for Canadian tax purposes, although you can only designate one principal residence for each year. For U.S. purposes, a home will only qualify if it is the place where you "regularly reside".

18.4.7 Other capital gains differences

Canada and the U.S. have very different rules with respect to the transfer of capital property to corporations, corporate reorganizations, mergers, windups, recapitalization, debt forgiveness, etc. If you are involved in such transactions, professional advice is essential, especially since both systems continuously change.

18.5 Minimum tax

Canada's minimum tax was discussed in 7.6. The U.S. alternative minimum tax (AMT) has the same general structure, but there are a number of important differences.

First, the U.S. AMT exemption is US$58,000 for married taxpayers filing jointly (or a surviving spouse) and US$40,250 for a single taxpayer. As well, the U.S. exemption is phased out for those with adjusted minimum taxable income over US$150,000 if married filing jointly (US$112,500 if filing as a single taxpayer).

Second, the U.S. AMT rate is calculated under a two-tier graduated rate schedule. A 26% rate applies to the first US$175,000 of alternative minimum taxable income over the AMT exemption amount, and a 28% rate applies to alternative minimum taxable income over US$175,000. The 28% rate comes into effect at an alternative minimum taxable income over US$87,500 for married individuals filing separate returns. For long-term capital gains, the maximum AMT rate is reduced to 15%. (The Canadian rate, including provincial tax, is about 23%.)

Watch out for U.S. minimum tax.

Third, the list of "AMT adjustments"—items added back to income for AMT purposes—is, of course, different between the two countries. For U.S. tax purposes, the list includes the standard deduction, itemized property and state taxes paid, oil and gas drilling costs, mining exploration and development costs, a portion of accelerated

---

Example

Sam is an unmarried U.S. citizen living and working in Canada. In 2004, his employment income is Cdn$65,000, and he makes Cdn$100,000 (US$70,000) in interest income.

Sam will pay Canadian tax on his employment income and on his interest income. For U.S. regular tax purposes, the employment income will be eligible for the foreign earned income exclusion, and the U.S. tax on the interest income will be fully offset by a foreign tax credit for the Canadian tax he pays on the interest.

For U.S. AMT purposes, however, Sam's income will be US$70,000, minus his $40,250 AMT exemption. The AMT liability will therefore be 26% of $29,750, or $7,735. Only 90% of this amount can be offset by foreign tax credits, so Sam will have to pay $774 in U.S. tax. This will be in addition to his Canadian tax liability. No Canadian foreign tax credit will be available, since the interest is Canadian-source income even though it is being taxed by the U.S.

---

depreciation, certain stock option benefits and various other specific deductions.

Fourth, the U.S. foreign tax credit can only be used to offset 90% of your AMT payable. This means that if your income (not counting income eligible for the foreign earned income exclusion) is higher than the AMT exemption level, you will almost always end up paying at least some tax to the United States.

As you can see, if your income is high enough, you may have to pay a certain amount of U.S. alternative minimum tax even though your income is fully taxed by Canada. One way to reduce this liability is to earn additional U.S.-source income. Canada will give you a foreign tax credit for regular U.S. tax paid on the U.S.-source income, but not for U.S. AMT payable on Canadian-source income.

18.6 Income earned by children

18.6.1 Effects on dependant deduction

If you claim a deduction for a dependent child (US$3,100) on your U.S. return, that child may not claim the regular personal exemption on his or her own tax return. The effect is that any income the child earns is taxed.

In Canada, there is no federal credit for dependent children. As a result, income earned by your children will not affect the tax you pay unless you pay Québec provincial tax (see 17.2.1).

18.6.2 Attribution rules

We discussed the Canadian attribution rules with respect to minor children in 5.2.3. The basic rule is that if you give or lend funds to your child, the income from those funds (but not the capital gains) will be taxed in your hands rather than the child's, until the child turns 18.

The U.S. tax system accomplishes the same general anti-income-splitting objective in a very different way. The income of the child is taxed in the child's hands, but may in part be taxed at the parent's marginal tax rate.

> Review income splitting arrangements to prevent double taxation.

The first US$800 of unearned income (roughly equivalent in meaning to Canadian "income from property") of a child under 14 is not taxed. The next US$800 is taxed as the child's income. Beyond US$1,600, if the child has no *earned* income (compensation for services rendered), any further unearned income will be taxed at the rate of the parent with the greater taxable income. So, beyond the $1,500 level, little is usually gained from a tax point of view by having a child under 14 earn investment income.

If certain requirements are met, the parent whose taxable income is used for calculating the child's tax rate may elect to include the child's income directly. This will eliminate the need to file a tax return for the child, and also lead to a better matching of incomes between the Canadian and U.S. tax systems.

Income splitting arrangements that are set up for Canadian income tax purposes can result in double taxation if you are not careful. For example, suppose you and your 13-year-old son are both U.S. citizens and your son has no income, and you lend funds to him with the intention of building up "secondary" income over time that will not be attributed back to you (see 5.3.5). The income on the funds you have loaned will be taxed in your hands under Canadian law, but in your son's hands (albeit at your marginal rate while the child is under 14) under U.S. law. Because different taxpayers are paying the tax, no foreign tax credit will be available and you may end up being taxed twice on the same income.

In this example, as long as your son is under 14, you can elect to include his unearned income on your return for U.S. tax purposes. That should solve the double taxation problem, since the income will be taxed in your hands under both systems.

Bear in mind that attribution problems may arise in certain cases if you and your spouse do not file a joint U.S. return (see 18.7.1). For example, if you give your spouse $100,000 to invest and the investment earns $10,000 in Canadian-source dividend income, you will pay Canadian tax on the income and your spouse will pay the U.S. tax. If you and your spouse file a joint U.S. return, all Canadian taxes will be combined for foreign tax credit purposes. But if you and your spouse do not file jointly, no foreign tax credit will be available because different taxpayers are taxable on the income.

18.7 U.S. filing requirements

18.7.1 Joint return or not?

For federal Canadian tax purposes, every taxpayer is distinct and must file separately. Combining the income of two spouses is only considered for certain specific purposes, such as eligibility for the Child Tax Benefit (see 2.3.1) and the GST credit (see 2.9.3). For Québec purposes, spouses have the option of filing joint returns in certain circumstances (see 17.1.2).

For U.S. tax purposes, you have the option of filing a joint return with your spouse. If one spouse has little or no income, this will usually result in less tax than if you file as "married filing separately".

For U.S. purposes, a joint return is mandatory (if you are married) if you wish to claim certain deductions and credits. The child care credit is one example. Another is the US$25,000 loss allowance for an owner who actively participates in rental real estate.

If you're married, file a joint return where appropriate.

If you do not have a spouse, your filing status will be one of "single", "head of household" or "surviving spouse", all of which have different implications for your U.S. tax return.

If your spouse is a U.S. citizen, the decision as to whether to file jointly can be made annually. If your spouse is not a U.S. citizen, the decision to file jointly can only be made once.

If your spouse is not a U.S. citizen and has no U.S.-source income, and thus is not subject to U.S. tax, consider filing a "married filing separate" return. As a "non-resident alien", your spouse's Canadian income will not be relevant for U.S. tax purposes. On the other hand, if your spouse has little income from any source but you are paying tax to the U.S., you may elect to include the spouse's income on your joint return. In this case, filing a joint return can be beneficial, as it will give you larger exclusions and wider tax brackets at the lower rates.

Note also that if you file jointly with a non-resident alien spouse, you must always file jointly unless the election to file jointly is revoked; but once revoked, the decision can never be made again (unless you have a new spouse).

18.7.2 Time requirements for filing

The requirements for filing Canadian tax returns were discussed in 9.1.

U.S. tax returns must normally be postmarked by April 15 each year.

If you are a U.S. citizen whose "tax home" (place of employment) and "abode" (place of residence) are *both* outside the U.S., your filing deadline is automatically extended to June 15 each year. You must attach a statement to your return identifying that you are eligible for this extension. You mail your U.S. tax return to the IRS in Philadelphia.

If you are unable to meet your U.S. filing deadline, you may file for an extension of the deadline to August 15. The extension will be granted automatically.

Even though you are permitted to file your return in June or August, you must pay your balance owing by April 15. Interest on any balance of taxes owing will run from April 15.

18.7.3 Estimated taxes

We discussed the Canadian tax instalment requirements in 9.2.2. The U.S. has parallel requirements, which are called payments of "estimated taxes".

Estimated tax payments are due quarterly, on April 15, June 15, September 15 and the following January 15. As with the Canadian system, you can generally choose either last year's tax or this year's tax as the basis for your quarterly estimated tax payments.

If you are basing your payments on the current year's tax, you need only pay 90% of the year's tax liability (regular tax or AMT) in estimated tax payments—22.5% each quarter. If you are using last year's tax, you must normally pay 25% of that amount each quarter (or 27.5% each quarter if your prior-year adjusted gross income exceeded $150,000). In order to use last year's tax, you must have filed a return in the previous year and the year must have been a 12-month period.

In either case, any balance still owing will be due with your tax return. No estimated tax payments are required if your total tax for the year is less than US$1,000.

If you do not make your estimated tax payments on time, non-deductible late payment penalties will apply.

18.7.4 Disclosure requirements

As well as filing a tax return, you must disclose a substantial amount of financial information under U.S. law.

First, you must disclose holdings in any non-U.S. corporations which you control directly or indirectly, or in which you have increased or decreased your interest. You must provide this information for each foreign corporation by filing a separate Form 5471, "Information Return with Respect to a Foreign Corporation". The IRS uses this information, among other things, to help determine your liability for tax on any undistributed income of closely-held non-U.S. corporations that earn passive income.

Similar reporting rules are now in place for investments in foreign partnerships and foreign disregarded entities. This information is disclosed by filing Form 8865, "Return of U.S. Persons with Respect to Certain Foreign Partnerships", and Form 8858, "Information Return of U.S. Persons with Respect to Foreign Disregarded Entities".

In some cases, a Canadian corporation's reporting year must be the calendar year for U.S. reporting purposes.

Second, you are required to file annually a "Report of Foreign Bank and Financial Accounts" form with the U.S. Department of the Treasury. This form is mailed separately from your tax return and is due by June 30. It is required if the total value of your foreign (non-U.S.) bank accounts, brokerage accounts, RRSPs, etc. exceeds US$10,000 at any time in the year.

As discussed in 18.8.4, reporting rules are also in place for certain gifts and bequests over $100,000 received in one year. Any transfers to and from foreign trusts (including loans) must also be reported by filing an "Annual Return to Report Transactions with Foreign Trusts and Receipt of Certain Foreign Gifts". If you are treated as the owner of a foreign grantor trust, you must report annually. The return is due at the same time as your U.S. personal tax return.

If you have a Canadian RRSP or RRIF, you may need to comply with certain U.S. reporting requirements — see 18.3.4.

Severe penalties apply under U.S. law for not complying with the above disclosure requirements.

18.7.5 U.S. passport renewals

If you apply for a U.S. passport, or a renewal of your passport, while living outside the U.S., you will be required to provide your Social Security Number and file an IRS information return. If you have not been regularly filing U.S. tax returns, you may receive a request to file from the Internal Revenue Service. Ignoring such requests can leave you liable to criminal penalties. In the future, the IRS hopes that legislation will be passed permitting the U.S. government to withhold renewal of your passport for non-filing of tax returns.

18.8 U.S. gift and estate taxes

U.S. gift and estate taxes are part of a complex tax system for property transfers that has no equivalent in Canada. The transfer tax applies to transfers made during your lifetime (gift tax) and at death (estate tax). Taxes are levied on a graduated scale based on the cumulative value of all gifts made during your lifetime and at death, ranging from 18% to 48% in 2004 on cumulative lifetime transfers over US$1.5 million.

The U.S. recently passed significant changes to its gift and estate tax rules. Among other things, the maximum estate tax rate will gradually decrease until it reaches the target rate of 45% in 2009. In 2010, the estate tax is repealed, though the gift tax will remain in place at 35%. The lifetime estate transfer amount is $1 million for 2003 and increases gradually to $3.5 million by 2009. (Unless further legislation is passed, these new gift and estate law changes are scheduled for repeal in 2010 and the rules that were in place before the changes will generally apply once again in 2011.)

In this section we discuss how the gift and estate tax rules apply to U.S. citizens residing in Canada. If you are a non-U.S. citizen who owns U.S. property, see 19.4.

18.8.1 Lifetime gift and estate tax credit

U.S. citizens are permitted a lifetime estate tax credit to offset the transfer tax on US$1.5 million for 2004. The estate exemption amount will gradually increase to $3.5 million in 2009.

U.S. citizens are also permitted a gift tax exemption, which is set at US$1 million for each year until 2009. Any exemption amount used for gifts reduces the amount available on death.

18.8.2 Gift tax

Canada does not have a gift tax, although the giver of a gift (except to a spouse) is deemed to have sold the property at its current fair market value, possibly leading to income tax on a resulting taxable capital gain (see 6.4.5).

The U.S. does have a gift tax, which applies only to those who make very substantial gifts. The *giver* is liable for the tax. Where the giver and recipient are spouses who are both U.S. citizens, no gift tax applies at all. Otherwise, if only the giver is a U.S. citizen, gift tax may apply.

The gift tax generally does not apply to gifts to charities, U.S. political parties, and directly to institutions to pay for another person's tuition or medical expenses.

Up to US$11,000 may be given tax-free each year to any one donee, and up to $114,000 to a spouse who is not a U.S. citizen.

Consider using the annual $11,000 U.S. gift tax exclusion to transfer wealth to children.

A common estate planning technique is to make use of the $11,000 annual gift tax exclusion to transfer wealth to children. However, for the gift to be eligible for the exclusion, the recipient must have the right to use the gift without restriction. In these cases, steps should be taken to ensure that an adult retains control over the assets while the child remains a minor such as opening a "Uniform Gift to Minors Act" account in the U.S. or establishing a formal trust (with certain powers for the child to ensure that the exclusion will apply).

The Canadian tax (if any) that applies on a gift is an income tax, while the U.S. tax is not. As a result, no foreign tax credit applies in either system for taxes of the other system. Caution must therefore be exercised if you are making large gifts. One further problem with gifts is that, for U.S. purposes, your cost base of property (plus a portion of the gift tax paid) will be carried through to the recipient of a gift, whereas on death, any property left to your beneficiaries is treated as acquired by them at its fair market value.

You must also watch out for the Canadian attribution rules, as outlined in Chapter 5.

The Canada-U.S. tax treaty does not provide any relief for U.S. gift tax, although you can elect to have a deemed disposition for U.S. purposes in order to match income recognition in the U.S. and Canada. Making this election would allow you to increase the property's cost base to its fair market value at the time the gift is made. However, making the election will not reduce any gift tax payable.

As discussed below in 18.8.4, U.S. recipients of gifts from foreign individuals must also report gifts over $100,000 in a calendar year.

18.8.3 Estate tax

The U.S. imposes estate tax on death of U.S. citizens based on the fair market value of the deceased's gross estate, which includes all worldwide assets owned at death, regardless of whether the assets pass outside the will.

If the gross estate exceeds $1.5 million in 2004, an estate tax return must be filed nine months after the date of death, even if no estate tax is payable. Under the U.S. rules, the executor of the estate is personally liable for any taxes and penalties owed by the estate until official clearance is granted by the IRS.

An unlimited marital deduction is provided for any amounts left to your spouse on death, if your spouse is a U.S. citizen. As a result, leaving all of your estate to your spouse will result in no estate tax applying on your death. This will cause one US$1.5 million exemption amount to be wasted, since only one US$1.5 million exemption on your combined estate would be available on your spouse's death.

Generally, a marital deduction is only permitted for property passing to the spouse outright with no restrictions on its use. But you may intend for the assets to be used by your spouse and pass to your children or other individuals on your spouse's death, even if, for example, your spouse remarries. Such property may be treated as "qualified terminal interest property", which is eligible for the marital deduction if an election is made on the estate tax return and certain other requirements are met.

If you hold property jointly with a non-U.S. citizen spouse or other individual, the value of the property's inclusion in your gross estate will be based on the proportionate initial contribution to purchase the property. As such, it is important to save receipts or other documentation relating to property purchased jointly with others.

Life insurance proceeds are subject to U.S. estate tax if the insured had a beneficial interest in the policy, such as a right to change beneficiaries, borrow against the policy or cancel the policy. Certain techniques are available to minimize the estate tax burden on life insurance proceeds, including the use of life insurance trusts and gifting plans. To use these strategies, advice from an estate planning professional is essential.

Some items in an individual's estate are subject to both U.S. income and estate taxes. These items include accrued compensation or commissions for personal services received after death, investment income, instalment sales, employment survivor benefits and retirement plans such as IRAs. Planning strategies may be available to reduce the resulting double taxation. For example, you could gift income-producing assets to individuals or trusts during your lifetime or bequeath specific assets to charities. Professional advice on implementing these strategies is recommended.

18.8.4 U.S. reporting rules for gifts and foreign trusts

U.S. citizens must file an annual gift tax return if any gifts made in the calendar year exceed the annual $11,000 exclusion, if you elect to split gifts with your U.S.-citizen spouse, or if any gifts are in trust. The return is due with your regular U.S. personal income tax return.

If you are a U.S. citizen and you transfer money or property to a foreign trust, or you receive a distribution from one, you must report the transfer to the IRS. The penalty for not complying with these reporting rules is 35% of the gross value of the money or property transferred, and additional penalties for continued failure can run up to 100% of the transferred amount.

> Beware of U.S. gift and foreign trust reporting rules.

U.S. citizens must also report each gift or bequest received in a year if the total of all gifts and bequests received from foreign persons in that year is more than US$100,000. Penalties for non-compliance are substantial.

If you are treated as the owner of a foreign grantor trust, you must file Form 3520A, "Annual Information Return for Foreign Trust with a U.S. Owner," each year by March 15 of the following year.

18.8.5 Generation-skipping tax

The U.S. imposes a special tax to ensure gifts and bequests made to grandchildren do not skip a level of transfer taxation as a result of bypassing the intermediate generation. The generation-skipping tax adds an additional transfer tax on transfers from grandparents to their grandchildren that results in the same net gift that would have resulted had the gift passed from grandparent to parent to grandchild.

A lifetime exemption of US$1.5 million is available to offset the generation-skipping tax. This exemption is separate from the lifetime exemption for estate and gift taxes discussed in 18.8.1. Making the election to use this exemption is extremely complex and should not be done without professional advice. Additionally, transfers to trusts having direct or contingent beneficiaries who are significantly younger than you should be made in consultation with a qualified tax adviser.

18.9 References

The following publications can be obtained (in person or by telephone request) from your nearest CRA Tax Services Office. Forms and guides may also be available from the CRA's Internet site at *www.cra-arc.gc.ca*.

Interpretation Bulletin IT-221R3, "Determination of an individual's residence status"
Interpretation Bulletin IT-270R2, "Foreign tax credit"
Interpretation Bulletin IT-395R, "Foreign tax credit—capital gains and capital losses on foreign property"
Interpretation Bulletin IT-506, "Foreign income taxes as a deduction from income"
Interpretation Bulletin IT-520, "Unused foreign tax credits—carryforward and carryback"
Form T2036, "Calculation of provincial foreign tax credit"
Form T2209, "Calculation of federal foreign tax credits"
Form T4056, "Emigrants and Income Tax"
Form T4055, "Newcomers to Canada"

The following may be obtained from any office of the Internal Revenue Service, and are generally available at U.S. embassy and consular offices, or from the IRS' Internet site at *www.irs.ustreas.gov*.

Publication 17, "Your Federal Income Tax"
Publication 54, "Tax Guide For U.S. Citizens and Resident Aliens Abroad"

Publication 514, "Foreign Tax Credit For Individuals"

Publication 521, "Moving Expenses"

Publication 523, "Selling Your Home"

Form 706, "United States Estate (and Generation-Skipping Transfer) Tax Return

Form 709, "United States Gift (and Generation-Skipping Transfer) Tax Return

Form 1040, "U.S. Individual Income Tax Return"

Form 1116, "Computation of Foreign Tax Credit"

Form 2350, "Application For Extension Of Time to File U.S. Income Tax Return"

Form 2555, "Foreign Earned Income"

Form 3520, "Annual Return to Report Transactions with Foreign Trusts and Receipt of Certain Foreign Gifts"

Form 3520A, "Annual Information Return of Foreign Trust With a U.S. Owner"

Form 3903, "Moving Expenses"

Form 3903F, "Foreign Moving Expenses"

Form 4868, "Application for Automatic Extension of Time to File U.S. Individual Income Tax Return"

Form 5471, "Information Return With Respect To A Foreign Corporation"

Form 6251, "Alternative Minimum Tax—Individuals"

Form 8833, "Treaty-Based Return Position Disclosure under Section 6114 or 7701(b)"

Form 8858, "Information Return of U.S. Persons with Respect to Foreign Disregarded Entities"

Form 8865, "Return of U.S. Persons with Respect to Certain Foreign Partnerships"

Form TD F 90-22.1, "Report of Foreign Bank and Financial Accounts"

If you visit or own property in the U.S.

- Avoid becoming a U.S. resident while visiting (19.1)

- If you own rental real estate in the U.S., elect the net rental income method (19.2.1)

- Sell real estate to a buyer who will occupy it as a principal residence (19.3.1)

- Apply for a U.S. "withholding certificate" on the sale of real estate (19.3.1)

- Consider using your Canadian principal residence exemption on the sale of your U.S. residence (19.3.2)

- Be cautious when acquiring shares in U.S. corporations (19.4.1)

- Leave property to your spouse or a qualified domestic trust (19.4.6)

- Mortgage property (non-recourse) to reduce the value of your U.S. real estate (19.4.6)

- Acquire property jointly with your spouse or another person (19.4.6)

- Split your worldwide assets with your spouse (19.4.6)

- Consider a split interest purchase with your child (19.4.6)

- Hold your U.S. property through a Canadian corporation (19.4.6)

- Hold your U.S. assets through a Canadian partnership that elects to be treated as a corporation in the U.S. (19.4.6)

- Sell U.S. property before death (19.4.6)

- Consider taking out life insurance to cover U.S. estate taxes (19.4.6)

In this chapter we discuss the United States taxes that apply to Canadian residents who are not U.S. citizens and who acquire U.S. investments such as stocks and real estate. (Taxation of U.S. citizens resident in Canada was covered in Chapter 18.) Such investments are taxed in four ways: on the income they generate; on their sale; on gift; and on death of the owner. We also discuss the "snowbird" rules that can make you resident in the U.S. for tax purposes.

In general, the interaction between the U.S. and Canadian tax systems can be highly complex. Cross-border transactions should not be undertaken without qualified professional tax advice.

19.1 Snowbirds—U.S. residency rules

If you spend a substantial portion of the year in the U.S., you may become a U.S. resident for tax purposes. If this happens you may be required to file U.S. tax returns and pay U.S. tax on your income from *all* sources, including Canada (except to the extent that you can claim foreign tax credits—see 19.3.2). If you accidentally become a U.S. resident for tax purposes, the tax cost can be substantial.

If you hold a green card, you have the status of a U.S. permanent resident and will be considered resident in the U.S. for tax purposes wherever you live.

> Avoid becoming a U.S. resident while visiting.

If your "physical presence" in the U.S. totals 183 days or more in the year, you will be deemed a U.S. resident. For this purpose, you must total up the number of days you spend in the U.S. in the current year, 1/3 of the days from the preceding year and 1/6 of the days from the second preceding year.

Example

Simone spends the winter each year in Miami and the fall, spring and summer in Montréal. For 2002, 2003 and 2004, she is physically in the U.S. for 150, 90 and 140 days respectively.

For 2004, Simone's "physical presence" calculation is $140 + (1/3 \times 90) + (1/6 \times 150)$, or 195. Since this figure exceeds 183, she is considered resident in the U.S. for 2004 (subject to the "closer connection" rule described below).

If you are deemed a U.S. resident under the "physical presence" test but the number of days you spend in the U.S. in the *current* year is less than 183, you can be treated as non-resident for purposes of U.S. tax if you can establish that you have a "closer connection" to Canada than to the U.S. To make this determination, the IRS will look at factors such as where your family, automobile and personal belongings are located, where your driver's licence was issued, where you are registered to vote, and where you derived the majority of your income for the year. This information is reported on Form 8840 (see 19.5), which is due by June 15 of the following year.

If your current year's days in the U.S. are 183 or more, or if you hold a green card, you can gain a measure of protection from the Canada-U.S. tax treaty if you can establish that under the treaty you are resident in Canada rather than the U.S. (This protection is not as broad as being treated as non-resident under the "closer connection" rule above, however.) For this purpose you would need to show that you have a permanent home in Canada and not in the U.S.; or, if you have a permanent home in both countries or neither, that your personal and economic relations are closer to Canada. You will have to file information with the IRS within certain time limits to be entitled to this treaty "tie-breaker" protection. Although you may not be subject to U.S.

income tax on your Canadian income, you are still required to follow the regular U.S. reporting rules, including reporting ownership of non-U.S. corporations, reporting transfers to and distributions from non-U.S. trusts and reporting receipts of foreign gifts and bequests. If you have a green card, filing on this basis may jeopardize your U.S. immigration status.

19.2 Income from U.S. sources

Certain U.S.-source income is subject to U.S. income tax or U.S. tax withholding or disclosure requirements even if you are not resident in the U.S.

19.2.1 Obtaining a U.S. Individual Taxpayer Identification Number (ITIN)

If you invest or perform services in the U.S., you may be asked to provide an Individual Taxpayer Identification Number (ITIN) for tax reporting and withholding purposes. The IRS issues ITINs to individuals who are required to have a U.S. taxpayer identification number but who do not have, and are not eligible to obtain a U.S. Social Security Number.

Some temporary ITINs issued before 1996 may have become invalid. If you have an ITIN issued before 1996, you may need to apply for a replacement ITIN.

New U.S. rules have made the process of applying for an ITIN more difficult and time-consuming. If you plan to invest or perform services in the U.S., consider seeking help from professional tax advisor in navigating the ITIN application process.

19.2.2 Rent from real estate

A withholding tax of 30% normally applies to the gross amount of any rent paid to a resident of Canada on real estate located in the United States. (Unlike withholding taxes on interest and dividends, this tax is not reduced by the Canada-U.S. tax treaty.)

> **Example**
>
> Leanne lives in Canada and owns a condominium in Texas. She rents out the condominium for the entire year, receiving US$10,000 in rent. Her mortgage interest, maintenance costs, property taxes and depreciation total US$8,000.
>
> Over the course of the year, 30% of the rent paid to Leanne, or US$3,000, should be withheld by her tenant and remitted to the IRS.

At the end of the year, Leanne may elect to file a U.S. tax return and to pay U.S. tax on her net rental income. In the example above, her net rental income would be only US$2,000 rather than US$10,000. She can then receive a refund for the withholding tax, to the extent it exceeds the tax payable on her U.S. return. However, note that state tax (and possibly a small amount of city tax) may be payable on rental income.

If you have any expenses (mortgage interest, maintenance, insurance, property management, property taxes, etc.), you will almost always want to elect the "net rental income" method. The amount subject to tax at your marginal rate will be substantially lower than the amount subject to 30% withholding.

> If you own rental real estate in the U.S., elect the net rental income method.

Once you've elected to file on a net basis, the election is permanent and you will be taxed on the net basis in future years. If you make the election, it applies to all of your U.S. rental real estate. Make sure you take into account the fact that the election can only be revoked in limited circumstances.

If you make the election, you can provide Form W8-ECI (see 19.5) to your tenant or agent, and 30% of the rent will not need to be withheld.

Depreciation must be claimed for U.S. income tax purposes. Unlike Canada's capital cost allowance system (see 11.2.7), depreciation is not a discretionary deduction in the U.S. Any allowable amount, regardless of whether you claim it, will reduce the property's cost base and increase the gain on its disposition.

19.2.3 Dividends and interest from U.S. corporations

Like rental payments, payments of dividends and interest by U.S. persons and corporations to residents of Canada are subject to U.S. withholding tax. The Canada-U.S. tax treaty limits the tax to 15% for dividends and 10% for interest in most cases. Certain interest may qualify for an exemption from U.S. tax.

You do not file a U.S. income tax return in respect of dividend and interest income on which the correct tax is withheld.

19.3 Sale of U.S. properties

19.3.1 Withholding tax (FIRPTA) on sale of real estate

If you sell real estate located in the U.S., a withholding tax of 10% of the sale price is normally payable under FIRPTA (the *Foreign Investment in Real Property Tax Act* of 1980). The tax withheld can be offset against the U.S. income tax payable on any gain you realize on the sale, and refunded if it exceeds your U.S. tax liability when you file your U.S. tax return to report the disposition.

If you are selling U.S. real estate for less than US$300,000, selling it to a buyer who intends to occupy it as a residence can be advantageous. Withholding under FIRPTA will not apply if the property is sold for less than US$300,000 and the purchaser intends to use it as a residence. For this

> Sell real estate to a buyer who will occupy it as a principal residence.

exception to apply, the purchaser must have definite plans to reside at the property for at least half of the time that the property is in use during each of the two years following the sale. The purchaser does not have to be a U.S. citizen.

Bear in mind that the gain on the sale will still be taxable in the U.S. A U.S. tax return must be filed for every disposition of U.S. real property.

Another way of reducing the FIRPTA withholding is to apply to the IRS before the sale for a "withholding certificate" on the basis that your expected U.S. tax liability will be less than 10% of the sale price. The certificate will indicate what amount of tax should be withheld by the purchaser rather than the full 10%. You must file the application before the sale's closing date.

Be sure to apply for a "withholding certificate" if you are making an instalment sale—otherwise, the 10% withholding will be required on the entire sale price up front.

> Apply for a U.S. "withholding certificate" on the sale of real estate.

Some states such as California and Hawaii have state withholding tax provisions that parallel FIRPTA.

19.3.2 Income tax on the sale of U.S. real estate

For income tax purposes, you must file a U.S. tax return to report the gain on the sale of U.S. real estate. You can then claim a credit for the FIRPTA tax withheld. The maximum U.S. tax rate on capital gains for assets held for more the 12 months is 15%. Regular graduated U.S. rates apply for assets held for less than one year. The effective highest Canadian rate is about 22.5% because Canada only taxes one-half of the gain (see 6.2.1). However, 100% of the gain is taxed for U.S. purposes.

If you have owned U.S. non-business real property and have been resident in Canada since before September 27, 1980, you can likely take advantage of the Canada-U.S. tax treaty (see 18.2.3) to reduce the amount of your gain

> **Example**
>
> Roxanne bought a cottage in the U.S. for personal use in 1978 for US$10,000. On January 1, 1985 it was worth US$30,000. In 2004, Roxanne sold the cottage for US$60,000.
>
> The U.S. will tax only US$30,000 of Roxanne's gain, which is the increase in value of the property since the beginning of 1985. State income tax may be based on a gain of either US$30,000 or US$50,000, depending on whether the state adheres to the Canada-U.S. tax treaty.

that is taxable in the U.S. In this case, only your gain accruing since January 1, 1985 will be taxed.

If you cannot establish a January 1, 1985 valuation, the gain accrued to that date is determined by assuming that the entire gain accrued equally over each month in the holding period.

To claim the benefit under the treaty, you will need to make the claim on your U.S. return and include a statement containing certain specific information about the transaction.

> Consider using your Canadian principal residence exemption on the sale of your U.S. residence.

U.S. tax on the sale of U.S. property will generate foreign tax that can be used to reduce the Canadian tax on the sale. (See 18.2.2 for an explanation of the operation of foreign tax credits.) If the property qualifies, you can shelter the amount of the gain taxed in Canada by claiming the Canadian principal residence exemption (see 6.4.2). However, using the exemption will proportionately reduce the foreign tax credit available to you for Canadian tax purposes.

19.3.3 Sales of U.S. stocks and bonds

As long as you are not a resident or citizen of the U.S., U.S. tax will normally not apply to sales of shares in U.S. corporations, whether public or private and no matter where they are traded.

However, if the majority of the corporation's assets are U.S. real estate, the corporation may be considered a "U.S. real property holding corporation" (unless it is a publicly traded company and you own less than 5% of the shares). In such a case, any gain on the sale of the shares of the corporation will be taxed by the U.S. in a manner similar to sales of real property.

19.4 U.S. estate taxes for Canadians

U.S. estate taxes can impose a very serious burden on the death of Canadians and other non-U.S. citizens who own U.S. stocks and real estate. We shall discuss federal estate taxes only; many states also have estate taxes, and these must be considered as well.

The rules discussed here only apply in situations where both the deceased and the surviving spouse are Canadian citizens and residents. If either spouse is a U.S. citizen or resident, the planning alternatives outlined in this section may not be appropriate.

19.4.1 Property subject to estate tax

U.S. estate tax applies to the property of Canadians that is "situated within the United States". This includes:

- real property located in the U.S.
- certain tangible personal property located in the U.S.

- shares of U.S. corporations, regardless of the location of the share certificates and regardless of where the shares are traded
- debts of U.S. persons, including the U.S. government (with specific exceptions)
- U.S. pension plan and annuity amounts (including IRAs).

U.S. estate tax could apply to any of your personal assets that are located in the U.S. at the time of your death. U.S. case law has established that the assets must be located in the U.S. with a degree of permanence, so the tax probably will not apply to jewellery or other items you might take with you on vacation. However, furniture and artwork in your Florida condominium, for example, may be subject to U.S. estate tax. For RRSPs, the location of the underlying property determines where the property is situated.

Assets normally excluded from the definition of property situated within the U.S. include: shares of a foreign (non-U.S.) corporation, regardless of where the corporation's assets are situated; U.S. bank deposits; certain U.S. corporate bonds that are publicly traded outside the U.S.; and certain debt obligations.

Be cautious when acquiring shares in U.S. corporations.

The "taxable estate" for estate tax purposes is the gross value of all of the deceased's property situated in the U.S., minus certain allowable deductions. The most significant deductions are:

- amounts left to the deceased's spouse if the spouse is a U.S. citizen
- amounts transferred to a "qualified domestic trust" (see 19.4.6)
- a deduction for a non-recourse mortgage (see 19.4.6) encumbering U.S. property
- a deduction for a share of the deceased's liabilities at time of death— including Canadian income taxes payable

Once the "taxable estate" has been determined, U.S. federal estate tax applies on the cumulative value of all taxable gifts made during your lifetime and at death, at graduated rates ranging from 18% to 48% in 2004 on cumulative lifetime transfers over US$2 million. These rates are scheduled to decrease gradually to target rates of 45% for estate tax and 35% for gift tax in 2009. Under current law, the estate tax is repealed in 2010 and reverts to its 2001 form in 2011, though these provisions will probably change before 2010. An applicable credit amount will then reduce this tax, as we shall see in 19.4.2.

19.4.2 Lifetime estate tax credit

Under U.S. domestic law, non-residents of the U.S. who are not U.S. citizens can apply an applicable credit amount of US$13,000 against the estate tax (if you are a U.S. citizen, see 18.8.1). This credit amount effectively exempts US$60,000 of the estate from taxation.

The Canada-U.S. tax treaty increases the U.S. applicable credit amount for residents and citizens of Canada from the US$13,000 allowed under U.S. law to US$555,800 in 2004 and higher in later years. This credit must be prorated by the value of the Canadian deceased's U.S. estate over the value of the deceased's worldwide estate (as determined under U.S. rules). The effective exemption amount is scheduled to increase gradually to $3.5 million in 2009. The estate tax is to be repealed for 2010; in 2011, the effective exemption amount of $1 million and the estate tax will return. The gift tax is not scheduled for repeal.

The proration of the credit means that Canadians will not be subject to U.S. estate tax unless the value of their worldwide gross estate exceeds US$1.5 million. It also means that wealthy Canadians who hold a relatively small proportion of their total estate in the United States will still be subject to substantial U.S. estate tax. These Canadians may, therefore, choose to avail themselves of the planning techniques discussed in 19.4.6.

Your estate must file a U.S. estate tax return if your property within the U.S. is worth over $60,000, even if no tax is payable. To benefit from the treaty benefits, you must disclose all of your worldwide assets to the IRS on this return.

19.4.3 Marital credit

A "marital credit" is available under the Canada-U.S. tax treaty if an estate tax marital deduction would have been available had the surviving spouse been a U.S. citizen. However, this credit will be capped at the lesser of the applicable credit amount allowed to the deceased's estate and the U.S. estate tax payable after other credits. This effectively allows a minimum $26,000 credit (i.e., 2 x $13,000) where U.S. property is transferred to a spouse on death.

The executor of the estate must elect to take advantage of this provision and must irrevocably waive the benefit of any estate tax marital deduction that may have otherwise been allowable. In effect, the executor must either claim the treaty marital credit or create a qualified domestic trust (but not both). The deadline for the election and waiver is usually nine months after the date of death.

19.4.4 Canadian credit for U.S. estate taxes

On death, Canada will normally tax the accrued capital gains in the deceased's estate (see 22.2.3). A foreign tax credit is available in Canada to offset foreign income taxes paid on foreign-source income. However, U.S. estate taxes are not income taxes. As a result, no foreign tax credit is available under Canadian domestic law to offset taxes on death.

Under the treaty, Canada permits U.S. estate tax on U.S. assets to be deducted from a Canadian resident's Canadian tax otherwise payable for the year of death. The credit will be limited to the Canadian tax attributable to the deceased's U.S.-source income for the year of death.

19.4.5 Special rules for smaller estates

If the value at death of the worldwide estate of a Canadian resident individual (other than a U.S. citizen) is less than US$1.2 million (determined under U.S. rules), the treaty narrows the range of U.S. assets on which estate tax may be levied to properties the gain on the sale of which would have been subject to U.S. income tax under the treaty. For this purpose, the definition of U.S. source income is expanded to include gains on deemed dispositions of U.S. securities.

Since the U.S. estate tax exemption amount was increased to US$1.5 million for 2004 (see 19.4.2), the treaty's rules for small estates are not currently relevant.

19.4.6 Ways to reduce your exposure to U.S. estate tax

Once you have determined which of your assets are subject to U.S. estate tax, there are a number of strategies you can put in place to reduce your estate's potential U.S. estate tax exposure.

Where property is left to a surviving spouse who is a U.S. citizen, or to a qualified domestic trust (QDOT), the estate tax can be deferred until the death of the surviving spouse.

> Leave property to your spouse or a qualified domestic trust.

To qualify as a QDOT, the trust instrument must provide that at least one trustee be a U.S. citizen or U.S. corporation, and that no distribution of capital may be made from the trust without the U.S. trustee being able to withhold U.S. estate tax. Any capital paid out of a QDOT will then become subject to estate tax. More stringent rules apply to QDOTs with assets exceeding US$2 million in value. A properly structured QDOT may qualify as a "spousal trust" for Canadian tax purposes (see 21.5.2).

Mortgage property (non-recourse) to reduce the value of your U.S. real estate.

A "non-recourse" mortgage is one that entitles the lender to have recourse only against the property mortgaged. That is, if you default on payment, the mortgagee can seize the mortgaged property, but cannot bring suit against you for the balance if the property is not worth enough to pay off the debt. A non-recourse mortgage outstanding on your U.S. real estate will reduce your equity in the property, and thus reduce the value of your taxable estate.

Acquire property jointly with your spouse or another person.

Another way you can reduce your estate tax exposure is by acquiring U.S. assets jointly with your spouse (or another person). For this to work, you and your spouse will each have to supply your own funds; you cannot simply give half of the interest in the property to your spouse, or give your spouse the funds to invest. Where assets are jointly held and it can be proven that each joint tenant paid for their interest with their own money, on the death of the first joint tenant, each tenant is deemed to own their share of the property. If it cannot be proven that each spouse paid for their own interest, the first joint tenant to die is deemed to own 100% of the property for purposes of determining the value of the taxable estate.

If you have each invested your own funds and you and your spouse jointly own a condominium worth US$200,000, for example, only US$100,000 of that value will form part of your estate on your death.

Split your worldwide assets with your spouse.

If your spouse has no assets or assets of minor value, consider having your spouse acquire full ownership of one or more of your U.S. assets, such as a vacation property, worth up to the US$1.5 million exemption amount. Seek professional tax advice before doing so, however, since the transfer could trigger the attribution rules or gift tax if your spouse does not use their own funds.

Consider a split interest purchase with your child.

In some situations, it may be beneficial for U.S. estate tax purposes for you to split your interest in an asset with your child. In this strategy, you would acquire a life interest in the property and your child would acquire a remainder interest with his or her own funds. The rules in this area are extremely complex—if you want to pursue this strategy, professional advice is a must.

A more obvious solution to U.S. estate tax is to hold any U.S. stocks and real estate in a Canadian corporation rather than personally. When you die, your corporation does not, and no U.S. estate tax applies to holdings in shares of a Canadian corporation. You have effectively converted the "location" of your assets from the U.S. to Canada. While this solution is often useful, it is fraught with pitfalls, and qualified professional advice should be obtained. Some possible problems that should be addressed include:

> Hold your U.S. property through a Canadian corporation.

- Beyond the initial setup costs, there are ongoing costs to maintaining a corporation, including legal and accounting fees, and capital taxes in some Canadian provinces.
- The acquisition of the U.S. assets by the corporation must be legally complete, and all corporate formalities must be observed. If it is determined that the corporation was only acting as an agent or mere title holder for you, estate tax can still apply to the property on your death.
- Any income earned by the corporation on its U.S. assets (such as interest, dividends, rent) will be subject to tax both when originally earned and when paid out to you in the form of dividends. The combined effect of the taxes may be higher than the tax you would pay if you held the assets directly.
- If the property is U.S. real estate that you already own personally, any accrued gain will normally be taxed by the U.S. when you transfer the property to the corporation.
- If the U.S. real estate is a personal use property, the accrued gains will generally be taxable in Canada at the time of its transfer to the corporation.
- If you or members of your family will be using the property for personal purposes, you may be taxed in Canada as having received a shareholder benefit from the corporation.
- If the property is sold after death and the funds distributed, the total income tax cost may be higher than the potential estate tax cost in certain cases.

The CRA recently changed its administrative policy of not assessing a taxable benefit to a shareholder of a "single purpose corporation", which is generally a corporation established for the sole purpose of holding residential real property in the U.S. for the shareholder's personal use and enjoyment. Single purpose corporations that existed before the policy change in May 2004 are exempt from this policy change until the property is sold or the shares of the corporation are transferred to other than a spouse or common-law partner. Because of this change, no new single purpose corporations should be established.

Instead of using a Canadian corporation, you might consider establishing a Canadian partnership with your adult child to hold your U.S. assets and have the partnership elect to be treated as a corporation for U.S. tax purposes. On your death (or your spouse's death), your partnership interest and the underlying assets can be transferred directly to your child. Since the U.S. will treat the partnership as a corporation, the assets held by it should bypass your estate entirely for U.S. estate tax purposes. And since Canada will treat the entity as a partnership, you can avoid some of the negative Canadian tax implications discussed above of holding U.S. property through a Canadian corporation. Again, this strategy is complex and should not be pursued without professional tax advice.

If you sell your U.S. assets (say, to a family member) before your death, and receive in exchange assets that are not "located in the U.S." (e.g., cash or a promissory note situated in Canada), you will have no U.S. assets left to form a taxable estate.

Hold your U.S. assets through a Canadian partnership that elects to be treated as a corporation in the U.S.

This step may be useful when death is anticipated within a short time period. For example, property could be sold to a child to whom you intend to leave the property anyway, in exchange for a bona fide promissory note. The note might then be left to your spouse or to another family member. If the note were left to the child, the sale may be treated as a gift and subject to U.S. gift tax.

On such a sale, U.S. and Canadian income tax will apply to any gain (the Canadian tax applying to one-half of the capital gain—see 6.2.1). A foreign tax credit will normally be available in Canada to offset part or all of the tax paid.

Sell U.S. property before death.

Be aware of the possible application of the Canadian attribution rules (see Chapter 5) where you have transferred property to your spouse or to a family member who is under 18. Also, make sure you do not take back debt (such as a promissory note) from someone resident in the United States, since certain debts of U.S. residents are generally considered to be property located in the U.S. Before undertaking any transaction, be sure to compare the tax consequences that will arise on death to the tax consequences that will arise on a transfer before death.

Consider taking out life insurance to cover U.S. estate taxes.

If you anticipate that substantial estate tax will apply on your death, consider taking out life insurance as a way of funding the payment of the tax without requiring the sale of your U.S. assets. Life insurance proceeds will not form part of your estate on death, even if provided by a U.S. insurer (although they will be included in your worldwide assets for purposes of determining the applicable credit amount discussed in 19.4.2). Bear in mind that premiums paid on a life insurance policy are not deductible for either Canadian or U.S. income tax purposes. Also, if the policy is with a U.S. insurer, have your professional adviser review the Canadian income tax implications of holding the policy.

19.5 References

The CRA publishes a booklet titled "Canadian Residents Going Down South", available (in person or by phone) from your nearest CRA Tax Services Office or via the Internet at *www.cra-arc.gc.ca*. Written jointly with the IRS, it includes information on U.S. tax laws.

The following forms and publications may be obtained by telephoning or writing to any office of the Internal Revenue Service (IRS). They may also be available at United States embassy and consular offices, or from the IRS' Internet site at *www.irs.ustreas.gov*.

Form 706NA, "United States Estate (and Generation Skipping Transfer) Tax Return: Estate of non-resident not a citizen of the United States"

Form 1040NR, "U.S. Non-resident Alien Income Tax Return"

Form W8-ECI, "Exemption from Withholding of Tax on Income Effectively Connected with the Conduct of a Trade or Business in the United States"

Form 8288-B, "Application for Withholding Certificate for Dispositions by Foreign Persons of U.S. Real Property Interests"

Form 8840, "Closer Connection Statement"

Form W-7, "Application for IRS Individual Taxpayer Identification Number"

Publication 515, "Withholding of Tax on Non-resident Aliens and Foreign Corporations"

Publication 519, "U.S. Tax Guide for Aliens"

Planning for your retirement

- Start planning and saving for retirement at least 15 years before you plan to retire (20.1)

- Consider topping up your RRSP and using the tax refund to pay down your mortgage (20.1)

- Prepare detailed cash flow forecasts to project changes in your expenses and sources of income as you get older (20.2.1)

- Reconsider your investment strategy as you near retirement (20.2.2)

- Split income by assigning CPP/QPP benefits to the lower-income spouse (20.3.1)

- Delay or defer income until 2005 where possible to minimize the OAS clawback (20.3.2)

- Aim for at least $1,000 of pension income for both spouses (20.3.5)

- Top up your RRSP before the end of the year in which you turn 69 (20.4.1)

- Convert your RRSP to a RRIF or annuity at the end of the year in which you turn 69 (20.4.6)

This chapter discusses a number of financial planning issues to consider as you plan your retirement. The decisions you make when planning your retirement can greatly affect your quality of life throughout your retirement and the financial resources you can make available to your heirs. We strongly recommend that you seek professional financial and tax planning advice. Since retirement planning and the estate planning issues discussed in Chapter 21 are closely related, you should consider developing your retirement and estate planning strategies at the same time.

20.1 Saving for your retirement

Most people can live comfortably in retirement on 70 to 80 percent of their pre-retirement income (adjusted for inflation). Meeting this target requires dedicated long-term planning. Generally, the principal sources of retirement income for Canadians are employer-sponsored pension plans, government pension plans and registered retirement savings plans (RRSPs), and other savings.

If you are a member of a personal or employer-sponsored pension plan (see 3.4), you should consider this as one potential source of retirement income, not as your total retirement fund. Similarly, you should not plan to rely too heavily on Old Age Security (OAS) or the Canada and Québec Pension Plans (CPP/QPP) since these government programs will not provide much more than subsistence level income.

Beyond these types of income, you'll probably have to develop resources on your own through other savings and investment strategies. If you don't start at least 15 years before you reach retirement age, you'll probably find yourself working longer than you had intended and/or unable to afford the retirement lifestyle you expect.

> Start planning and saving for retirement at least 15 years before you plan to retire.

By your mid- to late-forties, depending on your circumstances, you should generally find it easier to put larger amounts of funds toward your retirement nest egg: you will be entering your peak income-earning years, your children will be nearing independence, and most of your major lifestyle acquisitions (except maybe your home) will probably be bought and paid for. But don't wait until then—due to the exponential growth of your retirement investments through compounding, the earlier you can start saving for retirement, the better off you will be.

Your RRSP is one of the best available retirement savings vehicles. It allows you to set aside money and to defer the taxes you would otherwise pay on it. Try to contribute as much as possible, and do so early in the year so your contribution can earn tax-sheltered income for the entire year. In Chapter 3, we discussed the tax rules governing RRSPs and a number of strategies for maximizing your RRSP's growth, along with registered pension plans (RPPs) and other deferred income plans.

> Consider topping up your RRSP and using the tax refund to pay down your mortgage.

Building funds in your RRSP and building equity in your home should be two key components of your retirement savings plan. A commonly-asked question is whether you would be further ahead in the long run to maximize your RRSP contributions or to put the same funds toward paying down your mortgage (see 1.2.3). The answer depends on a variety of factors, including your mortgage's interest rate and remaining amortization period, your RRSP balances and types of investments, your marginal tax rate, the number of income-earning years you have left until you plan to retire, and the availability of other pension plan funds. To hedge your bets, consider taking advantage of both strategies by making maximum annual RRSP contributions and using the resulting tax refund to make a lump-sum mortgage payment.

20.2 Getting ready to retire

20.2.1 Assessing your financial situation

As you get close to retirement, you will need to update your net worth statement (see 1.1.2) to get a clear picture of your potential retirement income resources. You will also need to prepare new cash flow forecasts to reflect the upcoming changes in your financial situation and to determine your monthly disposable income. As in preparing a budget (see 1.1.3), your cash flow forecasts should list the amounts you expect to receive and pay out monthly.

You should prepare several cash flow statements to take into account changes in your expenses and sources of income as you get older. For example, preparing a statement at retirement will show cash flow changes resulting from your loss of employment income and your receipt of pension income; it should also reflect reduced employment-related expenses for items such as commuting and clothes and perhaps increased expenses for items such as travel and medical bills. Cash flow statements at ages 60 and 65 will reflect the impact of your CPP/QPP and Old Age Security benefits (see 20.3) on your finances. A further cash flow statement at age 69 or when you mature your RRSP should forecast RRIF or annuity income you will receive.

> Prepare detailed cash flow forecasts to project changes in your expenses and sources of income as you get older.

These detailed forecasts will show if your resources will be enough or if you will need to reduce your planned spending or sell assets to help meet your cash flow needs (see 20.2.3). The projections will also give you the information you need to make decisions such as when you should apply to receive CPP/QPP benefits (see 20.3.1), when and how much to withdraw from RRSPs and whether you should opt for an integrated pension (see 20.3.6).

You should review your retirement projections every one or two years to take into account any changes in your personal circumstances or goals, tax or pension law amendments, economic events and changes to any other assumptions on which your plan is based.

20.2.2 Reconsidering your investment strategy

In 1.1.4, we discussed the importance of determining your objectives and risk tolerance in developing your investment strategy. As you enter retirement, your investment objectives probably will change: instead of building your asset base, your aim will be to preserve or draw on your capital gradually so it will provide a steady and dependable source of income throughout your own and your spouse's lifetimes.

The closer you get to retirement, the less able you will be to replace substantial investment losses and the less risk you should tolerate. Consider changing your investment mix in the years leading up to your retirement so that a greater proportion of your wealth is invested in more secure, fixed income assets such as government or other high quality bonds, preferred shares and guaranteed investment certificates (GICs). Since your retirement could last 30 years or more, you will probably need to have some proportion of your portfolio invested in growth equities such as shares or other equities.

> Revise your investment strategy as you near retirement.

20.2.3 Planning for the sale of assets

On reaching retirement, you may need to reorganize your finances to meet your cash flow needs. This could involve selling some of your assets, withdrawing funds from your RRSP or selling your home. Before doing so, watch out for unintended consequences.

Many tax incentives and social programs are based on your net income for tax purposes (essentially your total income less certain deductions—see 2.1.1). The capital gains arising from asset sales or the income inclusion resulting from your RRSP withdrawals could significantly increase your net income and your tax bill for the year. If your net income is too high, some tax and social benefits will be reduced or eliminated. These include the federal age credit (see 20.3.4) and the Québec age and pension income credits (see 17.2.5). You could also wind up having to pay back some of your Old Age Security benefits for the current year and receiving reduced OAS cheques in July through June of the next year (see 20.3.2). A liability for minimum tax could also arise (see 7.6).

Before you sell your investments or dip into your RRSP funds, consider the following strategies for avoiding a significant income inclusion:

- Consider using resources that do not affect your income for tax purposes first. For example, withdraw from your savings account (without using your emergency fund; see 1.3.1) or certain fixed income investments before withdrawing from your RRSP.
- Spread your sales of assets such as shares and RRSP withdrawals over several years to avoid creating a large income inclusion in any one year.
- Instead of receiving your sales proceeds in one payment, consider making it part of the terms of sale that the proceeds are to be paid to you in equal instalments over five years. This will enable you to spread the income inclusion over the five years by claiming a capital gains reserve (see 6.5.1). Of course, you'll want to consider the risk of default of payment.
- Remember that selling your home or cottage will not affect your income for tax purposes if the property is eligible for the principal residence exemption (see 6.5.2).
- Instead of selling your home, consider a reverse mortgage whereby the lender pays you a fixed amount of money each month toward a mortgage that the lender holds on your property. When your home is ultimately sold, the lender will get back the total amount of its payments plus interest and you or your estate will be entitled to the remainder of the sale proceeds. Since a reverse mortgage is not a beneficial strategy for everyone, be sure to consult an independent financial planning professional before entering into such an arrangement.

20.2.4 Insurance coverage and other post-retirement benefits

As a retiree, your life insurance needs are somewhat different from those discussed in 1.3.2. While you will still want to be sure that funds will be available to cover your estate's tax liability arising on your death and to provide for your spouse and other dependants, you will likely have fewer debts to service and no need for coverage for loss of employment or self-employment income.

In reviewing your insurance needs, be sure to investigate the existing death benefit and the survivor's benefits available on your death. Many employers provide life insurance to their pensioners, although the amount may decrease over time. Some employers also pay a death benefit (see 22.3), which may help out your spouse financially.

You should also review your spouse's medical insurance coverage under your post-retirement benefits in the event of your death. Many survivors lose their entitlement to medical insurance coverage on their spouse's death and you should consider alternate arrangements in advance to ensure your spouse will have coverage after your death.

Since life insurance fills many important roles in estate planning, your review of your coverage on retirement should take place in the wider context of the issues discussed in 21.7. For example, you may wish to consider purchasing life insurance to fund a capital gains tax or other tax liability that may arise on your death.

20.2.5 Survivor's benefits

When you retire, if you are a member of a company pension plan, it will normally provide you with several choices regarding the payment of your pension after your death. These options may include a life-only benefit, a specified guarantee period, a surviving spouse benefit at amounts ranging from 50% to 100%, a 50% spousal benefit, or a combination of these options.

If you choose a specified guaranteed payment period of, say, five, 10 or 20 years, your company guarantees it will pay your pension for that period of time. If you die before the period is over, your pension cheque will be paid to your estate until the period expires.

If you choose a 100% joint and last survivor guarantee, the company will pay you a pension until you die and will continue to pay the same pension to your spouse until your spouse dies.

Under a 50% spousal benefit, your spouse will receive half of your pension upon your death. Most provinces require that the surviving spouse receive 50% (60% in some cases) of your pension amount upon your death, unless the spouse specifically renounces this entitlement in writing when you choose your pension option.

When you are assessing the various options, bear in mind that the longer the potential payout period, the lower the pension payment. For example, the monthly pension payment for a five-year guarantee period usually will be much higher than payments under a surviving spouse benefit option.

20.3 Government assistance for retirees

20.3.1 Canada Pension Plan/Québec Pension Plan benefits

Between the ages of 60 and 70, you can apply to begin receiving your monthly pension benefits under the Canada Pension Plan or Québec Pension Plan. To qualify to receive benefits before age 65, you must stop working by the end of the month before your CPP retirement pension begins and continue not to work in the month your CPP retirement begins, or your employment or self-employment earnings in the month your CPP retirement begins and the preceding month must be less than the average monthly annual pension payable at age 65 for the current year.

The amount of your CPP/QPP cheques will depend on how many years you have contributed to the plan, the amount of your contributions and the age at which you decide to start receiving your pension. CPP/QPP benefits are adjusted annually for inflation; the maximum monthly retirement benefit at age 65 was about $801 at the time of writing. These benefits are taxable as income.

Although you can apply to receive pension amounts as early as age 60, you will have to pay a penalty in the form of reduced benefits for receiving these amounts early. The penalty is 0.5% of your benefits otherwise payable at age 65 for every month (or 6% a year) before your 65th birthday that you collect CPP/QPP benefits and will apply to reduce your benefits for life. If you decide to apply for the benefits after age 65, your benefits will increase by 0.5% for every month after age 65 (up to age 70) that you do not collect CPP/QPP benefits and will effectively increase your benefits for life.

> **Example**
>
> Vanessa accepts an early retirement package from her company and decides that she wants to start receiving her CPP/QPP benefits at age 62. Since she will begin receiving her pension benefits 36 months before her 65th birthday, she estimates her monthly CPP/QPP pension benefits at $814 less $147 ($814 × 36 × 0.5%), for a total monthly pre-tax pension amount of $667.

To estimate your benefits, you may request a Statement of Contributions from Social Development Canada or the Régie des rentes du Québec.

Many factors will influence your decision about when to apply for your benefits. If you expect your expenses to be higher during the early part of your retirement, perhaps because you wish to travel, you may appreciate receiving benefits before age 65. On the other hand, if you do not need the funds to pay your living or other expenses, you may be better off delaying your application since the benefits will be included in your taxable income. Your life expectancy should also be considered—if you are expected to reach your late seventies and early eighties, you may benefit from starting to collect your CPP/QPP benefits at age 65.

The CPP/QPP also pays a death benefit equal to six months of regular CPP/QPP benefits to a maximum of $2,500; this amount is taxable to the estate or the survivor in the year received. The surviving spouse may also apply for a survivor's benefit under the CPP/QPP, which will be a percentage of the deceased's benefits based on the survivor's age and other factors. For example, if the surviving spouse is 65 and not receiving other CPP benefits, the survivor's benefit will generally be 60% of the deceased's CPP/QPP benefits.

You will need to apply for your CPP/QPP benefits at least six months before you wish to begin receiving them. CPP applications are filed with Human Resources Centres of Canada or over the Internet with Social Development Canada (see 20.6); QPP applications are filed with the Régie des rentes du Québec.

As a strategy for saving taxes through income splitting, you may direct that up to 50% of your CPP benefits be paid to your spouse, provided both of you are over age 60. If either of you does this, a portion of the other spouse's CPP is assigned automatically back to the first spouse.

> Split income by assigning CPP/QPP benefits to the lower-income spouse.

If both spouses are eligible for maximum CPP benefits, assignment will not change anything, since each will assign half of the maximum to the other. But if one has high CPP benefits and the other has low benefits or none, the assignment can effectively transfer up to half of the CPP income to the lower-income spouse. The amount that can be split is equal to the retirement pensions you both earned while together, to a maximum of 50%.

The attribution rules discussed in Chapter 4 specifically do not apply to an assignment of CPP benefits. If you and your spouse are both over 60, and you have higher CPP benefits and are in a higher tax bracket, you should consider such an assignment. This assignment might not be advantageous, however, if it affects your spousal tax credit claim (see 2.2.1).

CPP benefits can be assigned by completing a form available from Human Resources Development Canada; QPP benefits can be assigned by completing a form available from Régie des rentes du Québec.

If you are resident in the U.S. and you receive CPP/QPP benefits, see 20.3.3.

20.3.2 Old Age Security benefits and the OAS clawback

OAS benefits are a taxable pension available at age 65. Unlike CPP/QPP payments, which are based on prior contributions, your entitlement to the OAS benefit is based on your age and how long you have lived in Canada. To receive the maximum pension, you must have lived in Canada for 40 years or more after turning 18. Partial pension may be available if you lived in Canada for 10 or more years after turning 18. A social security agreement between Canada and another country may allow you to add your period of residence in the other country to your period of Canadian residence for purposes of determining your OAS entitlement.

OAS benefits are paid monthly and benefit rates are indexed quarterly for inflation. At the time of writing, the maximum OAS payment is about $463 per month. For high-income taxpayers, these payments are completely taxed back through a special tax, known informally as the "clawback". The tax reduces benefits for taxpayers whose net income (after most deductions such as RRSP contributions) is over $59,790. If your net income exceeds about $96,843, the clawback will apply to 100% of your OAS benefits. Spouses' incomes are not combined for purposes of the clawback; each taxpayer's income is considered separately.

The clawback tax on OAS benefits is deducted from your monthly benefits cheque. The amount withheld is based on your income in the prior two years. For example, for the first six months of 2004, your tax withheld was based on your 2002 income while your tax withheld for the last half of 2004 is based on your 2003 income. If too much tax is withheld, the excess will be applied to reduce your income taxes otherwise owing or refunded to you after you file your return for the year. If the tax withheld falls short of your liability, you will have to repay the difference.

> Delay or defer income until 2005 where possible to minimize the OAS clawback.

To minimize the clawback's potential effect, try to delay or defer recognition of income until the following year where possible. For example, if you are thinking about selling investments that have appreciated in value in 2004, consider waiting until 2005 to cash them in—preservation of your OAS benefits may well outweigh the returns you'll forgo by waiting a few months for the proceeds from your appreciated investments (provided their value does not decline in the meantime).

To start receiving your OAS benefits as quickly as possible after turning 65, you should file your application with Income Security Programs, Human Resources Development Canada at least six months before your 65th birthday. If you make your application after turning 65, it may be approved retroactively for up to one year.

If you are resident in the U.S. and you receive OAS benefits, see 20.3.3.

20.3.3 Cross-border payments of CPP/QPP, OAS and U.S. social security benefits

Under the Canada-U.S. social security agreement, U.S. residents who receive CPP/QPP or OAS benefits are not liable for Canadian withholding tax on these amounts. These benefits received by U.S. residents are taxable only in the U.S.

Similarly, if you are a resident of Canada and you receive U.S. social security benefits, no U.S. withholding tax applies on these amounts; 85% of the benefits are subject to Canadian tax.

20.3.4 Age credit

If you are 65 or older by the end of the year, you get an additional federal credit of up to $625 for 2004. This credit is linked to your income and is phased out by 15% of your net income over $29,124. Thus, the credit completely disappears once your net income reaches $55,240. (Your spouse's net income does not affect this calculation.) The Québec age credit is discussed at 17.2.5.

20.3.5 Pension income credit

You are entitled to a federal tax credit of 16% of your qualifying pension income, up to $1,000 of pension income for the year. A similar credit is available in Québec—see 17.2.5.

Qualifying pension income does not include Canada Pension Plan, Old Age Security or Guaranteed Income Supplement payments. It basically means private pension income received through a life annuity. If you are 65 and over or are receiving payments as a result of your spouse's death, it also includes annuities out of an RRSP or a deferred profit-sharing plan, a payment out of a RRIF (see 20.4.4), or the income portion of a regular annuity.

To make the most of this credit, you should aim to have at least $1,000 of qualifying "pension income" annually, plus another $1,000 for your spouse if possible.

> Aim for at least $1,000 of pension income for both spouses.

20.3.6 Integrating government assistance with your pension benefits

Many pension plans offer the choice of an integrated or normal pension. An integrated pension takes into account the approximate amount of government assistance payments you will receive over the course of your retirement, providing higher payments in the first retiring years and lower payments when you become entitled to receive CPP/QPP payments (see 20.3.1) and/or OAS payments (see 20.3.2).

If you choose the integrated pension, you will normally have the same monthly income before and after age 65 (unless you decide to apply for CPP/QPP before then). Maintaining a consistent level of income before and after you start receiving your OAS and CPP/QPP benefits can help keep your income in a lower tax bracket and avoid having your government payments taxed back or reduced.

20.4 Maturing your RRSP

In Chapter 3, we discussed the tax rules and some planning ideas regarding RRSPs. This section discusses your options for maturing your RRSP. There are basically four routes for getting your money out of an RRSP—you must make use of one of the options described below by the end of the year in which you turn 69. Note that life income funds discussed in 20.4.5 are only available in respect of locked-in RRSPs.

20.4.1 RRSP contributions at age 69 and after

If you turn 69 and must wind up your RRSP in 2004, remember that you only have until December 31, 2004 (and not March 1, 2005) to make a contribution to your RRSP for 2004. If your spouse hasn't yet reached age 70, you can continue making deductible contributions to a spousal RRSP as long as you have earned income in the previous year or unused RRSP contribution room carried forward from prior years.

> Top up your RRSP before the end of the year in which you turn 69.

If you have earned income (generally salary and wages—see 3.1.3) in 2004, this will create new RRSP contribution room for 2005. But if you turned 69 in 2004, you must contribute your 2005 amount before you wind up your RRSP at the end of 2004. If you have contributed your maximum amount for 2004 and your $2,000 penalty-free overcontribution, your additional contribution will attract a penalty tax of 1% per month. But the penalty will only apply for the period between the date of the overcontribution and January 1, 2005—after that, your 2005 deduction room will be available. The tax savings from your 2005 RRSP deduction will probably far outweigh the penalty, especially if you make your overcontribution in December 2004.

20.4.2 RRSP maturity option #1—Withdraw the funds and pay the tax

The first, and easiest, way to cash out your RRSP is simply to withdraw the funds in a lump sum. The amount withdrawn from the RRSP is included in your income for the year in which you do so. It is taxed as ordinary income, just as if it were salary, even if some of the value of the RRSP represents capital gains (which outside an RRSP are normally only partially taxed and, in some cases, could be entirely exempt). A percentage to cover income tax will be withheld at source by the financial institution and remitted to the CRA (and Revenu Québec if appropriate) on your behalf (see 3.2). You will then report the income and the amount of tax withheld on your annual income tax return and either receive a refund or, if not enough tax was withheld, pay the difference.

20.4.3 RRSP maturity option #2—Purchase an annuity

The second method is to purchase an annuity, which will provide you with a steady income stream over the life of the annuity. The RRSP proceeds will not be taxed immediately; the annuity payments will be taxed as you receive them. (As discussed in 20.3.5, up to $1,000 per year of the income may be effectively exempted through the pension income tax credit.)

There are three general kinds of annuities, each of which can be tailored through a variety of options to suit your needs: "term-certain", payable to you or your estate for a fixed number of years; "single life", payable to you as long as you are alive; and "joint and last survivor life", payable as long as either you or your spouse is alive. Other features may include a guaranteed term as part of a life annuity, indexing for inflation, reduction of payment on the death of your spouse, reduction of payment when Old Age Security payments begin, and so on. Unless you purchase a life annuity with a guaranteed period or a survivor option, your annuity dies with you and no residual balance will be left to your heirs.

If you are interested in converting your RRSP to an annuity, you should discuss the available options, and their effect on the monthly annuity payment you receive, with your life insurance agent or trust company. Prevailing interest rates must also be considered to determine whether annuities alone, or a combination of annuities and RRIFs, might provide greater flexibility and returns.

20.4.4 RRSP maturity option #3 – Convert your RRSP to RRIF

The third option for maturing your RRSP is to convert it into a Registered Retirement Income Fund, or RRIF. A RRIF is somewhat like an RRSP, in that you can have it invested in various kinds of securities. However, you must withdraw at least a "minimum amount" from the RRIF each year and report what you withdraw for tax purposes. (Again, currently up to $1,000 per year of such income may be effectively exempted through the pension income tax credit, as explained in 20.3.5.)

The amount that must be withdrawn from the RRIF is a fraction of the value of the RRIF at the beginning of the year that increases gradually each year based on your age, levelling out at 20% once you turn 94. You may use your spouse's age for the calculation of your RRIF minimum withdrawal amounts instead of your own. Doing so may allow you to extend the tax deferral on the funds in the plan if your spouse is younger than you are.

20.4.5 RRSP maturity option #4 – Convert locked-in RRSP to LIF or LRIF

A life income fund (LIF) provides an alternative to a life annuity when certain individuals, who were formerly members of a registered pension plan, terminate employment or plan membership. The LIF is an option for individuals who have previously transferred pension funds to a locked-in RRSP (see 3.3.2).

A LIF is a RRIF for tax purposes (see 20.4.4) with additional restrictions. Generally, LIFs are available for pension and locked-in funds, subject to federal and provincial pension laws. Like any other RRIF, a minimum amount must be withdrawn each year. As well, under a LIF there is a maximum amount that can be withdrawn each year. In some provinces, the remaining balance of funds in the LIF must be used to purchase a life annuity by December 31 of the year in which the individual turns 80.

You may also want to consider a life retirement income fund (LRIF), now available in many provinces. If you hold a LRIF, you usually will not be required to purchase an annuity at age 80, and the maximum amount available for withdrawal typically will have some reference to the investment earnings remaining in the fund.

A LIF or LRIF can offer an attractive alternative to a life annuity option. The alternatives for accessing pension monies and locked-in funds are evolving and changing in jurisdictions across the country. Contact your financial adviser to determine which options are available to you.

20.4.6 What's the best option?

By the end of the year in which you turn 69, you will have to decide what to do with your RRSP. While your personal cash flow needs should be your primary concern, your decision should take into account your overall investment and estate planning goals. A straight withdrawal will rarely be the best option, since you will be taxed on the total income in the current year—and none of it will be eligible for the pension tax credit (see 20.3.5).

> Convert your RRSP to a RRIF or annuity at the end of the year in which you turn 69.

Instead, if you wish to retain some control over the investment of your RRSP funds, you should purchase a RRIF (see 20.4.4). If you prefer simply to have a steady monthly income that you don't have to worry about, you could contact your life insurance agent and purchase an annuity (see 20.4.3).

A RRIF will give you more flexibility than an annuity in establishing the amount withdrawn each month, although you must still withdraw a monthly minimum. LIFs also offer flexibility within a range of minimum and maximum monthly withdrawals.

If you are maturing your RRSP, consider the effect of the tax brackets on your income. Your main goal, of course, is to ensure that you have enough income each month to meet your needs. If you can satisfy those needs with a longer-term payout that keeps your income below the high-tax brackets, you may be financially better off.

20.5 Cross-border retirement planning

If you have lived and worked in Canada and the U.S. (or in another country) and you are considering which country you want to live in after you retire, your retirement planning will be quite complex. In addition to two sets of income tax rules, you will have to consider differences in your health care coverage, government-assisted investment vehicles and how your assets will be taxed at death. Beyond your lifestyle goals, the taxation of your investment and pension income in Canada and the U.S. should be a key factor in your decision about where to retire.

If you have lived and worked in both countries, you may have built up retirement assets on both sides of the border. These assets can include RRSPs (see Chapter 3), U.S. Individual Retirement Accounts (IRAs) (see 18.3.4), Canadian company pensions (see 3.4), U.S. company pension plans (also known as 401(k) plans) and a variety of other types of plans. You may have paid into both the Canada/Québec Pension Plan and "FICA", the U.S. social security plan.

Retirement planning in cross-border situations involves the same retirement planning steps discussed in 20.1: you need to assess your net worth, outline your goals and objectives, review your cash flow requirements now and in retirement, and determine your sources of retirement income. You will also need to consider the usual areas of risk management (including disability and life insurance), taxation, investment strategies and estate planning. Due to differences between the laws of the two countries, planning opportunities may be available to minimize your overall tax liability and maximize your retirement assets and cash flow. But without proper advice, double taxation can result, especially on death.

As we saw in 20.2, retirement planning typically involves the preparation of financial projections to incorporate outside sources of retirement income such as government and employer pensions and to determine which assets should be accessed and in what order to maximize your retirement income. Before these projections can be prepared, you will need to review the rules for withdrawal of funds from the various Canadian and U.S. tax-sheltered plans. The tax treatment of withdrawals from these funds will vary depending on their status under the tax laws of Canada and the U.S. The same income may be taxable in both countries and, in certain cases, a foreign tax credit will be available to minimize or even eliminate double taxation (see 18.2.2).

When you are deciding whether to retire in the U.S. or in Canada and developing your retirement plan, you will need to address the following questions. The answers will depend on your particular situation; professional advice is strongly recommended.

- What is your tax status in each country and how are you taxed as a result? Is this the best result from a tax perspective? Do you have any choices?
- How will your RRSP be taxed as a non-resident of Canada? Can you still contribute to your RRSP if you do not live in Canada? If you do not return to Canada, should you withdraw your RRSP in a lump-sum?
- Will your expenses be higher in Canada or in the U.S.?
- How will you pay for your health care coverage? How does your provincial medicare coverage compare to your U.S. coverage, if any?
- How will your U.S. tax-deferred plans be treated for Canadian tax purposes if you are resident here?
- Can you transfer the funds in your U.S. plans to an RRSP? Is this beneficial?
- How do the CPP and the U.S. social security pensions interact in your situation? Can you collect two separate pensions and when should you start collecting them?

- Is it more advantageous to hold U.S. or Canadian-denominated investments? Should you adopt a different investment strategy depending on the country of retirement?

In creating your estate plan for the distribution of your assets on death, you will need to review the laws of both Canada and the U.S. in detail. From a tax perspective, residing in the U.S. at death or simply holding U.S. property can be costly. For a detailed discussion of U.S. estate taxes on death, see 19.4.

20.6 References

Old Age Security and Canada Pension Plan application kits are available (in person or by telephone request) from Social Development Canada (SDC). You can apply for CPP online at the SDC web site at www.sdc.gc.ca. At this web site you can also find several booklets and fact sheets about the Old Age Security program, the Canada Pension Plan and the retirement income system.

You can obtain the following publications (in person or by telephone request) from your nearest CRA Tax Services Office. Forms and guides may also be available from the CRA's Internet site at *www.cra-arc.gc.ca.*

Interpretation Bulletin IT-500R, "Registered Retirement Savings Plans— Death of an annuitant"
Information Circular 72-22R9, "Registered Retirement Savings Plans"
Information Circular 78-18R6, "Registered Retirement Income Funds"
Guide, "RRSPs and Other Registered Plans for Retirement"
Guide, "When You Retire"

CHAPTER 21

Estate planning

- Make a will, or review your existing will (21.2)
- Take steps to minimize probate fees (21.4)

  Consider the advantages of establishing one or more family trusts (21.5.3)

- Take action before the 21st anniversary of a trust's creation to minimize the impact of a deemed disposition of all of a trust's capital property (21.5.3)
- If you are 65 or older, consider setting up an "alter ego" or "joint partner" trust (21.5.5)
- Look into the potential benefits of an estate freeze (21.6.2)
- Make sure you have sufficient life insurance (21.7)
- Plan for the succession of your business (21.8)

  Consider a pre-paid plan to finance your funeral and cemetery arrangements (21.10)

Careful estate planning can help you minimize the taxes arising on death and leave as much as possible to your beneficiaries. In this chapter, we provide some estate planning strategies that you may want to consider. Keep in mind that estate planning can be extremely complicated, and depends very much on your personal situation and goals. It should be undertaken in conjunction with the development of your retirement plan, as discussed in Chapter 20. Professional advice is highly recommended. If you or your spouse is not Canadian, much of our commentary in this chapter will not apply to your situation; if you or your spouse is a U.S. citizen, see Chapter 18.

21.1 What is estate planning?

The goal of estate planning is to achieve the state of financial affairs you desire either at your death or later in your life when you wish to transfer family property to others. Like your financial plan (see Chapter 1), your estate plan should not be something you do once, then file away. Rather, it is a continual process that may evolve to meet changing family circumstances and wishes concerning who inherits your estate. You should give serious consideration to your estate plan at least every five years.

Estate planning may involve more than merely creating or changing the terms and features of a will. For example, you should also consider the way you hold assets. Whether you own your assets personally, through a family trust or through a holding company has important estate planning implications. Like other aspects of estate planning that evolve with changing circumstances, you may wish to periodically consider whether the structure of your asset holdings remains appropriate for your estate planning goals.

21.2 The will

21.2.1 Purpose of a will

The will is a key element of estate planning. It allows you to provide for an orderly distribution of your assets in accordance with your desires and in a way that minimizes the tax burden on your estate and your beneficiaries. Depending on your circumstances, having more than one will may be advantageous—for example, multiple wills can help reduce probate fees (see 21.4) or facilitate the administration of your estate if you have assets in different countries.

Your will's primary function is to specify where and when your assets are to be distributed. You may want to leave specific properties (e.g., jewellery, furniture or shares in your business) to specific beneficiaries. You may want to leave a stated sum of money to certain people or to named charities (make sure you get the correct legal name of the charity). You will also want to specify a "residual" beneficiary, who will get everything left in the estate after your specific bequests are satisfied.

The way you choose to direct assets to beneficiaries is influenced by several factors. For example, you may wish to simply leave everything directly to your spouse. Alternatively, you may want to use a "spousal trust" that, as we'll see in 21.5.2, can offer certain tax advantages and a measure of protection from potential creditors without any loss in flexibility for your surviving spouse. As discussed in 22.2.3, there will be no tax on the accrued capital gains on your property when the property is transferred to your spouse or a spousal trust, provided your spouse or spousal trust obtains ownership and unfettered rights to the property.

If you do not make a will, provincial law will determine how your assets are distributed. The result can vary significantly, depending on where you reside at the time of death. In Ontario, for example, the law provides that the surviving spouse gets the first $200,000 of the estate and divides any additional amounts with the deceased's children in accordance with a formula. However, in Alberta, the surviving spouse is only entitled to the first $40,000, with the balance of the estate divided among the surviving spouse and the deceased's children under a formula.

Note also that, in some provinces, family law can effectively override the instructions in your will. In Ontario, for example, your spouse can elect to ignore the will and take the amount of money due to him or her under the "net family property" rules (see 21.3). If this is done, your estate may lose the benefit of the capital gains rollover described in 22.2.3.

If you have specific desires as to who should have custody of or guardianship over your children after your death and while they are under 18, you can put these desires into your will for consideration by the courts. However, in some provinces, this designation is not binding.

While in some provinces an entirely handwritten will may be valid, it is strongly advisable to have your will prepared or reviewed with the assistance of a lawyer, or a notary in Québec, and a tax adviser to ensure it meets your wishes and takes tax and family law considerations into account.

Periodic reviews of your will are necessary to ensure that your estate plan is consistent with changes in the tax law, which occur regularly, as well as any changes in provincial family law and succession law.

Changes in your own personal circumstances such as the birth of a child or a change in marital status could also necessitate a change to your will. For example, in many jurisdictions, a will becomes void if you marry after making the will, unless it was made in contemplation of the marriage. On the other hand, a will may not become void after a divorce.

If you do not make a will or if your will is invalid, the process of obtaining court approval for distribution of your assets may be cumbersome and expensive. Your representative or heirs must apply to the court to appoint an administrator (also called an "estate trustee") to administer and distribute the estate in accordance with a formula set out in legislation.

As discussed in 1.3.4, consider also executing powers of attorney in the event you become unable to act by reason of disability or mental incompetence—one for decisions related to your finances and one for decisions related to your personal care. If, for example, you become mentally disabled, the continuing powers of attorney would enable the named "attorney" to act in your stead. You may wish to give the powers of attorney to the same person you name as your executor, such as your spouse.

21.2.2 Choosing your executor and estate trustee

In your will, you should designate one or more persons as your executor and estate trustee. The person should be someone you can trust to take charge of your affairs and distribute your assets in accordance with your desires as set out in your will. The executor and estate trustee will normally apply to the court for "letters probate" (see 21.4), which will give court approval for the executor to take over your property, manage it and distribute it to your beneficiaries.

The responsibilities of your executor and estate trustee include determining the assets and liabilities of the estate, filing all income tax returns for you and the estate (including any foreign succession duty or tax returns) and paying the debts (including all taxes) outstanding at the date of your death.

Ideally, you should choose an executor and estate trustee who is familiar with your personal situation. Often the executor will be your principal beneficiary (such as your spouse). Sometimes this may not be appropriate, however, because of a possible conflict of interest with other beneficiaries.

You should consider naming an alternate executor and estate trustee in case your executor dies before you do. Otherwise your estate may be handled by the executor of your executor's estate. Naming an alternate executor and estate trustee is also important in case the named executor is either unable to or chooses not to act. This can avoid costly court proceedings.

If you are an executor and estate trustee yourself, see Chapter 22 for a discussion of your role and responsibilities.

21.2.3 Will planning to minimize your estate's tax liability

There are many tax-oriented clauses that can be included in a will to help minimize tax liability. The will should include a provision granting executors and trustees broad authority to make or join in any election, designation or allocation under tax legislation. This will ensure that your executor can use benefits such as the principal residence designation and capital gains exemption. The following clauses should also be considered:

- forgiveness of certain loans made to family members
- a discretionary power permitting trustees to determine which assets are to form the trust property of spousal or other trusts
- a reminder to your executors that if you have not made your maximum RRSP contribution at the time of your death, one should be made by your estate to your spouse's RRSP before the required deadline.

In your will, you can name the beneficiary of your RRSP, deferred profit-sharing plan, death benefits and life insurance proceeds. Alternatively, these plans and policies usually allow for naming a beneficiary directly within the plan documents. While designating beneficiaries directly in the plan documents may reduce probate costs, there may also be implications for spousal rights under family law.

Note that your estate may have to pay tax on the full value of your RRSP on your death if you designate as the beneficiary of your RRSP someone other than your spouse or (as of 1999 and under a special election after 1995) your financially dependent children (see 22.4). If you are planning to make a charitable gift through your will, instead of donating cash, consider donating publicly traded securities, mutual funds or segregated funds of a life insurance company in order to minimize taxes payable at death (see 8.3.2).

21.3 Family law

Provincial family law can have a significant impact on your estate planning. Every province has legislation to protect the interests of spouses on marriage breakdown. This legislation may apply on death as well. We'll use Ontario family law for purposes of this discussion. The laws of each province are different, however, and professional advice should be obtained.

On marriage breakdown, Ontario's *Family Law Act* provides for an equal division of "net family property", which includes almost all property acquired during the marriage and the increase in the value of property owned at the time of the marriage. Business assets, shares in a privately-held or public corporation and investments are typically all included in "net family property". Each spouse's assets are totalled and an equalizing payment is required, so that each spouse ends up with half of the value of the net family property.

The above provisions apply on death as well. The surviving spouse may elect to take an equalizing payment for one-half of the difference in net family property rather than whatever has been left to him or her under the deceased's will. Clearly, such rules can interfere with estate planning, and should be considered when making a will.

Spouses can agree to have these provisions of the *Family Law Act* not apply by signing a "domestic contract". Separate independent legal advice for each spouse is required before signing such a contract.

21.4 Probate fees

Probate fees are charged by the courts in each province (except Québec) to grant letters probate which confirm that the deceased's will is valid and the executor has the authority to administer the estate.

The probate charge generally applies to the total value of an estate's assets at the time of death, without any deduction for debts other than those encumbering real property. In some cases, the assets can be distributed and the estate wound up without probate but probate is generally required before third parties such as financial institutions (e.g., banks, investment dealers) will release property to the executor or estate trustee. If there is no will, probate is still required because the court has to confirm that an executor has been appointed to distribute the deceased's property as required by law.

Probate fees are highest in Ontario and British Columbia, where they are 1.5% and 1.4%, respectively, of the value of the estate in excess of $50,000 (with lower rates applying the the value below $50,000). In Nova Scotia, the top rate is 1.3% of the value of the estate over $100,000 (with progressive flat rates applying to values below $100,000). In other provinces the top rates are typically 0.4% to 0.7% of the value of the estate. Québec levies a nominal flat fee that is not based on the estate's value. Alberta has progressive flat rates based on the estate's value to a maximum of $400. The probate fees for large estates in other provinces can be substantial as there is no maximum.

Property held by two people as "joint tenants" with right of survivorship (rather than as "tenants in common") is not subject to probate, since on the death of one joint tenant the property does not form part of the estate but simply becomes wholly owned by the other.

> **Example**
>
> Jonah, who lives in Ontario, dies in 2004. His estate consists of a house worth $500,000, with a $200,000 mortgage on it, $100,000 in personal effects, and the shares of his business, worth $1 million. He also owes $80,000 on a personal line of credit to the bank at the time of his death.
>
> The value of Jonah's estate for probate purposes is $1,400,000. The house is counted as $300,000 (i.e., minus the mortgage), and his other assets are $1,100,000. The $80,000 debt is not deducted. The fee for probating Jonah's will is $20,500 (calculated as 0.5% of the first $50,000, plus 1.5% of the balance of $1,350,000).

The following techniques can reduce the cost of probating your estate. Note, however, that any planning to reduce probate fees must take numerous other issues (such as family law, income tax effects, land transfer tax, GST and other sales taxes) into account—professional advice is strongly recommended.

- If you are leaving property to your spouse (or another person), consider holding the property as joint tenants with your spouse (or that other person) with a right of survivorship. On your death, the property will pass automatically to the other joint tenant and will not form part of your estate. Note that there may be immediate adverse tax consequences if you transfer the property to a joint tenant who is someone other than your spouse. Also, there are some situations where a joint tenancy will be severed on death by provincial legislation.
- Try to keep certain assets out of the estate. This is quite practical in the case of life insurance and RRSPs issued by life insurance companies, where beneficiaries (other than the estate) can be designated in the RRSP plan documents or in the life insurance policy. Also consider transferring property during your lifetime, either directly to your intended beneficiaries or to a trust. Again, take care that this does not result in the premature recognition of accrued capital gains.
- Change the location of property to a jurisdiction where probate fees are low or fixed through the use of a holding company incorporated in the lower-fee jurisdiction. You would then prepare a separate will dealing with the shares of that company.

- If you own real estate with no mortgage, and you also owe money (perhaps on a personal line of credit or on a debt secured by other assets), consider having the debt converted to a mortgage or charge on the real estate. It may then reduce the value of the real estate for probate purposes.
- If you have certain assets that can be passed to beneficiaries without probate, such as shares in a private company, you may be able to reduce probate fees by making a secondary will that only includes these assets. Your executor would then apply for probate on the primary will but not the secondary one.
- If you are age 65 or over, two types of trust—"alter ego" and "joint partner" trusts—can help you keep assets out of your estate and reduce its value for probate purposes without giving up your right to those assets during your lifetime—see 21.5.5.

21.5 Trusts

21.5.1 What is a trust?

A trust is an arrangement whereby one or more persons (the trustees) hold legal title to property (the trust property) for the benefit of other persons (the beneficiaries). The person who creates the trust and puts ("settles") property into it is called the settlor.

> Brian is leaving the country to work in Africa for several years. He gives Paul $120,000 to hold in trust for Brian's two teenagers, Dianne and Darryl. Brian draws up a trust agreement that allows Paul to use the trust funds to pay for Brian's children's education, to invest the funds not yet used, and to pay half of the capital of the trust to each child when he or she turns 23.
>
> In this example, Brian is the settlor, Paul is the trustee and Dianne and Darryl are the beneficiaries. Paul will have legal ownership of the $120,000, but he is required to use it only for Dianne and Darryl's benefit and not for his personal use. If the trust document permits, he can pay himself a fee for his services as trustee.

Example

There is no legal requirement that the settlor and the trustee be different people. (In the example above, Brian could simply declare and document that he is holding funds in trust for his children, and a trust would be created.) Similarly, the settlor and the beneficiary can be the same person. (This is what happens when you put funds into a self-directed RRSP, for example. You are the settlor and beneficiary, and a trust company is the trustee of your assets—see 3.1.6.) However, the choice of settlor, trustee and beneficiaries will affect the taxation of the trust and its beneficiaries. For example, there are a number of attribution rules that apply to trusts, including those outlined in Chapter 5. Careful planning is required.

Note that the mechanics and terminology of trusts are somewhat different in Québec, which is governed by the province's *Civil Code* rather than by the common law that governs the rest of Canada.

21.5.2 What kinds of trusts are there?

A trust can be set up during the settlor's lifetime (as in the example above). Such a trust is called an *inter vivos* (Latin for "among the living") trust.

A trust can also be created by the settlor's will, in which case it is called a testamentary trust.

A trust for the settlor's spouse that meets certain conditions is a "spousal trust." The principal conditions are that all of the income of the trust must be paid to the spouse during the spouse's lifetime, and that none of the capital can be distributed to anyone other than the spouse during the spouse's lifetime. (After the spouse's death, however, the income and capital can be distributed to someone else, such as the settlor's children.) Such a trust can be either testamentary or *inter vivos*. A transfer of property from the settlor to a spousal trust does not trigger tax on any accrued capital gain; instead the property passes at the settlor's tax cost, and any capital gain is taxed only when the trust eventually disposes of the property or the spouse dies (see 22.2.3).

Note that if your will creates a trust, that trust will be separate from your estate. The estate is taxed as a trust for as long as it takes to wind up your affairs and distribute your assets. A trust set up in your will, on the other hand, can be designed to continue for many years beyond your death.

In all, there are as many as two dozen types of trusts in use today. Each meets a purpose or addresses an aspect of tax or common law. For a discussion of two new kinds of trusts, called "alter ego" and "joint partner" trusts, see 21.5.5.

21.5.3 How is a trust taxed?

A trust is a separate person for income tax purposes. The trustee(s) must file a T3 trust tax return (and a TP-646 Québec trust return in some cases) and pay tax on the trust's income. A trust is generally taxed as an individual, but is not eligible for the personal credits (see Chapter 2). A testamentary trust pays tax at the same marginal rates as individuals (see 5.1), but an *inter vivos* trust pays tax at a flat rate—the top rate of combined federal and provincial tax for individuals (about 45%).

Consider the advantages of establishing one or more family trusts.

The trust's income includes its income from carrying on business (see Chapter 11), from taxable capital gains (see Chapter 6) and from investments (interest, dividends, rent, etc.—see Chapter 7), calculated as if the trust were a living individual. Amounts that are payable or paid to beneficiaries are deducted from the trust income, and the beneficiaries report such income on their tax returns, subject to the attribution rules discussed in Chapter 4.

Certain kinds of income, such as capital gains and dividends, preserve their character when flowed through to a beneficiary. Thus, such income can be treated as capital gains (see Chapter 6) or as dividends (see 7.1.2) on the beneficiary's tax return. Other income loses its character as it flows through a trust.

A special election called the "preferred beneficiary election" is available where a beneficiary is disabled (as defined for tax purposes in 2.5.1). This election allows the trust and a certain kind of beneficiary to agree that the trust's income will be taxed in the beneficiary's hands so that, in a later year, the income can be paid out by the trust to the beneficiary free of tax.

Other special tax rules allow income and capital gains to be taxed in the trust even if these amounts have been paid out to the beneficiary during the year. This can be beneficial if the trust has unused losses from previous years that can offset this income. For certain testamentary trusts, this election may also save taxes if the beneficiary would otherwise be subject to tax at a higher rate than the trust.

In your will, you can provide a separate testamentary trust for each beneficiary. This will allow each trust to benefit from lower graduated rates of tax for the income retained in such a trust.

Every 21 years a trust (other than a spousal trust — see 21.5.2) is deemed to dispose of all of its property, so that accrued capital gains are taxed as if the assets have been sold. Before the end of each 21-year period, consult a professional adviser to determine whether steps can be taken to minimize the impact of this deemed disposition.

> Take action before the 21st anniversary of a trust's creation to minimize the impact of a deemed disposition of all of a trust's capital property.

21.5.4 The benefits of setting up a family trust

A trust offers tremendous flexibility in structuring your affairs and controlling the future use of your property. The powers of the trustees can be strictly limited and defined; or they can be given full discretion as to when and whether to pay income or distribute capital to the beneficiaries, how to manage the trust property and when to wind up the trust.

Setting up the trust while you are alive can also provide several advantages:

- by making yourself a trustee, you can keep control of the trust assets (such as shares of your business)
- by getting the assets out of your estate, you can reduce probate fees (see 21.4)
- because the assets will not be in your estate, they will not form part of the public record that anyone can examine in the court office

- income splitting may be possible, depending on the application of the attribution rules (see Chapter 4).

A trust can also be useful as part of an estate freeze plan (see 21.6). In many cases, you may not know at the time you set up the freeze how you will want the growth allocated among your children. You may also not yet want to give them direct ownership in the business. In such an event you should consider setting up a family trust and having the trust subscribe for the "growth" common shares (or, preferably, have them gifted to the trust). If you are the trustee and have discretion as to how to allocate the income and capital of the trust, you can decide several years later (or even in your will) which of your children should inherit the business. This may also provide some protection for your children against family law legislation (see 21.3). If you have already established such a plan, ensure that its benefits will not be neutralized by the income-splitting tax on certain income received by minors (see 5.2.4).

An *inter vivos* trust can offer benefits over a power of attorney or applying to the court to appoint a guardian in the event of incapacity. As we saw in 1.3.4, a power of attorney allows you to designate a person who will take control of your financial affairs if you become incapacitated due to illness or injury. Potential advantages of trusts over powers of attorney include the following:

- Unlike a power of attorney, the trust agreement is a comprehensive document that sets out the trustee's specific duties and powers.
- A higher standard of fiduciary duty applies to a trustee than to an attorney.
- The trust survives death, but a power of attorney does not.
- Property held under the trust agreement can be managed by the trustees in the event of incapacity without the settlor's involvement, thereby offering protection against third party abuse, since the settlor does not have independent control of his or her assets.
- A power of attorney may not be adequate to manage assets outside of your own province—each province and state in North America has different legislation. The authority of a trustee acting on behalf of a trust would be more readily recognized by a foreign bank or other institution.

21.5.5 Alter ego and joint partner trusts

Two types of trusts, called "alter ego" and "joint partner" trusts, may be useful as substitutes for wills and powers of attorney and can produce significant benefits in terms of avoiding probate fees and easing difficulties for your survivors or your business while your estate is being settled.

If you are age 65 or over, an alter ego trust can help you keep assets out of your estate without giving up your right to those assets during your lifetime. Under the terms of such a trust, all of the income and capital of the trust property will be held and used for your benefit alone. Income and capital gains generated by the trust property will be taxable in your hands, as they would be if you continued to own the assets personally. On your death, the alter ego trust document performs the same function as a will would have by setting out how the trust assets should be distributed.

A joint partner trust works the same way. Spouses (or common law or same-sex partners) can transfer assets to the trust and remain its only beneficiaries during their lifetimes. No income tax will arise when the property is transferred to the trust and all of the income and capital gains of the trust property will be taxable in the partners' hands during their lifetimes. Be cautious of the attribution rules discussed in 5.2, which may cause the income to be taxed in the settlor's hands.

> If you are 65 or older, consider setting up an "alter ego" or "joint partner" trust.

If you plan to transfer qualified small business corporation shares or qualified farm property to an alter ego or joint partner trust, keep in mind that the $500,000 capital gains exemption (see 6.3) for these types of property cannot be used by these trusts. To overcome this, you may want to elect out of the rollover provisions to trigger a capital gain and claim the capital gains exemption at the time you transfer the property to the trust.

On the death of the settlor of an alter ego trust or the second partner of a joint partner trust, the trust will be deemed to have disposed of its assets at fair market value, and any capital gains will be taxed in the trust's hands.

For alter ego and joint partner trusts, the deemed realization at fair market value discussed in 21.5.3 will not occur every 21 years but is deferred until the day on which the settlor or surviving partner dies.
If the trust continues to exist, a deemed disposition will occur every 21 years after the death of the settlor (for alter ego trusts) or surviving partner (for joint partner trusts).

However, note that since alter ego and joint partner trusts are *inter vivos* trusts, they pay tax at the highest marginal rate applicable to individuals. As such, trust income does not benefit from graduated rates of tax and any capital gains that arise on the deemed disposition resulting from the settlor's death may bear more income tax in the estate than it would if taxed in the hands of the deceased.

21.6 Estate freezing

21.6.1 What is an estate freeze?

"Estate freezing" is the term used to describe steps taken to fix the value of your estate (or some particular asset) at its present value, so that future growth will accrue to the benefit of others, such as your children (or to a trust for your children) and not be taxed on your death. Several provisions of the *Income Tax Act* are designed to facilitate this type of planning.

Estate freezing is most often used when you own a business that your family will continue to own after your death and that you expect will increase in value in future years. Your children may be involved in running the business. Even if they are not, you may want them to own it after your death.

21.6.2 How do you freeze an estate?

There are many different approaches to an estate freeze, some of them very complex. The following example is one of the simplest types:

> **Example**
>
> Lucas owns all of the common shares of his business, X Corp. His original share investment in X Corp. was $100, and it is now worth $1 million. Lucas expects it to increase in value significantly over the next several years. Lucas has two children, both in their early 20s, who work in the business.
>
> First, Lucas exchanges his common shares of X Corp. for 1,000 new preferred shares (a step that can be taken without triggering any income tax). The preferred shares are voting shares. They are also retractable at any time, at his option, for $1,000 per share. In other words, Lucas can demand that the corporation pay him $1 million for his shares at any time.
>
> Each of Lucas' children then subscribes for 50 new common shares in X Corp., paying $1 per share. Since X Corp. is worth $1 million, and Lucas' preferred shares are retractable for $1 million, the common shares have negligible value at the moment.
>
> Over the next few years, the value of X Corp. rises to $1.5 million. Now Lucas' preferred shares are still worth only $1 million, but the common shares are worth $500,000. Lucas has thus transferred the post-freeze "growth" in the corporation to his children at no tax cost to him.
>
> Note also that since Lucas' preferred shares are voting shares, he has kept control of the corporation. Lucas has 1,000 votes and his children together have only 100.

The mechanics of an estate freeze are complex, and there are numerous income tax rules that have to be considered. The basic concept, however, is generally as outlined above. Often you will set up a holding company and a family trust (see 21.5.4) as part of the freeze, rather than having your children subscribe directly for shares in the operating company.

An estate freeze can significantly reduce the tax payable on your death, if the value of your business is "frozen" sufficiently early. The value of the business will be fixed at the time of the freeze, so the tax on the subsequent capital

> Look into the potential benefits of an estate freeze.

appreciation will be deferred until your children sell the business (or until their deaths). You can also multiply the availability of the capital gains exemption for certain small business shares (see 6.3.1), if it is still available when your children eventually dispose of the shares. At the same time, you do not need to give up control of the business.

You can also continue to receive income from the corporation, either by declaring dividends on the preferred shares, or by drawing a salary if you continue to work in the business.

If you use a trust to acquire the common shares, you can retain flexibility with respect to allocating the shares of the business among your children later.

At the time you set up the freeze, you can trigger part or all of the accrued capital gain on your shares to date. This may allow you to use your $500,000 capital gains exemption (see 6.3.1), for example. Be aware of the various restrictions on claiming the exemption (see 6.3.3).

Depending on how the freeze is structured, you can achieve income splitting (see Chapter 5) by directing income into the hands of your children for tax purposes. Note that certain attribution rules do not apply if your corporation qualifies as a "small business corporation" (see 6.2.3) or your children have reached the age of 18 (see 5.2.6). However, existing arrangements may be affected by the income-splitting tax on certain income received by minor children (see 5.2.4).

Whether an estate freeze is useful to you will depend very much on your business, your financial position, your future plans and your goals. Qualified professional advice should be obtained before this type of planning is undertaken.

21.7 Life insurance

Life insurance plays many roles in estate planning. For example, it can:

- provide replacement income for your dependants
- provide a fund for emergency expenses or children's education in future years
- pay for final expenses such as funeral costs
- assist in funding the succession of a business in a closely-held corporation
- fund capital gains tax liability that arises on death (see 22.2.3)

- allow you to accumulate funds on a tax-sheltered basis to supplement retirement income.

Insurance proceeds received on the death of the life insured are not taxable. Similarly, the premiums you pay for your life insurance are generally not tax deductible.

If your corporation is the beneficiary of a policy on your life, the corporation may be able to distribute the life insurance proceeds to your estate and other shareholders without any tax applying.

> Make sure you have sufficient life insurance.

Your need for insurance will change as factors such as your income, investment portfolio and dependants change. Therefore, a regular review of your coverage is important.

There are many different life insurance products available. These products can generally be divided into two types: term insurance and permanent insurance.

Term (or "pure") insurance policies usually have lower premiums at younger ages. You are paying the cost of insuring against the risk of your death in the current year, and nothing more. As long as you continue to pay the premiums, your coverage will continue; many policies guarantee renewal without additional medical evidence. However, the cost of premiums will increase dramatically in later years for normal renewable policies. Most term policies terminate at age 70 to 75, which is lower than the current average life expectancy, though many companies offer "term to age 100"-type policies, which can be acquired for level premiums over life.

A permanent insurance policy (often called "whole life" or "universal life") combines pure insurance coverage with an investment fund. As a result, the cost of premiums is often much higher than term insurance. However, many permanent insurance policies offer fixed premiums for guaranteed maximum terms (say, 10 or 20 years). At the end of the term, the policy is often fully paid up. The policy can be designed so that the investment fund or cash surrender value accumulates tax-free. Such a fund can be borrowed against or "cashed out" in later years. However, doing so will have a tax cost.

Permanent insurance products are usually desirable for the following purposes:

- capital gains tax funding
- estate equalization (to allow for an even distribution of your estate, such as where you wish to leave business assets to beneficiaries active in a family business and non-business assets to those family members not active in the business)

- business succession planning
- long-term, tax-effective investment strategies.

When buying insurance, consider who should be the beneficiary. If your estate is the beneficiary, the insurance proceeds will form part of your estate on your death, and will be subject to any claims that creditors have on your estate. The proceeds will also be subject to probate fees (see 21.4 above). You may therefore want to have the insurance proceeds payable directly to your spouse or another beneficiary, in order to bypass the estate. The investment fund or cash surrender value of a policy can also be protected from creditors during your lifetime where certain beneficiaries are named.

21.8 Business succession

If you own and manage a business, it could well be your family's largest asset. After your death, the business may be crucial for meeting your family's financial needs. Taking steps to ensure your business's ongoing profitability and management can be just as important as considering the planning opportunities available to minimize taxes on your death.

One of the first issues you must resolve is what will happen to the business when you die. You could plan for the business to be kept in the family, sold to a buyer outside the family, or liquidated. The option you choose will depend on things such as the nature of the business, the likelihood of its continued success after your death, and the abilities of your family members and/or key employees to run the business's operations.

> Plan for the succession of your business.

If the family is not capable or does not want to run the business, it may be in everyone's best interests to sell or liquidate the business on or before your retirement. If some family members are quite active in managing the business while others are not, dividing ownership equally among your family might seem fair but it could disrupt the business and create tension in the family. Often in these cases, you could use other family assets or life insurance to ensure fairness for all family members.

If you decide to keep the business in the family, you should seek professional advice to help you decide whether to transfer ownership during your lifetime or on death, who will receive the business's shares and in what proportion, whether the shares will be gifted or sold, and the most tax-effective way to structure the transfer.

If you do not own 100% of your company's shares, the transfer of its legal control may be addressed by a carefully drafted shareholders' agreement (see 14.4).

Life insurance owned by you or your company can facilitate the sale of your shares of the company and help to fund any tax liability arising on death. The tax rules may allow you to maintain certain tax advantages associated with life insurance-funded arrangements if your company was the beneficiary of a life insurance policy held for this purpose held on or before April 25, 1995, or if there was an agreement in place at that time relating to the disposition of your shares.

21.9 Planning for the succession of wealth

In some cases where a family business has been sold, the family's largest asset after the sale is the net sale proceeds. In other cases, wise investment decisions have resulted in the accumulation of significant wealth. Since the bulk of such estates may ultimately accrue to your children, you should assess the age at which they should have access to this wealth and whether controls or restrictions should be placed on the use of these resources for certain periods of time.

Inter vivos and testamentary family trusts (see 21.5.4) can facilitate the transfer of wealth to children over pre-determined ages. Such trusts are also useful in situations where the child is dependent by reason of mental or physical infirmity. They can also be beneficial if your children lack an appreciation for the value of money or if you wish to safeguard assets from family law legislation.

If you will be passing on a sizeable estate to your children, you should consult with your legal and tax advisers to develop a plan to transfer the wealth into their hands.

21.10 Pre-paid funeral and cemetery arrangements

Planning and paying for your funeral and cemetery arrangements in advance can go a long way toward easing the stress on your survivors at a difficult time. Many funeral and cemetery service providers offer plans through which you can deposit funds as pre-payment for their services.

Consider a pre-paid plan to finance your funeral and cemetery arrangements.

To help Canadians finance these arrangements, the tax rules provide a special tax exemption for the interest earned on eligible pre-paid amounts. Like the deferred income plans discussed in Chapter 3, the sooner you contribute to a pre-paid funeral or cemetery arrangement, the longer your funds will benefit from the effect of tax-free compounding of interest.

You can contribute up to $35,000 to an arrangement that covers both funeral and cemetery services. If the funeral and cemetery services will be provided by separate businesses, you can contribute up to $15,000 to an arrangement that covers only funeral services and up to $20,000 to an arrangement that covers only cemetery services. The funds in your account can be used to cover your own funeral and cemetery arrangements or those of anyone you choose; the limits only restrict the amount that any one person can contribute to such plans over his or her lifetime.

Although the amounts of your lump-sum or periodic contributions are not tax-deductible, any interest income earned on the deposited amounts will not be subject to tax while they are in the plan. If you withdraw the funds and use them for other purposes, any amounts in excess of your total contributions will be taxable in the year of withdrawal.

Any amounts left over after the funeral and cemetery expenses have been paid for will be refunded to the contributor or the contributor's estate. The tax payable on the refund is calculated with a formula that ensures that only the fund's investment income is subject to tax.

21.11 References

There is little published information on estate planning that is easily understood by the layperson. As well, every individual's case is different. Consult a qualified tax professional for advice.

The CRA publishes the following publications, which are available (in person or by telephone request) from your nearest CRA Tax Services Office. Forms and guides may also be available from the CRA's Internet site at *www.cra-arc.gc.ca.*

Guide, "T3 Trust Income Tax and Information Return"
Interpretation Bulletin IT-531, "Eligible funeral arrangements"
Brochure, "When You Retire"

If you are an executor or estate trustee

- Take steps to minimize the tax burden on the estate (22.1.3)
- Consider realizing selected capital gains and losses on assets left to a spouse or spousal trust (22.2.2)
- Consider filing separate income tax returns to multiply credits (22.2.3)
- Obtain a clearance certificate before distributing assets (22.2.4)
- Watch out for the effects of foreign estate taxes (22.5)

If you are an executor or estate trustee, your responsibilities for the deceased's estate include filing all tax returns required and ensuring that all taxes have been paid. To fulfil these responsibilities, you will need to know about the tax rules that apply on death. In this chapter, we provide an overview of these rules and some steps you may be able to take to minimize the taxes owed by the deceased and the estate.

22.1 What happens on death?

When a person dies, the executor or administrator of the person's estate (called the "estate trustee") is responsible for taking charge of the individual's affairs and distributing assets as set out in his or her will. The executor's responsibilities include determining the assets and liabilities of the estate, filing all income tax returns for the deceased and the estate, paying the debts outstanding at the date of the individual's death (including all taxes), and letting the beneficiaries know which of the amounts they receive from the estate are taxable.

If there is no will or the will is invalid, provincial law will determine how the deceased's assets are distributed. The deceased's representatives or heirs must apply to the court to appoint an administrator to administer and distribute the estate according to a formula set out in legislation.

22.1.1 Applying for probate

The executor will normally apply to the court for "letters probate", which will give court approval for the executor to take over the deceased's property, manage it and distribute it to the beneficiaries of the estate.

Probate fees are charged by the courts in each province (except Quebec) to grant letters probate. The probate charge generally applies to the total value of an estate's assets at the time of death, without any deduction for debts other than those encumbering real property (see 21.4 for estate planning steps you may be able to take to minimize probate fees).

22.1.2 Notifying government agencies

If the deceased received Canada Pension Plan (CPP) or Old Age Security (OAS) payments, the executor or legal representative should contact Social Development Canada to cancel the deceased's benefits and determine the death benefits due to a surviving spouse or the estate.

22.1.3 Post-mortem tax planning

Tax planning does not necessarily cease on death. There may be many opportunties for post-mortem planning available to the deceased's estate to lessen the tax burden on the estate or the deceased taxpayer to the benefit of the beneficiaries. Post-mortem planning begins shortly after death and is usually complete within the first year.

For example, in certain circumstances, more than one income tax return may be filed for the deceased taxpayer (see 22.2.4). If the deceased had an RRSP, the executor may be able to make a contribution to a spousal RRSP before the deadline (60 days after the end of the year of death).

In more complicated situations, the deceased's representative may choose to wind up a corporation during the first fiscal period of the estate, or make certain elections relating to capital losses arising in the estate (see 22.2.3).

If you are an executor and estate trustee, you should seek advice on how to minimize the tax burden on the estate that has been left under your care. If you do not, you could be sued by the beneficiaries. The courts have found executors liable for failing to take active steps to structure the estate's affairs to minimize income tax.

22.2 Taxes on death

22.2.1 Tax payable by the estate

When a person dies, the executor must file a "terminal return" for the deceased to report income up to the date of death. Although the regular T1 and Québec TP1 return forms are used, there are a number of special rules for these returns. For example:

- charitable donations, which can normally be claimed for the year of donation or carried forward to future years (see 8.1), can be carried back and claimed in the year prior to death (subject to the limits discussed in 8.1), if not of use in the terminal return
- medical expenses paid, which can normally be claimed for a 12-month period ending in the year (see 2.7.1), can be pooled for any 24-month period that includes the day of death
- the full amount of the deceased's RRSP (see 3.1) or RRIF (see 20.4.4) is brought into income for the year of death, unless the beneficiary of the plan is the deceased's spouse or certain

dependants (see 22.4); if the funds are not transferred to the spouse's own RRSP or RRIF, the spouse must report the funds as income for tax purposes

- any balance borrowed by the deceased from an RRSP under the Home Buyers' Plan (see 3.3.6) or Lifelong Learning Plan (see 3.3.7) and not yet repaid must be included in income unless an election is made to have the liability assumed by the surviving spouse
- minimum tax (see 7.6) does not apply to the year of death
- capital property not left to a surviving spouse (either outright or through a trust) is deemed disposed of at its fair market value, resulting in either a capital gain or a capital loss (see 22.2.3)
- capital losses, which are normally only allowed to offset capital gains (as discussed in 6.2.2), may be deducted from other income (except to the extent you have previously claimed the capital gains exemption)
- certain kinds of income earned but not received by the deceased before death can be reported on a separate return (against which the deceased's personal credits can be claimed a second time) (see 22.2.3)

The terminal return for the deceased is due by the usual deadline (see 9.1.1) or six months after death, whichever is later. For example, if the date of death is March 10, 2004, the deceased's 2004 return is due by April 30, 2005.

A similar extension is allowed for filing of the return for the year before the year of death if the individual dies before the return's normal due date. Continuing our example above, the deceased's 2003 tax return would be due by September 10, 2004 instead of the usual April 30, 2004 deadline. Any balance of tax owing is due on April 30 of the year after the year of death or six months after death, whichever is later.

If the deceased person was paying tax by instalments, no further instalment payments have to be paid after his or her death. The only instalments required are those that were due before the date of death, but not paid.

Note that life insurance proceeds received as a result of an individual's death are not subject to income tax. Life insurance is discussed in more detail in 21.7.

If you are an active or retired partner of a professional partnership, see 16.2.6.

22.2.2 Estate returns

Any income earned after death will be subject to tax as part of the estate. The estate is treated as a separate person that must file a return as a trust each year until all of the assets are distributed. (Sometimes this distribution can take several years, but normally an estate can be wound up within one year.) Any income paid to beneficiaries of the estate may be taxed in their hands directly, instead of in the estate.

22.2.3 Capital gains on death

Canada has no federal estate tax or inheritance tax, nor do any of the provinces. To the extent you simply have cash in the bank and you leave it to your family, there will be no tax to pay at all (other than probate fees, discussed in 21.4).

Many people, however, have capital assets such as stocks, real estate and jewellery. As a general rule, capital assets are deemed for tax purposes to have been sold at their fair market value immediately before death, thus triggering a capital gain on all of the increase in value that has accrued since the assets were purchased. This prevents gains from accruing indefinitely without ever being taxed. The normal capital gains rules apply to this deemed disposition, together with the availability of exemptions, such as the $500,000 capital gains exemption (see 6.3).

> **Example**
>
> Jane dies in March 2004. Her only capital assets are her house, which has a cost base of $50,000 and is now worth $600,000; a diamond ring, which has a cost base of $5,000 and is now worth $10,000; and a stock portfolio, which has a cost base of $10,000 and is now worth $100,000.
>
> The house will be deemed sold at fair market value just before Jane's death, but there will be no capital gain because it was her principal residence. The ring and the stocks will also be deemed sold at their current values, for a total gain of $95,000. One-half of the capital gain, or $45,000, will be taxed as a taxable capital gain on Jane's terminal return.

Any accrued capital losses are also realized at death. If you own depreciable property, recaptured capital cost allowance or a terminal loss may also be triggered.

The main exception to the "deemed disposition" rule is the case in which you leave assets to your spouse (including a common-law or same-sex spouse—see 2.2.1) or to a spousal trust (a trust that meets certain requirements, as outlined in 21.5.2). In such a case, you are deemed to have sold your assets immediately before your death at their cost, so no capital gain results, as long as your spouse or a spousal trust obtains ownership and unfettered rights to the property. Your spouse (or the trust) then inherits that cost for tax purposes along with the assets.

When your spouse (or the trust) sells the assets, or on your spouse's death, the full capital gain or loss from your original purchase price will be taxed.

There is, however, a special rule under which an estate trustee may elect to realize a capital gain or loss on a property-by-property basis when assets are left to a spouse (or a spousal trust) on the deceased's death. This election may be beneficial if the estate trustee elects to trigger a capital gain in order to use loss carryforwards or a capital gains exemption. Alternatively, triggering a capital loss may recover tax in the year prior to death, since capital losses in the year of death may be carried back to the immediately preceding year and used against any income, except to the extent that the deceased previously claimed the capital gains exemption (see 6.3).

If you are an active or retired partner of a professional partnership, see 16.2.6.

22.2.4 Separate income tax returns

The executor or legal representative must file an ordinary income tax return reporting the income of the deceased from January 1 of the year of death to the date of death. In certain circumstances, the executor may exclude specific types of income from the ordinary return and report them on separate, optional income tax returns.

Certain tax credits such as the age credit, the basic personal tax credit, the spousal tax credit, the equivalent-to-spouse tax credit, the dependant tax credit and the caregiver credit that apply in the ordinary return for the year of death may also

> Consider filing separate income tax returns to multiply credits.

be deducted in each of the separate returns filed. Certain other tax credits and certain deductions may be used in either the separate returns or the ordinary return or split between the returns.

The executor may choose to file up to three separate returns aside from the ordinary return. These optional returns are for income from:

- rights or things
- a business as a partner or proprietor
- a testamentary trust.

Rights or things are amounts that were not paid at the time of death and that, had the person not died, would have been included in his or her income when received. There are rights and things from employment and other sources such as certain investments.

If the deceased was a partner or sole proprietor of a business, business income may be reported on a separate return if the fiscal period of the business was not the same as the calendar year and the death occurred after the end of the fiscal period, among other conditions. The executor may use this return to report income for the time from the end of the fiscal period to the date of death.

Similarly, if the deceased was a beneficiary of a testamentary trust and the trust does not report its income on a calendar year basis, income from the end of the trust's fiscal period to the date of death may be reported on a separate return, if applicable. Income from *inter vivos* trusts does not qualify for this special treatment.

22.2.5 Clearance certificates

Obtain a clearance certificate before distributing assets.

As executor or legal representative, you may want to get a clearance certificate from the CRA before you distribute all of the property under your control. A clearance certificates indicates that all taxes for which the deceased is liable have been paid. If you do not get a certificate, you will be liable for any tax the deceased owes. A clearance certificate covers all tax years to the date of death. A separate clearance certificate is needed for a trust such as a spousal trust, which is deemed to have disposed of its assets immediately before the spouse's death.

22.3 Death benefits

A death benefit is an amount paid in recognition of a deceased employee's service. Death benefits may be paid by the deceased's employer to the surviving spouse, other family members or to the estate. Up to $10,000 of such benefits may be received tax-free.

The first $10,000 of death benefits paid in respect of any one employee is exempt from tax. The employee's spouse gets the exemption; to the extent there is no spouse or the spouse receives less than $10,000 and other taxpayers receive such funds, any remaining amount of exemption can be split among the other recipients. "Spouse" includes common-law and same-sex spouses who meet the criteria outlined in 2.2.1.

Note that life insurance proceeds are completely different from death benefits, and are not taxed at all when received.

22.4 RRSPs and RRIFs

On death, a taxpayer is normally taxed on the entire amount of any RRSPs or RRIFs, except where the funds are left to the taxpayer's spouse or financially-dependent child, in which case they are included in the spouse's or child's income (see 22.2.1). To the extent the funds come from an RRSP, they can be transferred to the spouse's own RRSP or RRIF for a deduction that offsets the income inclusion. The spouse can also use these funds to acquire an annuity. To the extent the funds come from a RRIF, if the spouse is named as a successor annuitant to the RRIF, the payments under the deceased's plan will continue to be paid to the spouse. If the spouse is named as beneficiary of the RRIF, amounts under the deceased's plan can be transferred to the spouse's own RRSP or RRIF, or he or she can use the funds to acquire an annuity.

If the RRSP or RRIF funds are left to a dependent child or grandchild, the RRSP or RRIF funds can either be taxed in the hands of the child or grandchild or used to buy a term annuity to age 18. The executor should obtain professional advice on these matters.

22.5 Foreign estate taxes

If you own assets in other countries, estate, inheritance or succession taxes of those countries (or their states or provinces) may apply on your death.

Estate taxes and succession duties imposed by other jurisdictions are not normally eligible for a foreign tax credit in Canada, even though you may have a Canadian income tax liability as a result of the deemed disposition described in 22.2.3. Double taxation can result. You may need to plan for this ahead of time.

> Watch out for the effects of foreign estate taxes.

If you are a U.S. citizen, see our discussion of U.S. estate tax in 18.8.1.

If you are not a U.S. citizen but own assets legally located in the U.S., including real estate, debts owed to you by U.S. citizens or shares in U.S. corporations, see the planning techniques discussed in 19.4.6.

22.6 References

The CRA publishes the following publications, which are available (in person or by telephone request) from your nearest CRA Tax Services Office. Forms and guides may also be available from the CRA's Internet site at *www.cra-arc.gc.ca*.

Interpretation Bulletin IT-210R2, "Income of deceased persons—periodic payments"

Interpretation Bulletin IT-212R3, "Income of deceased persons—rights or things" and Special Release IT-212R3SR

Interpretation Bulletin IT-234, "Income of deceased persons—Farm crops"

Interpretation Bulletin IT-278R2, "Death of a partner or retired partner"

Interpretation Bulletin IT-305R4, "Testamentary spousal trusts"

Interpretation Bulletin IT-313R2, "Eligible capital property—Rules where a taxpayer has ceased carrying on business or has died"

Interpretation Bulletin IT-349R3, "Intergenerational transfers of farm property on death"

Interpretation Bulletin IT-407R4, "Disposition of cultural property to designated Canadian institutions"

Interpretation Bulletin IT-508R, "Death benefits"
Guide, "Preparing Returns for Deceased Persons"
Guide, "T3 Trust Income Tax and Information Return"
Guide, "Death of an RRSP Annuitant"
Guide, "Death of a RRIF Annuitant"
Guide, "What to Do Following a Death"

Appendices

Appendix I
Federal and Provincial Income Tax Rates and Brackets for 2004

	Tax Rates	Tax Brackets	Surtax Rate	Threshold
Federal	16.0%	Up to $35,000		
	22.0	35,001 – 70,000		
	26.0	70,001 – 113,804		
	29.0	Over 113,804		
British Columbia	6.05%	Up to $32,476		
	9.15	32,477 – 64,954		
	11.7	64,955 – 74,575		
	13.7	74,576 – 90,555		
	14.7	Over 90,555		
Alberta	10.0%	All income		
Saskatchewan	11.0%	Up to $36,155		
	13.0	36,156 – 103,300		
	15.0	Over 103,300		
Manitoba	10.9%	Up to $30,544		
	14.9	30,545 – 65,000		
	17.4	Over 65,000		
Ontario	6.05%	Up to $33,375		
	9.15	33,376 – 66,752	20%	$3,856
	11.16	Over 66,752	36	4,864
Québec	16.0%	Up to $27,635		
	20.0	27,636 – 55,280		
	24.0	Over 55,281		
New Brunswick	9.68%	Up to $32,183		
	14.82	32,184 – 64,368		
	16.52	64,369 – 104,648		
	17.84	Over 104,648		
Nova Scotia	8.79%	Up to $29,590		
	14.95	29,591 – 59,180		
	16.67	59,181 – 93,000		
	17.50	Over 93,000	10%	$10,000
Prince Edward Island	9.8%	Up to $30,754		
	13.8	30,755 – 61,509		
	16.7	Over 61,509	10%	$5,200
Newfoundland	10.57%	Up to $29,590		
	16.16	29,591 – 59,180		
	18.02	Over 59,180	9%	$7,032

Appendix II

Federal and Provincial Non-refundable Tax Credits for 2004[a]

	Federal	B.C.	Alta.	Sask.	Man.
Tax rate applied to credits	16.0%	6.05%	10.0%	11.0%	10.9%
Basic personal	$8,012	$8,523	$14,337	$8,264	$7,634
Spousal/partner and wholly dependent person[b]	6,804	7,298	14,337	8,264	6,483
Income threshold	*680*	*730*	*0*	*826*	*648*
Age 65 and over[c]	3,912	3,822	4,022	3,912	3,728
Income threshold	*29,124*	*28,450*	*29,942*	*29,124*	*27,749*
Age supplement	–	–	–	1,033	–
Disability[c]	6,486	6,392	6,668	6,486	6,180
Dependants:					
18 and under	–	–	–	2,582	–
Under 18 and infirm[d]	3,784	3,729	3,890	3,784	3,605
18 and over and infirm	3,784	3,729	3,890	3,784	3,605
Income threshold	*5,368*	*5,940*	*5,519*	*5,368*	*5,115*
Caregiver	3,784	3,729	3,890	3,784	3,605
Income threshold	*12,921*	*12,622*	*13,284*	*12,921*	*12,312*
Pension[c]	1,000	1,000	1,111	1,000	1,000
Medical threshold[e]	1,813	1,772	1,865	1,813	1,728
Canada Pension Plan[f] (max)	1,831	1,831	1,831	1,831	1,831
Employment Insurance (max)	772	772	772	772	772
Education[g]					
Full time – per month	400	200	445	400	400
Part time – per month	120	60	133	120	120
Tuition fees[g]					
Interest paid on student loans[h]					
Charitable donations (see 8.1)					

	Ont.	N.B.	N.S.	P.E.I.	Nfld.
Tax rate applied to credits	6.05%	9.68%	8.79%	9.8%	10.57%
Basic personal	$8,043	$7,756	$7,231	$7,412	$7,410
Spousal/partner and wholly					
dependent person[b]	6,830	6,586	6,140	6,294	6,055
Income threshold	*683*	*659*	*614*	*629*	*606*
Age 65 and over[c]	3,927	3,787	3,531	3,619	3,482
Income threshold	*29,238*	*28,193*	*26,284*	*26,941*	*25,921*
Age supplement	–	–	–	–	–
Disability[c]	6,499	6,279	4,293	5,400	5,000
Dependants:					
18 and under	–	–	–	–	–
Under 18 and infirm[d]	3,791	3,663	2,941	3,015	2,353
18 and over and infirm	3,791	3,663	2,386	2,446	2,353
Income threshold	*5,390*	*5,197*	*4,845*	*4,966*	*5,057*
Caregiver	3,791	3,663	4,176	2,446	2,353
Income threshold	*12,971*	*12,509*	*11,661*	*11,953*	*11,500*
Pension[c]	1,112	1,000	1,000	1,000	1,000
Medical threshold[e]	1,821	1,755	1,637	1,678	1,614
Canada Pension Plan[f] (max)	1,831	1,831	1,831	1,831	1,831
Employment Insurance (max)	772	772	772	772	772
Education[g]					
Full time – per month	433	400	200	200	200
Part time – per month	130	120	60	60	60
Tuition fees[g]					
Interest paid on student loans[h]					
Charitable donations (see 8.1)					

Notes

(a) The table shows the dollar amounts of all federal and provincial non-refundable credits for 2004 (except for Québec's, which are outlined on the following pages). In order to determine the credit value, each dollar amount must be multiplied by the tax rate shown, which is the lowest tax rate that applies in that jurisdiction. For example, the federal basic personal credit amount of $8,012 is multiplied by 16% to determine the credit value of $1,282.

Income earned by the taxpayer or dependant, as applicable, in excess of the income thresholds shown in the tables serves to reduce the availability of the credit on a dollar-for-dollar basis. The only exception to this is the age credit, which is reduced by 15% of the taxpayer's income in excess of the threshold.

(b) The spousal/partner credit may be claimed for a common-law partner as well as for a spouse. Taxpayers who are single, divorced or separated and who support a dependant in their home may claim the wholly dependent person credit. The credit can be claimed for dependants under the age of 18 who are related to the taxpayer, for the taxpayer's parents or grandparents, or for any other infirm person who is related to the taxpayer.

(c) These credits are transferable to a spouse or common-law partner. The amounts available for transfer are reduced by the excess of the spouse's or partner's income over the basic personal credit amount. The disability credit is also transferable to a supporting person other than a spouse or partner; however, in this case, the amount of the credit is reduced by the excess of the disabled person's income over the basic personal credit amount.

(d) The credit for a dependant with a disability under the age of 18 is reduced by certain child and attendant care expenses claimed in respect of the dependant.

(e) The medical credit is calculated based on qualified medical expenses exceeding 3% of net income or the threshold indicated in the table, whichever is less.

(f) Self-employed taxpayers can deduct 50% of their Canada or Québec Pension Plan premiums in calculating net income. The balance is claimed as a credit.

(g) The tuition credit is calculated based on tuition and mandatory ancillary fees paid for the calendar year. Both the tuition and education credits are transferable to a spouse or common-law partner, parent or grandparent. The maximum amount transferable for both federal and provincial purposes is $5,000 (indexed for inflation for some provinces) less the excess of the student's income over the basic personal credit amount. Any amounts not transferred may be carried forward by the student and claimed in future years.

(h) Interest paid on student loans is eligible for both a federal and provincial credit. The credit must be claimed by the student, but can be carried forward for five years.

Québec Personal Tax Credits for 2004

Tax rate applied to credits[a]	20%
Basic personal	$6,275
Amount transferred from one spouse to another[b]	—
Person living alone or with dependant[c]	1,115
Age 65 and over[c, d]	2,200
Single parent[e]	1,380
Dependent children[e]	
First	2,765
Second and subsequent	2,550
Other related dependants over 18[e]	2,550
Dependant in full-time attendance at a post-secondary school[e, g]	1,755
Disability[d, h]	2,200
Infirm dependants over 18[f]	6,275
Pension[c, d, i]	1,000
Québec Pension Plan[j] (max)	1,831
Employment Insurance (max)	772
Health Services Fund	1,000
Union and professional dues[k]	
Tuition fees[l]	
Interest paid on student loans[m]	
Medical expenses[n]	
Charitable donations (see 17.2.9)	

Notes

(a) The table shows the dollar amounts of Québec non-refundable credits for 2004. The credit rate of 20% for 2004 is applied to the dollar amounts shown in the table to determine the credit value. For example, the basic personal credit amount of $6,275 is multiplied by 20% to determine the credit value of $1,255.

Many of these credits are income-tested. "Family income" means the total income of both spouses/partners. "Net family income" means the total income of both spouses/partners minus $27,635. The net income calculation is the same under both the general and simplified systems (see 17.1.2).

(b) The spousal/partner credit and the transfer of the unused portion of a spouse's/partner's disability credit is now replaced with a new mechanism for the transfer of the unused portion of all non-refundable credits from one spouse/partner to the other (under the general and simplified systems). The deduction related to the transfer can only be claimed after all other non-refundable credits have been accounted for in calculating the individual's income tax otherwise payable. There is no wholly dependent person credit in Québec.

(c) The amounts for a person living alone, age 65 and over, and pension income are added together and reduced by 15% of net family income (see note (a)).

(d) These credits are transferable to a spouse or a common-law partner. The amounts available for transfer are reduced by any income tax payable by the spouse or partner.

(e) The amounts for a single parent, dependent children and dependent post-secondary students are added together and reduced by the amount of the dependant's net income.

(f) The amounts for other related dependants and infirm dependants are reduced by the amount of the dependant's net income.

(g) The amount for a dependant attending a post-secondary school, which is available for up to two semesters per year per dependant, may only be claimed by a supporting person.

(h) The disability credit is transferable to a supporting person. The amount available for transfer is reduced by any income tax payable by the dependant.

(i) The pension credit is calculated based on the lesser of eligible pension income and $1,000.

(j) Self-employed taxpayers can deduct 50% of their Québec or Canada Pension Plan contributions in calculating net income (under either the general or the simplified system). The balance is claimed as a non-refundable credit.

(k) The credit for union and professional dues is calculated based on the annual fees paid in the year. The portion of professional dues relating to liability insurance is allowed as a deduction and is not included in calculating the credit.

(l) The tuition credit is calculated based on tuition, professional examination and mandatory ancillary fees paid for the calendar year. The credit is not transferable, but may be carried forward to future years by the student.

(m) Interest paid on student loans but unclaimed in a particular year may be carried forward indefinitely.

(n) The medical credit is calculated based on qualified medical expenses in excess of 3% of family income (see note (a)).

Index